BRIDGES TO
LITERATURE

McDougal Littell

Evanston, Illinois • Boston • Dallas

READING • FLUENCY • LITERATURE • VOCABULARY

Author

Jane Greene Literacy Intervention Specialist; Reading, Writing, Language, Evaluation Consultant to schools nationwide; author of *LANGUAGE! A Literacy Intervention Curriculum.* Dr. Greene established the underlying goals and philosophy, advised on the tables of contents, reviewed prototypes, and supervised the development of the assessment strand.

English Language Advisor

Judy Lewis Director, State and Federal Programs for reading proficiency and high-risk populations, Folsom, California; Editor, *Context,* a newsletter for teachers with English learners in their classes. Ms. Lewis reviewed selections for the program and provided special guidance on the development of EL notes.

Consultant

Olga Bautista Reading Facilitator, Will C. Wood Middle School, Sacramento, California. Ms. Bautista provided advice on reading, pacing, and EL instruction during the development phase and reviewed final prototypes of both the Pupil Edition and Teacher's Edition.

ISBN 13: 978-0-618-90587-4   ISBN 10: 0-618-90587-1

Printed in the United States of America.

1 2 3 4 5 6 7 8 9—DCI—12 11 10 09 08 07

BRIDGES TO
LITERATURE

Level III

12 Reader's Choice LONGER SELECTIONS FOR INDEPENDENT READING

Student Resources

 Some selections available on the Reading Coach CD-ROM

Not According to Plan

Unit 1
Fiction

You've checked your list. You've made your plans. Who knew that you would get lost?

Life is full of surprises. So are some stories. In this unit, you will read stories that contain unexpected events. These stories are fiction—writing that comes from the imagination.

All fiction contains four key parts:
- **Characters:** the people or animals in the story
- **Plot:** what happens in the story
- **Setting:** where and when the story happens
- **Theme:** the writer's message about life or human nature

The Tell-Tale Heart

by Edgar Allan Poe, adapted by Sue Ellis

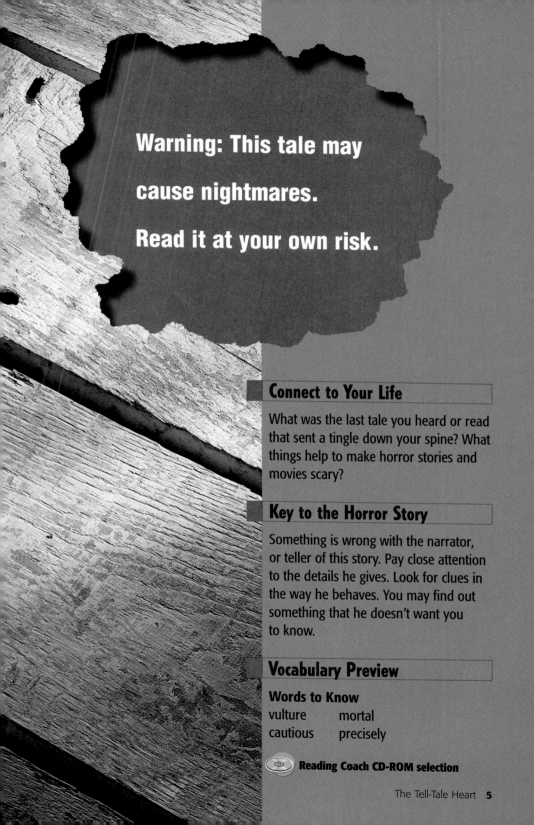

Warning: This tale may cause nightmares. Read it at your own risk.

Connect to Your Life

What was the last tale you heard or read that sent a tingle down your spine? What things help to make horror stories and movies scary?

Key to the Horror Story

Something is wrong with the narrator, or teller of this story. Pay close attention to the details he gives. Look for clues in the way he behaves. You may find out something that he doesn't want you to know.

Vocabulary Preview

Words to Know
vulture   mortal
cautious   precisely

Reading Coach CD-ROM selection

FOCUS _____
The narrator wants to explain something about himself. Find out what it is.

True! Nervous—very, very dreadfully nervous I had been and am! But why will you say that I am mad? The disease had sharpened my senses. It did not destroy them or make them dull. Above all, my sense of hearing was acute! I heard all things in heaven and in the earth. How then am I mad? Listen! Observe how calmly I tell you the whole story.

acute
(ə kyo͞ot′)
sharp

10 It is impossible to say how I first got the idea. But once I did, it haunted me day and night. I had no reason. I loved the old man. He had never wronged me. He had never insulted me. I didn't want his gold. I think it was his eye. Yes, it was his eye! He had the eye of a vulture—a pale blue eye, with a film over it. Whenever it looked at me, my blood ran cold. And so, very gradually, I made up my mind to take the life of the old man, and get rid of the eye forever.

vulture
(vŭl′ chər)
n. bird that eats dead things

THINK IT THROUGH
What does the narrator want to do? Why?

FOCUS _____
The narrator tries to carry out his plans. Read to find out what happens.

20 Now this is the point. You think I'm mad. Madmen know nothing. But you should have seen me. You should have seen how wisely I went about my work.

I was so careful! I showed such foresight! I was so cautious!

cautious

(kô′ shəs)

adj. very careful

I was never kinder to the old man than during the whole week before I killed him. Every night, about midnight, I turned the latch of his door and opened it—oh, so gently! Then when I opened it just enough for my head, I would put in a lantern. The lantern showed no light; its sides were

30 closed. I moved it slowly, very slowly, so that I might not disturb the old man's sleep. It took me an hour to place my whole head within the opening so far that I could see him as he lay upon his bed. And then, so cautiously—cautiously (for the hinges creaked)—I would open the lantern. One single thin ray of light from the lantern would fall on the old man's vulture eye. I did this for seven long nights—every night at midnight— but the eye was always closed. So it was

40 impossible to do my work; for it was not the old man who annoyed me, but his Evil Eye. And every morning, when the day broke, I went boldly into his room. I spoke bravely to him, calling him by name in a hearty tone, inquiring how he had spent the night. He had no reason to suspect that I had been looking in on him while he slept.

REREAD

Try to picture this scene in your mind. Why couldn't the narrator kill the old man?

inquiring

(ĭn kwīr′ ĭng)

asking

On the eighth night I was even more cautious in

50 opening the door. The minute hand of the watch moves more quickly than mine did. Never before that night had I felt my own power and wisdom. I could scarcely contain my feelings of triumph. There I was, opening the door little by little, and he was not aware of me. Perhaps he heard me, for he moved on the bed

suddenly, as if startled. Now you may think that I drew back—but no. His room was as black as pitch with the thick darkness (for the shutters were closed, through fear of robbers). So I knew that he could not 60 see the door opening, and I kept pushing it, steadily, steadily.

I had my head in, and was about to open the lantern, when my thumb slipped on the side of the lantern, and the old man sprang up in the bed, crying out, "Who's there?"

I kept quite still and said nothing. For a whole hour I did not move a muscle, and in the meantime I did not hear him lie down. He was still sitting up in the bed listening. Presently I heard a slight groan, and I 70 knew it was the groan of mortal terror. It was the sound of fear—from the bottom of the soul. I knew it well myself. Many a night I have felt those same terrors. I knew what the old man felt, and pitied him, although I chuckled in my heart. I knew that he had been lying awake ever since the first slight noise, when he had turned in the bed. His fears had been continuing to grow upon him. He had been trying to talk himself out of them, but he could not. He could 80 feel—although he could not see or hear it—my head's presence in his room.

mortal
(môr′ tl) *adj.* extreme; almost threatening death

THINK IT THROUGH

What happens on the eighth night? How is it different from the first seven nights?

The narrator hears something. How does this sound affect
what he does?

When I had waited a long time, very patiently,
without hearing him lie down, I decided to open a
little—a very, very little—crack in the lantern. So I
opened it—you cannot imagine how carefully—until a
single dim ray, like the thread of the spider,
shot out from the crack and fell precisely
upon the vulture eye.

It was open—wide, wide open—and I
90 grew furious as I gazed upon it. I saw it
perfectly clearly—all a dull blue. It had a
hideous veil over it that chilled the very

precisely
(prĭ sīs′ lē)
adv. exactly

hideous veil
(hĭd′ ē əs vāl′)
ugly covering

center of my bones. But I could see nothing of the old man's face or body, for I had directed the ray as if by instinct, precisely on that eye.

And now have I not told you that what you mistake for madness is only the extreme sharpness of my senses? Now, I say, there came to my ears a low, dull, quick sound, such as a ticking clock makes when covered in cotton. I knew that sound too well too. It was the beating of the old man's heart.

REREAD
How is the sound of the clock like the sound of the old man's heart?

But even yet I kept still. I scarcely breathed. I held the lantern motionless. I tried to see how steadily I could keep the ray upon the eye. Meanwhile the awful drumming of the heart increased. It grew quicker and quicker, and louder and louder every instant. The old man's terror must have been extreme! It grew louder, I say, louder every moment!—do you hear me well? I have told you that I am nervous: so I am. And now at the dead hour of night, amid the awful silence of that old house, this strange noise began to terrify me. Yet, for some minutes longer I stood still. But the beating grew louder, louder! I thought the heart must burst. And now a new fear seized me—the sound would be heard by a neighbor! The old man's hour had come! With a loud yell, I threw open the lantern and leaped into the room. He shrieked once—once only. In an instant I dragged him to the floor, and pulled the heavy bed over him.

REREAD
What causes the narrator to carry out his deed?

But for many minutes, the heart beat on with a muffled sound. This, however, did not worry me; it would not be heard through the wall. Finally it stopped. The old man was dead. I removed the bed and looked at the corpse. Yes, he was stone,

stone dead. I placed my hand upon the heart and held it there many minutes. There was no beating. He was stone dead. His eye would trouble me no more.

130   If you still think me mad, you will think so no longer when I describe how I hid the body. The night was ending, and I worked fast but in silence. First I cut up the corpse. I cut off the head and the arms and the legs. I then took up three boards from the floor of the room and hid the body parts. Then I replaced the boards so cleverly and carefully that no human eye— not even *his*—could have noticed anything wrong. There was nothing to wash out—no stain of any kind, not even blood. I had been too cautious for that. A
140 tub had caught all—ha, ha!

THINK IT THROUGH

What does the narrator do? How does he feel about it?

FOCUS

The police arrive. Read to find out how the narrator covers up his crime.

When I ended my work, it was four o'clock—still dark as midnight. As the bell sounded the hour, there came a knocking at the street door. I went down to open it with a light heart—for what had I now to fear? Three men entered who introduced themselves as police officers. A shriek had been heard by a neighbor during the night. The neighbor had called the police, and they had come to search the house.

    I smiled—for what had I to fear? I welcomed the
150 gentlemen. The shriek, I said, was my own in a dream. The old man, I mentioned, had gone to the

country. I took my visitors all over the house. I told them to search—search well. I led them, finally, to his room. I felt so confident that I brought chairs into the room and told them to rest here. I myself boldly put my chair upon the very spot under which I'd buried the corpse of the victim.

THINK IT THROUGH
How does the narrator react when the police arrive? How do you explain this reaction?

FOCUS
Something unexpected happens. Read to discover what the narrator reveals.

The officers were satisfied. My manner had convinced them. I was totally at ease. They sat, and
160 while I answered cheerily, they chatted. But soon, I felt myself getting pale and wished they were gone. My head ached, and I heard a ringing in my ears: but still they sat and still chatted. The ringing became more distinct; it continued and became more distinct. I talked more freely to get rid of the feeling, but it continued and got clearer—until, finally, I found that the noise was not within my ears.

distinct
(dĭ stĭngkt′)
clear

I now grew very pale; but I talked faster and
170 louder. Yet the sound increased—and what could I do? It was *a low, dull, quick sound—much like a ticking clock sounds when covered in cotton.*

REREAD
Where has the narrator used these words before?

I gasped for breath—and yet the officers didn't hear it. I talked more quickly, more emotionally; but the noise steadily increased. Why wouldn't they leave? I paced the floor, as if excited by the conversation—but the noise kept increasing. What could I do? I foamed—I raged—I swore. I swung my chair and scraped it on the boards, but the noise arose again and continually increased. It grew louder— louder—louder! And still the men chatted pleasantly and smiled. Was it possible that they didn't hear it? No, no! they heard!—they suspected—they knew! They were laughing at my horror! This I thought and this I think. But anything was better than this agony. I could not bear those smiles any longer! I felt that I must scream or die—and now—again—listen! louder! louder!—

"Villains!" I shrieked. "Pretend no more! I admit the deed!—Tear up the planks—here, here! It is the beating of his hideous heart!"

THINK IT THROUGH

1. What does the narrator end up telling the police?
2. What may have caused him to tell them this? Explain.
3. Do you think the heart was really beating at the end? Explain your answer.
4. How does the narrator show that he's mad? Use details from the story to support your answer.

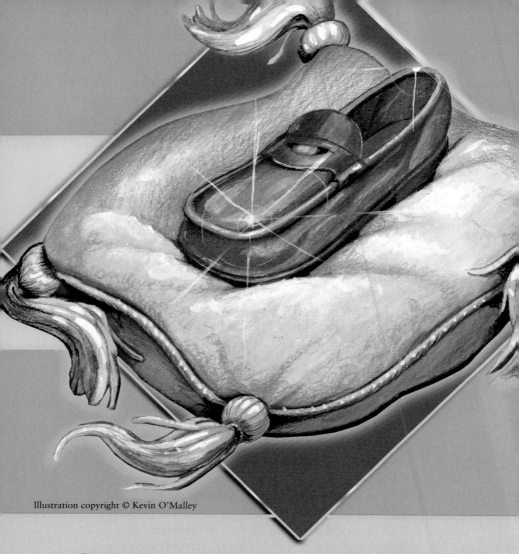

Illustration copyright © Kevin O'Malley

ONCE UPON A TIME, A HANDSOME PRINCE RETURNED A POOR GIRL'S LOST SLIPPER. THEY LIVED HAPPILY EVER AFTER. NOW MEET THE ONLY ONE IN THE WORLD WHO FITS INTO A CERTAIN SCUFFED-UP LOAFER.

Cinder Edna

BY ELLEN JACKSON

Connect to Your Life

Is there really such a thing as living happily ever after? Share your opinion with a partner.

Key to the Modern Fairy Tale

The first Cinderella tale was told long ago. There are hundreds of versions of Cinderella tales. "Cinder Edna" was written only a few years ago. It mixes old things with new. As you read about Cinder Edna, think about how well she fits your ideas about the original Cinderella.

Vocabulary Preview

Words to Know

cinders	dainty	profile
spunky	elegant	

Cinderella and Cinder Edna are neighbors with similar lives. Read to find out how they are different.

Once upon a time there were two girls who lived next door to each other. You may have heard of the first one. Her name was Cinderella. Poor Cinderella was forced to work from morning till night, cooking and scrubbing pots and pans and picking up after her cruel stepmother and wicked stepsisters. When her work was done, she sat among the cinders to keep warm, thinking about all her troubles.

cinders
(sĭn′ dərz)
n. ashes

10 Cinder Edna, the other girl, was also forced to work for her wicked stepmother and stepsisters. But she sang and whistled while she worked. Moreover, she had learned a thing or two from doing all that housework—such as how to make a tuna casserole sixteen different ways and how to get spots off everything from rugs to ladybugs.

Edna had tried sitting in the cinders a few times. But it seemed like a silly way to spend time. Besides, it just made her clothes black and sooty. Instead when the housework was done, she kept warm by mowing
20 the lawn and cleaning parrot cages for the neighbors at $1.50 an hour. She also taught herself to play the accordion.

Even with her ragged, sooty clothing Cinderella was quite beautiful.

Edna, on the other hand, wasn't much to look at. But she was strong and spunky and knew some good jokes—including an especially funny one about an anteater from Afghanistan.

spunky
(spŭng′ kē)
adj. having spirit or courage

THINK IT THROUGH
What is the biggest difference between the two girls?

Illustration copyright © Kevin O'Malley

FOCUS

Notice how Cinderella and Cinder Edna solve their problem.

30 Now, one day the king announced that he would give a ball and that all the ladies of the land were invited. Cinderella's stepsisters set about choosing what they would wear. All day they ordered Cinderella around as they made their preparations.

Cinder Edna's stepsisters were excited, too. On the evening of the ball they trimmed their toenails and flossed their teeth. They put on their most beautiful

gowns and drove away, leaving Edna behind to clean
up after them.

40   Cinderella sat among the cinders and sighed. "Oh
how I wish I had a fairy godmother who could change
these rags into a beautiful gown so that I, too, could
go to the ball."

    No sooner said than done. Cinderella *did* have a
fairy godmother, and she just happened to be passing
by. With a wave of her magic wand, she changed
Cinderella's rags into a beautiful gown. On
Cinderella's incredibly tiny feet appeared a
pair of dainty glass slippers.

50   Cinder Edna didn't believe in fairy
godmothers. Instead she had used her cage-
cleaning money to put a dress on layaway
for just these kinds of occasions.

    "And my comfortable loafers will be perfect for
dancing," she said as she slipped them onto her feet.

    Meanwhile Cinderella's big, bright eyes brimmed
with tears. "But, Fairy Godmother, how will I get to
the ball?"

    The fairy godmother was surprised that her
60 goddaughter couldn't seem to figure anything out for
herself. However, with another wave of the wand, she
changed a pumpkin into a carriage, six white mice
into horses, and a stray rat into a coachman.

    "Be sure to leave before midnight," she warned
Cinderella as she helped her into the
elegant carriage.

    Cinder Edna took the bus.

dainty
(dān′ tē)
adj. beautiful in a delicate way

elegant
(ĕl′ ĭ gənt)
adj. classy

THINK IT THROUGH

The girls have different personalities. How does this show in how they handle problems?

> Find out what effect Cinderella and Cinder Edna have on those they meet.

When Cinderella arrived at the ball, everyone thought she was a princess. The king's son Randolph
70 was taken with her great beauty. He asked her to dance, but Cinderella could only sway a bit to the music. She was afraid of mussing her hair, and she knew those fragile glass slippers would break if she danced too hard.

REREAD
What do you learn about Cinderella from these details?

Just then Cinder Edna entered the room. She made straight for the refreshment table and poured herself some punch. It was Randolph's princely duty to greet everyone, so he came over to say hello.
80 "What's it like, being a prince?" Edna asked, to make conversation.

"Quite fantastic," said the prince. "Mostly I review the troops and sit around on the throne looking brave and wise." He turned his head so that Edna could see how handsome his chin looked from the right side.

"Borrring," thought Edna.

"Excuse me, but we recycle plastic around here," said a little man with glasses and a warm smile.

"Just ignore him," said Randolph. "He's only my
90 younger brother, Rupert. He lives in a cottage in the back and runs the recycling plant and a home for orphaned kittens."

REREAD
How are the princes different?

Cinder Edna immediately handed Rupert her cup.

"Would you like to dance?" asked Rupert.

Cinder Edna and Rupert danced and danced. They did the Storybook Stomp and the Cinnamon Twist.

Illustration copyright © Kevin O'Malley

They did the Worm and the Fish. They boogied and woogied. At last they stopped for a round of punch. Edna learned that Rupert (1) loved tuna casserole, (2) played the concertina, (3) knew some good jokes.

concertina
(kŏn′ sər tē′ nə)
small accordion

She told him the one about the anteater from Afghanistan and he told her the one about the banana from Barbados.

They were deep in a conversation about gum wrappers and rusty tin cans when the clock began to strike twelve.

"Oh," cried Cinderella, running for the door. "The magic spell disappears at midnight."

110 "Oh, oh," cried Cinder Edna, running for the door. "The buses stop running at midnight!"

Randolph and Rupert ran after the two girls.

"Wait! Wait!" they called. But it was too late.

As the girls vanished into the night, the two princes ran smack-dab into each other on the palace steps.

Whap! They landed with a thud. Rupert's glasses went flying and broke into a million pieces on the cement.

"Look what you made me do!" said Randolph.

120 "Now she's gone—the only girl I ever loved."

"Well, didn't you get her name?" asked Rupert impatiently. "The one I love is named Edna."

"Gee, I forgot to ask," said Randolph, scratching his head.

THINK IT THROUGH

How does each prince react to the girl he has met?

FOCUS

The future begins to unfold for the two couples. Read to find out what happens to each couple.

As Rupert got up he stumbled over something. When he leaned close to look, he saw two shoes lying side by side on the steps. One was a scuffed-up loafer. The other was a dainty glass slipper. "These definitely should be recycled," he said.

130   "No! No!" said Randolph. "This is how we'll find them. We'll try these shoes on all the women in the kingdom. When we find the feet that fit these shoes, we'll have found our brides-to-be!"

Rupert looked at his brother with disbelief. "That is positively amazing," he said, "the most amazingly dumb idea I've ever heard. You could end up married to a midget. I have a much better idea." But Randolph wouldn't listen. He ran to his room to get his beauty sleep.

140   The next day he put his plan into action. He went to every house in the kingdom, trying to cram women's feet into the glass slipper.

Rupert, too, put his plan into action. First he looked up all the Ednas in the palace directory. Then he visited them and asked each one this question: "How many recipes do you know for tuna casserole?"

Randolph soon became discouraged. All the feet he saw were either too large, too wide, too long, or adorned with electric pink toenail

150   polish.

> **adorned**
> (ə dôrnd')
> decorated

Rupert, too, was discouraged. While some Ednas could name tuna casserole with pecan sauce, and others could name tuna casserole with sour cream and rice, no one could name more than seven kinds of tuna casserole.

Finally Randolph got to Cinderella's house. The cruel stepsisters were eager to try on the glass slipper, but, of course, it didn't fit either of them.

Suddenly Randolph noticed a woman in

160   rags, sitting forlornly among the cinders in the corner. Something about her seemed familiar.

> **forlornly**
> (fər lôrn' lē)
> sadly

"Oh, Miss. Why don't you try this on?" he suggested. With trembling hands, Cinderella tried on the glass slipper. It fit perfectly!

Randolph swept her up in his arms and carried her away to the palace so that they could be married.

Meanwhile Rupert reached Cinder Edna's house. Her wicked stepsisters wanted to try on the loafer, but
170 Rupert wouldn't let them because they weren't named Edna.

At that moment, Cinder Edna came in from mowing the lawn. Her heart almost stopped when she saw Rupert. He blinked nearsightedly at her.

Without his glasses Cinder Edna looked something like a large plate of mashed potatoes.

"Are you, let's see . . . Ashes Edna?" he asked, peering closely at his list of names. "No, I
180 already talked to her." He wasn't sure these Ednas with an extra name counted, but he had already tried the just plain Ednas.

"*Cinder.* Cinder Edna," she said.

"Oh. Well, can you name sixteen different kinds of tuna casserole?"

"Of course," she said, and she began to name them. She rattled off fifteen different kinds, including tuna casserole with pickled pigs feet, and then she stopped. What was the last one anyway?

190 "Only fifteen," said Rupert, turning to go.

"Well, maybe I can't name sixteen kinds of tuna casserole," said Edna. "But I *do* know a great joke about a kangaroo from Kalamazoo."

Rupert stopped in his tracks.

"My love!" he said. He gave her a kiss. "Will you marry me?"

> **nearsightedly**
> (nîr' sī' tĭd lē)
> in a way showing that he is unable to see objects clearly

> **REREAD**
> Why does Rupert realize she's the right Edna?

Illustration copyright © Kevin O'Malley

Soon after that, Randolph and Ella (she dropped the cinder part) and Rupert and Edna (she did the same) were married in a grand double ceremony.

200   So the girl who had once been known as Cinderella ended up in a big palace. During the day she went to endless ceremonies and listened to dozens of speeches by His Highness the Grand Archduke of Lethargia and the Second Deputy Underassistant of

Underwear. And at night she sat by the fire with nothing to look at but her husband's perfect profile while he talked endlessly of troops, parade formations, and uniform buttons.

profile
(prō' fīl')
n. side view of a face

And the girl who had been known as
210 Cinder Edna ended up in a small cottage with solar heating. During the day she studied waste disposal engineering and cared for orphaned kittens. And at night she and her husband laughed and joked, tried new recipes together, and played duets on the accordion and concertina.

Guess who lived happily ever after.

THINK IT THROUGH

1. What happens to Cinderella and Randolph? What happens to Cinder Edna and Rupert?
2. Which couple do you think lives happily ever after? Explain your opinion.
3. Which character in this tale is your favorite? Why?

THE NO-GUITAR BLUES

by Gary Soto

Fausto needs money for the guitar of his dreams. Then along comes a dog that eats orange peels. How will the dog fit into Fausto's plan?

Have you ever tried to convince your parent that you really need extra money? What was the answer? If he or she said no, what did you do?

Key to the Short Story

This story takes place in Fresno, California. The time is probably the 1980s, when the TV show *American Bandstand* was very popular. This show inspired many teenagers to form rock bands and to dream about becoming famous.

Vocabulary Preview

Words to Know
mission   turnover   secondhand
distracted   deceitful

 Reading Coach CD-ROM selection

Fausto makes his first attempt to get money for a guitar. Find out what happens.

The moment Fausto saw the group Los Lobos on "American Bandstand," he knew exactly what he wanted to do with his life—play guitar. His eyes grew large with excitement as Los Lobos ground out a song while teenagers bounced off each other on the crowded dance floor.

He had watched "American Bandstand" for years and had heard Ray Camacho and the Teardrops at Romain Playground, but it had never occurred to him
10 that he too might become a musician. That afternoon Fausto knew his **mission** in life: to play guitar in his own band; to sweat out his songs and prance around the stage; to make money and dress weird.

mission
(mĭsh′ ən)
n. special duty

Fausto turned off the television set and walked outside, wondering how he could get enough money to buy a guitar. He couldn't ask his parents because they would just say, "Money doesn't grow on trees" or "What do you think we are,
20 bankers?" And besides, they hated rock music. They were into the *conjunto* music of Lydia Mendoza, Flaco Jimenez, and Little Joe and La Familia. And, as Fausto recalled, the last album they bought was *The Chipmunks Sing Christmas Favorites.*

conjunto
(kôn hōōn′ tô)
old-fashioned style of Mexican music

REREAD
Why will Fausto have a problem getting a guitar?

But what the heck, he'd give it a try.
He returned inside and watched his mother make tortillas. He leaned against the kitchen counter, trying to work up the nerve to ask her for a guitar. Finally,
30 he couldn't hold back any longer.

"Mom," he said, "I want a guitar for Christmas."

She looked up from rolling tortillas. "Honey, a guitar costs a lot of money."

"How 'bout for my birthday next year," he tried again.

"I can't promise," she said, turning back to her tortillas, "but we'll see."

Fausto walked back outside with a buttered tortilla. He knew his mother was right. His father was a
40 warehouseman at Berven Rugs, where he made good money but not enough to buy everything his children wanted. Fausto decided to mow lawns to earn money, and was pushing the mower down the street before he realized it was winter and no one would hire him. He returned the mower and picked up a rake. He hopped onto his sister's bike (his had two flat tires) and rode north to the nicer section of Fresno in search of work. He went door-to-door, but after three hours he managed to get only one job, and not to rake leaves. He was
50 asked to hurry down to the store to buy a loaf of bread, for which he received a grimy, dirt-caked quarter.

THINK IT THROUGH
Whom does Fausto ask for a guitar? What is the result?

FOCUS
Read to find out how a dog gives Fausto a new idea.

He also got an orange, which he ate sitting at the curb. While he was eating, a dog walked up and sniffed his leg. Fausto pushed him away and threw an orange peel skyward. The dog caught it and ate it in one gulp. The

dog looked at Fausto and wagged his tail for more.
Fausto tossed him a slice of orange, and the dog
60 snapped it up and licked his lips.

"How come you like oranges, dog?"

The dog blinked a pair of sad eyes and whined.

"What's the matter? Cat got your tongue?" Fausto
laughed at his joke and offered the dog another slice.

At that moment a dim light came on inside Fausto's
head. He saw that it was sort of a fancy dog, a terrier
or something, with dog tags and a shiny collar. And it
looked well fed and healthy. In his neighborhood, the
dogs were never licensed, and if they got sick they
70 were placed near the water heater until they got well.

This dog looked like he belonged to rich people.
Fausto cleaned his juice-sticky hands on his pants and
got to his feet. The light in his head grew brighter. It
just might work. He called the dog,
patted its muscular back, and bent down
to check the license.

"Great," he said. "There's an address."

REREAD
What do you
think Fausto
plans to do?

The dog's name was Roger,
which struck Fausto as weird
80 because he'd never heard of
a dog with a human name.
Dogs should have names
like Bomber, Freckles,
Queenie, Killer, and
Zero.

Fausto planned to take
the dog home and collect
a reward. He would say
he had found Roger
90 near the freeway.
That would

scare the daylights out of the owners, who would be so happy that they would probably give him a reward. He felt bad about lying, but the dog *was* loose. And it might even really be lost, because the address was six blocks away.

THINK IT THROUGH

What does Fausto decide to do? How does he seem to feel about his plan?

FOCUS

Read to find out what happens when Fausto meets Roger's owners.

Fausto stashed the rake and his sister's bike behind a bush, and, tossing an orange peel every time Roger became distracted, walked the
100 dog to his house. He hesitated on the porch until Roger began to scratch the door with a muddy paw. Fausto had come this far, so he figured he might as well go through with it. He knocked softly. When no one answered, he rang the doorbell. A man in a silky bathrobe and slippers opened the door and seemed confused by the sight of his dog and the boy.

> **distracted**
> (dĭ străk′ tĭd)
> *adj.* not paying attention

"Sir," Fausto said, gripping Roger by the collar. "I found your dog by the freeway. His dog license says
110 he lives here." Fausto looked down at the dog, then up to the man. "He does, doesn't he?"

The man stared at Fausto a long time before saying in a pleasant voice, "That's right." He pulled his robe tighter around him because of the cold and asked Fausto to come in. "So he was by the freeway?"

"Uh-huh."

"You bad, snoopy dog," said the man, wagging his finger. "You probably knocked over some trash cans, too, didn't you?"

120 Fausto didn't say anything. He looked around, amazed by this house with its shiny furniture and a television as large as the front window at home. Warm bread smells filled the air and music full of soft tinkling floated in from another room.

"Helen," the man called to the kitchen. "We have a visitor." His wife came into the living room wiping her hands on a dish towel and smiling. "And who have we here?" she asked in one of the softest voices 130 Fausto had ever heard.

REREAD

How do the husband and wife greet Fausto?

"This young man said he found Roger near the freeway."

Fausto repeated his story to her while staring at a perpetual clock with a bell-shaped glass, the kind his aunt got when she celebrated her twenty-fifth anniversary. The lady frowned and said, wagging a finger at Roger, "Oh, you're a bad boy."

"It was very nice of you to bring Roger home," the 140 man said. "Where do you live?"

perpetual clock
(pər pĕch' ōō əl klŏk')
clock that runs without stopping

"By that vacant lot on Olive," he said. "You know, by Brownie's Flower Place."

The wife looked at her husband, then Fausto. Her eyes twinkled triangles of light as she said, "Well, young man, you're probably hungry. How about a turnover?"

"What do I have to turn over?" Fausto asked, thinking she was talking about yard work or something like turning trays of dried raisins.

turnover
(tûrn' ō' vər)
n. fruit-filled pastry

150　"No, no, dear, it's a pastry." She took him by the elbow and guided him to a kitchen that sparkled with copper pans and bright yellow wallpaper. She guided him to the kitchen table and gave him a tall glass of milk and something that looked like an empanada. Steamy waves of heat escaped when he tore it in two. He ate with both eyes on the man and woman who stood arm-in-arm smiling at him. They were strange, he thought. But nice.

> **empanada**
> (ĕm' pä nä' dä)
> meat-filled
> Mexican pastry

160　"That was good," he said after he finished the turnover. "Did you make it, ma'am?"

"Yes, I did. Would you like another?"

"No, thank you. I have to go home now."

As Fausto walked to the door, the man opened his wallet and took out a bill. "This is for you," he said. "Roger is special to us, almost like a son."

Fausto looked at the bill and knew he was in trouble. Not with these nice folks or with his parents but with himself. How could he have been so
170　deceitful? The dog wasn't lost. It was just having a fun Saturday walking around.

> **deceitful**
> (dĭ sēt' fəl)
> *adj.* full of lies

"I can't take that."

"You have to. You deserve it, believe me," the man said.

"No, I don't."

"Now don't be silly," said the lady. She took the bill from her
180　husband and stuffed it into Fausto's shirt pocket. "You're a lovely child. Your

parents are lucky to have you. Be good. And come see us again, please."

THINK IT THROUGH
How does Fausto react to Roger's owners?

FOCUS
Read to see how the reward makes Fausto feel.

Fausto went out, and the lady closed the door. Fausto clutched the bill through his shirt pocket. He felt like ringing the doorbell and begging them to please take the money back, but he knew they would
190 refuse. He hurried away, and at the end of the block, pulled the bill from his shirt pocket: it was a crisp twenty-dollar bill.

"Oh, man, I shouldn't have lied," he said under his breath as he started up the street like a zombie . He wanted to run to church for Saturday confession, but it was past four-thirty, when confession stopped.

> **zombie**
> (zŏm′ bē)
> one who is almost lifeless

He returned to the bush where he had hidden the rake and his sister's bike and rode home
200 slowly, not daring to touch the money in his pocket. At home, in the privacy of his room, he examined the twenty-dollar bill. He had never had so much money. It was probably enough to buy a secondhand guitar. But he felt bad, like the time he stole a dollar from the secret fold inside his older brother's wallet.

> **secondhand**
> (sĕk′ ənd hănd′)
> *adj.* used; not new

Fausto went outside and sat on the fence. "Yeah," he said. "I can probably get a guitar for twenty. Maybe at a yard sale—things are cheaper."
210 His mother called him to dinner.

The next day he dressed for church without anyone telling him. He was going to go to eight o'clock mass.

"I'm going to church, Mom," he said. His mother was in the kitchen cooking *papas* and *chorizo con huevos*. A pile of tortillas lay warm under a dishtowel.

> *papas*
> (pä′ päs)
> potatoes

> *chorizo con huevos*
> (chô rē′ zô kôn wä′ vôs)
> Mexican dish of sausage and eggs

"Oh, I'm so proud of you, Son." She beamed, turning over the crackling *papas*.

His older brother, Lawrence, who was at the
220 table reading the funnies, mimicked, "Oh, I'm so proud of you, my son," under his breath.

At Saint Theresa's he sat near the front. When Father Jerry began by saying that we are all sinners, Fausto thought he looked right at him. Could he know? Fausto fidgeted with guilt. No, he thought. I only did it yesterday.

Fausto knelt, prayed, and sang. But he couldn't forget the man and the lady, whose names he didn't even know, and the *empanada* they had given him. It
230 had a strange name but tasted really good. He wondered how they got rich. And how that dome clock worked. He had asked his mother once how his aunt's clock worked. She said it just worked, the way the refrigerator works. It just did.

Fausto caught his mind wandering and tried to concentrate on his sins. He said a Hail Mary and sang, and when the wicker basket came his way, he stuck a hand reluctantly in his pocket and pulled out the twenty-dollar bill. He ironed it between his palms,
240 and dropped it into the basket. The grown-ups stared. Here was a kid dropping twenty dollars in the basket while they gave just three or four dollars.

THINK IT THROUGH
What does Fausto do with the money? Why?

FOCUS _____

Is Fausto's dream of a guitar over? Read on to see what happens.

There would be a second collection for Saint Vincent de Paul, the lector announced. The wicker baskets again floated in the pews, and this time the adults around him, given a second chance to show their charity, dug deep into their wallets and purses and dropped in fives and tens. This time Fausto tossed in the grimy quarter.

250   Fausto felt better after church. He went home and played football in the front yard with his brother and some neighbor kids. He felt cleared of wrongdoing and was so happy that he played one of his best games of football ever. On one play, he tore his good pants, which he knew he shouldn't have been wearing. For a second, while he examined the hole, he wished he hadn't given the twenty dollars away.

    Man, I coulda bought me some Levi's, he thought. He pictured his twenty dollars being spent to buy
260 church candles. He pictured a priest buying an armful of flowers with *his* money.

    Fausto had to forget about getting a guitar. He spent the next day playing soccer in his good pants, which were now his old pants. But that night during dinner, his mother said she remembered seeing an old bass guitarron the last time she cleaned out her father's garage.

guitarron
(gē tä rôn')
Mexican guitar

36

"It's a little dusty," his mom said, serving his
favorite enchiladas, "But I think it works. Grandpa
270 says it works."

Fausto's ears perked up. That was the same kind the
guy in Los Lobos played. Instead of asking for the
guitar, he waited for his mother to offer it to him. And
she did, while gathering the dishes from the table.

"No, Mom, I'll do it," he said, hugging her. "I'll do
the dishes forever if you want."

It was the happiest day of his life. No, it was the
second-happiest day of his life. The happiest was
when his grandfather Lupe placed the guitarron,
280 which was nearly as huge as a washtub, in his arms.
Fausto ran a thumb down the strings, which vibrated
in his throat and chest. It sounded beautiful, deep and
eerie. A pumpkin smile widened on his face.

"OK, *hijo*, now you put your fingers like
this," said his grandfather, smelling of
tobacco and aftershave. He took Fausto's
fingers and placed them on the strings.
Fausto strummed a chord on the guitarron, and the
bass resounded in their chests.

> **hijo**
> (ē' hô)
> son

290 The guitarron was more complicated than Fausto
imagined. But he was confident that after a few more
lessons he could start a band that would someday play
on "American Bandstand" for the dancing crowds.

THINK IT THROUGH

1. How does Fausto get a guitar?
2. Do you think Fausto was right to give the money to the church? Why or why not?
3. How do you think Fausto is feeling when he offers to wash the dishes forever? Explain.

Courage
Counts

Nonfiction

Once someone ran from slavery when there was no clear way out. Once a woman became the first female chief of her tribe. Once someone took chances so that others could have better lives. What did these people have in common? Courage.

Nonfiction is writing about real people, places, and events.

- **Biography:** This is an account of a person's life written by another person.

- **True Account:** This is a real-life incident in someone's life that reads like a story.

A SLAVE

BY VIRGINIA HAMILTON

Into Bondage (1936), Aaron Douglas. Oil on canvas 60 3/8" x 60 1/2". In the collection of the Corcoran Gallery of Art, Washington, DC. Museum Purchase and partial gift from Thurlow Evans Tibbs. The Evans-Tibbs Collection.

Detail of *Into Bondage* (1936), Aaron Douglas.

SLAVES HAD
HEARD OF
SECRET PLACES
ALONG THE WAY
TO FREEDOM.
DISCOVER HOW
ONE MAN FINDS
HIS WAY TO THE
UNDERGROUND
RAILROAD.

Connect to Your Life

What do you know about slavery in America's past? What did freedom mean to slaves? Have a partner make a word web for either the word *slavery* or *freedom*. Make and fill in your own web for the other word. Then compare and contrast your webs.

Key to the True Account

"The Underground Railroad" got its name because of the actions of a runaway slave. His name was Tice Davids. As you read his true story, notice that in some parts, the type is italic. Think of these words as "voices" from the past that Tice Davids is remembering.

Vocabulary Preview

Words to Know

plantation	settlement
revived	rails

Tice Davids has reached a life-changing moment. Read about the action he takes.

The underground road was named for the deed of an actual man born a slave who one day ran away from slavery. It became the name given to all the secret trails that led north, and to the system of human helpers against slavery—black, white, and red—who braved prison and even death to lead the running-aways to freedom.

running-aways
runaway slaves

Tice Davids inspired the first use of the term "underground road." On a day in 1831

10 that seemed ordinary, full of pain and hard work for him, Davids discovered that he had changed. He wondered how it had happened that on this day he could not bear to be a slave a moment longer.

It was time for him to make his way north. And so he ran.

Tice knew where he was going. There were Friends across the Ohio River, waiting. North would be somewhere there, and on and on. Word of that had come to

Friends
Quakers, members of a religious group that was against slavery

20 him on the plantation. Whispers about liberty had made their way through the servants' quarters and on to the fields. They spread on the wind down to the riverbank. Tice had an idea of what it was to be free. It meant that he might rest without fear covering him like a blanket as he slept. It meant that nobody could buy or sell him.

plantation
(plăn tā′ shən)
n. large farm in the South where workers raised crops

Not all those who were slaves had the daring to escape. It wasn't that Tice was without fear. But, like

30 others before him, given the chance, he'd take it.

There were those, black and free, who combed the riverbank, looking to help the running-aways. And there were certain Presbyterian ministers from the South who had formed a new church and had settled in the counties of southern Ohio. They were known to be friends of slaves. Like ever-present eagles with fierce, keen eyes, they too watched the great river for the running-aways.

Trusted to be a good servant, Tice had taken his life into his own hands and had run. And now he hurried, running.

Detail of *Into Bondage* (1936), Aaron Douglas.

THINK IT THROUGH

Where is Tice going? Who did he think might help him?

FOCUS

Tice's journey has begun. Find out how Tice deals with the problems he faces.

"*Look for the lantern!*" That had been the urgent message passed along the slave quarters for those who would run at night.

"*Listen for the bell!*" Word was that the lone, distant sound of a bell clanging could be heard from across the wide river—when the wind was right. Other

times, the bell seemed to clang up and down the shore. The river might be covered in fog. And hidden deep in the mist on the shore, a running-away could clearly
60 hear the bell. He could follow its ringing all the way over and to a safe house .

safe house
secret place used to hide escaped slaves

Tice Davids would have to find a way across the great water if he was ever to be free. With luck he might find a usable boat or raft along the shore. What would he do if there was nothing to ride across on?

Capture for him was unthinkable, and he kept on running.

"Heard tell that on the other side, a slave is no
70 *longer such. They say that on the other side of the wide water, a slave is a free man."*

That was the word and the truth that all Kentucky slaves believed. He kept that in mind as he ran. He looked back, knowing what he would see. There were the planter and his
80 men, coming after him. The slave owner. Some called him master; Tice wouldn't when he could avoid it.

Friends, waiting across the river, was the word he could count on. If only he could get to the Friends!

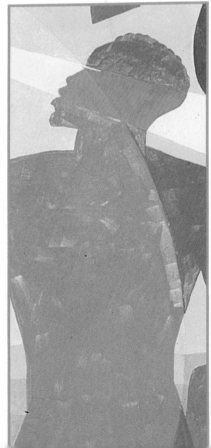

Detail of *Into Bondage* (1936), Aaron Douglas.

He had been running for some time. Almost as
90　though he were dreaming, he lifted one leg and then the
other. Whatever had possessed him to try to break out?

Now he was at the Kentucky shore and it was
empty. There was no boat to row, no raft to pole. The
distant Ohio shore seemed farther than far. There was
nothing for it but to swim.

Tice waded into the water, tired out before he
began. The cold wet of the river shocked
him, revived him. He knew to calm himself
down and soon got his mind in hand. He
100　began moving his arms, swimming in clean,
long strokes.

revived
(rĭ vīvd′)
v. refreshed; past
tense of *revive*

About halfway across, Tice thought he
heard a bell. The sound gave him
strength and he swam gamely on.

REREAD
How does Tice
show courage in
crossing the
river?

It took the slave owner time to locate a
skiff, but a small boat was found at last. He and his
men shoved off and gave chase. The slave owner
never let his slave out of his sight. Even when Tice
staggered from the water onto the Ohio shore, the
110　owner glared through the mist and pinpointed the
dark, exhausted figure.

"Think we have him now," he said. He blinked to
get the wet from his eyes. It was one blink too many.
Tice Davids was gone. Disappeared!

"It's not believable," the owner said. "I saw him
before my eyes and now he's gone. Vanished! It's not
possible, but there it is."

THINK IT THROUGH
What does Tice do that is so surprising to the slave owner?

> What happens to Tice? Read to find out how the search ends.

The slave owner searched the shore every which way. He looked into ditches. He and his men beat 120 the bushes and crept into caves and gazed up into trees. They poked the haystacks in the fields. They talked to people in the slavery-hating settlement at Ripley, Ohio, and they had their suspicions. But not one of the townsfolk would admit to having seen anybody running away. The Kentucky slave owner never again saw Tice Davids.

settlement
(sĕt′ l mənt)
n. small community

"Well, I'm going home," he said finally. He and his men crossed the river again and returned to Kentucky. 130 "Only one way to look at it," he told everyone at home, shaking his head in disbelief. "Tice must've gone on an underground road!"

Tice Davids made his way north through all of Ohio, all the way to Sandusky, on Lake Erie. There, at last, he settled, a free man—and the first to travel the underground road.

Later, the underground road took on an inspiring new name in honor of the amazing steam trains on parallel rails then coming into 140 their own in America: *the Underground Railroad!*

rails
(rālz)
n. two steel bars that form train tracks

Those who guided the running-aways along the highly secret system of the Underground Railroad had the cleverness to call themselves "conductors," the name used on the steam railway trains. The safe houses and secret hiding places known to the conductors were called "stations" and "depots," after railway stations and

railway depots. Eventually, Tice Davids became a
150 conductor on the Underground Railroad, helping
other running-aways escape.

THINK IT THROUGH

1. Why was Tice Davids able to escape? Use evidence
   from the selection to support your answer.
2. When Tice reached freedom, he could have left
   danger behind. Why do you think he chose to
   become a conductor on the Underground Railroad?
3. What advice would Tice have given to a slave who
   had not yet decided to run?

Detail of *Into Bondage* (1936),
Aaron Douglas.

Wilma Mankiller

by Linda Lowery

An old saying states, "You can't go home again." Wilma Mankiller proved the saying wrong. She returned to her home and became its chief.

Connect to Your Life

Recall the last time you found yourself in a strange place. How long did it take you to get used to it? Make a list of what made the place different. With a partner, talk about the kinds of adjustments you had to make.

Key to the Biography

This biography describes major happenings in the life of Wilma Mankiller. She belongs to the Cherokee Nation of Oklahoma. The Cherokee once lived happily in the southeastern sections of the country. Then came the winter of 1838–1839. U.S. soldiers forced more than 17,000 Cherokee people to leave their homeland. This event became known as the Trail of Tears. As you read, pay close attention to the details about this event. Although Wilma wasn't born until more than a century later, notice the effects the event has on her life.

Vocabulary Preview

Words to Know

coyotes	council
bugles	swirling

 Reading Coach CD-ROM selection

Young Wilma Mankiller finds herself in a new place. Read to find out how the differences there affect her.

San Francisco, 1956

Wilma Mankiller dove under the covers. It was warm and safe under the handmade quilt. Outside, screams of wild animals echoed off the walls. This was Wilma's first night in San Francisco, California, and she was afraid.

She knew the sound of wolves. The sound outside was not wolves. She knew the sound of coyotes. It was not coyotes.

> **coyotes**
> (kī ō′ tēz)
> *n.* small animals that are similar to wolves

10 When she woke up the next morning, still yawning from too little sleep, Wilma found out what had made the animal screams. It was something she had never heard back home in Oklahoma. It was the sound of police sirens.

San Francisco was full of things Wilma had never seen or heard of before. People disappeared from her hallway in boxes called elevators.

A view of the city of San Francisco

A view of the Oklahoma plains

All night long, flashy lights blinked on and off outside her window. Everything seemed strange and frightening, so different from home.

In her mind, Wilma traveled back to her grandfather's land on Mankiller Flats, in Oklahoma. Her family was happy there, living close to other Cherokee families. They had springwater to drink, woods full of deer and foxes, and a home her father had built.

But Wilma's father, Charley Mankiller, often worried about money. Money never went very far when there were nine children to raise. He wanted to give them the best schools, the best home, the best life he could.

When Wilma was ten, the United States government came up with a plan for Indian families. They promised houses and jobs to families who would move to cities. At night, in their house on Mankiller Flats, Wilma and her brothers and sisters pressed their ears against the bedroom door, listening. Their parents talked about moving. They talked about cities

like Chicago, New York, and Detroit. Would the
40 schools be better in the city? Would life there be
happier for their children?

Moving sounded awful to Wilma. Her parents,
however, decided it was a good idea. In October
1956, the family moved away from Mankiller Flats.

As they left, Wilma watched very hard out the car
window. She wanted to remember everything about
the home she loved: the colors of the birds, the shapes
of the trees, the sounds of the animals.

THINK IT THROUGH
Why is moving to San Francisco such a major change for
Wilma?

FOCUS
Read to discover what helps Wilma get used to her new
surroundings.

In her new home, colors and shapes and sounds
50 were scary—and mean too. When Wilma's new
teacher called her name in school, the class laughed.
To Cherokees, "Mankiller" was a special title, given
to someone who protected the tribe. To the kids in
school, it was a joke. They teased her about how she
talked. They thought she dressed strangely.

When Wilma walked home from school,
she saw signs in shop windows. They
said, "NO DOGS, NO INDIANS."
Wilma felt as if she had moved to the far
60 side of the moon.

REREAD
What does a sign
like this say
about some
people in
Wilma's new
city?

To comfort herself, Wilma thought about home: the
hawks soaring in the sky, the whispers of the wind in
the treetops.

She also thought of other Cherokees who had struggled through hard times. About 150 years ago, many Cherokee people were forced to move far from home. It was a terrible journey. It is called the Trail of Tears. Wilma remembered the story the way she had heard it many times from her father and her relatives.

The Trail of Tears, 1838

70 Years ago, Wilma's family told her, no Cherokees lived in Oklahoma. Their home was the southeast. How they loved that land! Soft rain fell on the hills. Apples, plums, and peaches grew on the trees.

But white settlers wanted the green land of the southeast. President Andrew Jackson decided that white settlers were more important than the Indians who lived there. In 1830, the president signed the Indian Removal Act.

It was a law. It said that all Cherokees had to leave
80 Georgia and Alabama, North Carolina and South

Cherokee Movement to Oklahoma, 1838–1840

Carolina, Tennessee and Virginia. The Cherokees refused. They loved their home.

So, in 1838, President Van Buren sent in the army. Soldiers dragged Cherokees from their log cabins. Soldiers loaded Cherokees onto wagons. Soldiers shot Cherokees who tried to get away.

The bugles sounded. The wagons began rolling away. Children stood up and waved good-bye to their mountain homes. The
90 Cherokees traveled 1,200 miles west, through rain, sleet, and snow. When wagons broke down, some people had to walk.

bugles
(by͞oo′ gəlz)   *n.* horns that are shorter than a trumpet

In the next two years, about 17,000 Cherokees were sent west. Four thousand died on the way. The army left the Cherokees on land that later became Oklahoma. There were no houses, no churches, and no schools.

Many mothers and fathers, children and grandparents, were sick from the
100 trip. They had nothing left but the spirit within them. Because of that spirit, they survived.

REREAD
How do you think this move affected the people who lived through it?

Wilma had always kept the story of the Trail of Tears in her heart. She was the great-great-great-granddaughter of the people who had cried on that trail. In San Francisco, Wilma cried too. There, she felt lucky about only one thing. The Cherokee people who had been shipped to Oklahoma never got to go back home. Wilma knew that one day, she would go
110 home again.

THINK IT THROUGH
How does Wilma compare her move to the Trail of Tears?

> Wilma does return to Mankiller Flats. Read to see what new challenges she finds there.

Home Again in Oklahoma, 1977

It took her over twenty years, but Wilma did go home. By then, in 1977, she had two daughters, Gina and Felicia. She packed them up and moved back to Mankiller Flats.

It felt wonderful to be near Cherokee friends again. She was happy to watch the robins and bluebirds from her porch. She heard the coyotes howl in the moonlight, and she wasn't afraid.

Wilma soon got a job with the Cherokee Nation.
120 Cherokees are people of two nations: the United States and the Cherokee Nation. The government in Washington, D.C., makes all the big decisions in the United States. The government in Tahlequah, Oklahoma, makes all the big decisions in the Western Cherokee Nation.

Wilma's job was to visit Cherokee people all over eastern Oklahoma. Many were poor. They had no lights in their houses and no water. Wilma helped them make their homes safer and better. One day in
130 1983, Wilma was on her way to work. She drove down a dirt road, thinking. The chief of the Cherokee Nation had offered her a job yesterday. He wanted her to be his assistant and run for deputy chief. What an honor to be asked! This was the second highest job in the Cherokee Nation.

> **honor**
> (ŏn′ ər)
> sign of great respect

But Wilma was a quiet person. To become deputy chief, she would have to win an election. She did not like talking to crowds. She didn't
140 want to be on television. "No," she had told the

chief. Chief Swimmer had been disappointed. "Think about it," he said. Now, as she drove along, she wondered if she had made the right decision.

Suddenly, she saw something through the oak trees. She stopped her station wagon and stared out the window. There sat an old, broken-down bus. Curtains hung in the windows. Laundry sagged on the line. Was this really someone's home?

REREAD

Try to picture this scene in your mind. What kind of life do you think the people who live here lead?

150   Wilma got out of her car and walked closer. She could see that a family lived inside.

The bus had no roof. What happens when it rains? she wondered.

Deep inside her, something tugged at Wilma. When she was a girl, the United States government had promised a better life for Indians in San Francisco. They broke their promise. If Wilma were deputy chief, she would have power to help change the lives of Cherokee people. She knew she would keep her
160   promises.

Stones flew as Wilma drove to Chief Swimmer's house. She had something to tell him. Her time to be a leader had come. She would run for deputy chief.

THINK IT THROUGH
Why doesn't Wilma want the job of deputy chief? What changes her mind?

FOCUS ────────────────────────────────
New problems come from an unexpected place. Read to find out how Wilma tries to solve them.

Wilma got right to work. She swallowed her shyness and talked to crowds of people. She asked them to vote for her. The Cherokee people had always

Cherokee dancers at Chehaw National Indian Festival

been grateful for Wilma's work. They had given her
warm welcomes when she visited.

170 But suddenly people were unfriendly, even angry.
Something was very wrong. Wilma could feel it. Soon
the truth came out. People were talking behind
Wilma's back.

"We Cherokees never had a woman as deputy
chief," they said. "It's a job for a man," they said.
Wilma was shocked. What a strange idea! In history,
Cherokee women had always been treated the same as
men.

Women were medicine healers. Women
were warriors. Women were council
180 members. How could anyone say only men
make good leaders? Had the Cherokees
picked up this idea from white people?
Wilma thought so.

council
(koun' səl)
n. body of
people elected to
plan, discuss, or
give advice

When white settlers came to America,
they brought new ideas with them. Some of their
ideas were good. Some were not. One idea was that
men were more important than women. Wilma set
out to prove that this idea was wrong. In her
speeches, she never talked about being a woman. She
190 only talked about her hopes and dreams for the
Cherokee people. She promised to get money for
houses, hospitals, and children's centers. She promised
to help her people make their towns better.

The trouble did not stop. Neither did Wilma.
Someone slashed the tires on Wilma's car. Strangers
shouted mean words on the phone. Someone
threatened to kill her. Everything around
her was swirling like a whirlwind. But
inside, Wilma kept still. She reached deep
200 down for strength. Long ago, her people
had survived the Trail of Tears. When she
was young, Wilma had survived San Francisco. Wilma
and the people who cried on the trail had survived
because they knew the
Cherokee Way.

swirling
(swûr' lĭng)
v. moving with a
twisting motion

You do not think about
the bad things. You think
about the good. Even if you
feel you will never make it,
210 you move ahead. It is called
"being of good mind." If
she practiced the Cherokee
Way, Wilma knew she
could survive—and win—
this election. Finally, the
Cherokee people went to

Wilma Mankiller standing before the
seal of the Cherokee Nation

the polls to vote. They voted for Chief Swimmer and Wilma Mankiller. On August 14, 1983, Wilma became the first Cherokee woman ever to be deputy chief. But that was only the beginning.

When Chief Swimmer was given a job in Washington, D.C., Wilma became chief.

It was 1985 when Wilma sat down at the chief's desk for the first time. "You look very natural sitting there," someone said. People hugged Wilma. They cried tears of happiness for her.

Wilma knew her job as chief would be hard work. But she was not frightened. She felt as if all the Cherokee people who had walked the Trail of Tears were with her. Their strength was her strength, just as it had been when she was a girl in San Francisco. Wilma had come home to Oklahoma. Now she was Chief Mankiller, the first woman chief in Cherokee history.

polls
(pōlz)
places where votes are cast

THINK IT THROUGH

1. Before she got the job, Wilma Mankiller faced both inner and outer conflicts, or problems. List both the inner and outer problems she overcame.
2. Review the different hardships Wilma Mankiller faced. Why did she succeed?
3. What qualities helped Wilma become a good leader? Use details from the text to support your choices.

Cesar Chavez:

Civil-Rights Champion

by Nancy Lobb

Connect to Your Life

Think of an example of unfair treatment in the world today. If you could, how would you solve that problem? What small step could you take in the near future? Discuss your responses with a classmate.

Key to the Biography

This selection is about a famous leader. Chavez organized Mexican-American farmworkers to fight for more rights. You'll come across some names of a few organizations. They will usually be shown in a shorter form of capital letters. You will see the names of other famous leaders. As you read, recall what you may know about their lives and work.

Vocabulary Preview

Words to Know

nonviolent	fasts
union	tactics
motto	

How can the powerless become powerful? Cesar Chavez spent his life finding the answers.

A saint. A hero. The Mexican-American Dr. Martin Luther King, Jr. All these things have been said about Cesar Chavez.

Chavez was a civil-rights leader. He led *La Causa,* the farmworkers' fight for their rights. Chavez won great gains for farmworkers.

Cesar Chavez was born in 1927 near Yuma, Arizona. In 1938 his family could not pay their taxes. So, they lost their farm. With many others, they left

10 for California, where they had heard there was work.

The Chavez family became migrant workers. They traveled from farm to farm, picking crops. They lived in labor camps. Home might be a tent, or it might be a one-room shack. For sure there would be no running water and no bathroom.

The life of the migrant workers was hard. Most of the work was "stoop labor." That meant the pickers had to bend over all day to pick the crops. They were paid very little.

20 Some farmers even cheated the workers out of the little they earned. The workers could not speak English. So there was little they could do to fight back. They also feared being sent back to Mexico. Life there was even harder.

The Chavez children went to school when they could. Chavez later said he went to over sixty-five grade schools "for a day, a week or a few months." Chavez finished eighth grade. This was far more education than most migrant children got.

30 But Chavez also taught himself. He was always reading. He loved the works of Mahatma Gandhi and

Dr. Martin Luther King, Jr. From these men he learned the idea of nonviolent protest.

> **nonviolent**
> (nŏn vī′ ə lənt)
> *adj.* not using force as a way of getting results

THINK IT THROUGH

How was Cesar like the other children of migrant workers? How was he different?

FOCUS

As a young man, Cesar began to tackle the problems of farmworkers. Learn how he first attracted attention.

During World War II, Chavez served in the Navy. When he returned, he married his girlfriend, Helen. They began working on a farm near San Jose with seven other family members. Later Chavez figured out that the nine workers put together were making twenty-three cents an hour!

40 Chavez joined the Community Service Organization (CSO). This group was working to help Mexican Americans better themselves.

Chavez worked in the fields by day. At night he worked to get Mexican Americans to register to vote. In just two months he signed up 4,000 workers.

The farm owners found out what Chavez was doing. They were afraid he would make trouble. So they fired him. Chavez began working full time for the CSO. He held meetings 50 to talk with workers. More workers joined the CSO.

> **REREAD**
> Find two events that led to changes in Cesar's life.

Chavez worked ten years for the CSO. Then in 1962 he left the group. Chavez wanted to form a farmworkers union. The CSO did not. So Chavez went out on his own.

> **union**
> (yōōn′ yən)
> *n.* organized group of workers

Chavez, his wife, and eight children moved to
Delano, California. Using their life savings of $1,200,
they formed the National Farm Workers
60 Association (NFWA). This group later
became the United Farm Workers
(UFW).

Workers were glad to sign up. Their
motto was the phrase "¡Sí, se puede!"
("Yes, it can be done!") This was the
beginning of Chavez's life work.

> **motto**
> (mŏt′ ō)
> *n.* sentence that
> expresses the
> group's goals

> **REREAD**
> Do you think this
> is a good motto?
> Explain.

Only three years later, the NFWA gained
the world's attention. It joined a strike, or *huelga,*
against grape growers in the Delano area. It was this
70 huelga that brought fame to Chavez.

Strikes, fasts , and marches. With these
tools, Chavez proved that farmworkers had
power. Together they could bargain with
farmers for better wages and working
conditions.

> **fasts**
> (făsts)
> *n.* periods of
> time without
> food

THINK IT THROUGH
Why do you think the farmworkers followed Cesar?

FOCUS
Read to find out what kind of leader Cesar became.

It all began when Filipino grape pickers struck for
higher wages. The NFWA joined in. The strike was to
go on for five years.

The story of Chavez and the migrant workers soon
80 reached the ears of all America. Newspapers and TV
spread the story of *La Causa.* In 1966 ten thousand
people from all over the United States marched on the

Cesar Chavez speaks from the steps of the California Capitol in Sacramento.

state capital in Sacramento. Still the grape growers would not give in.

Chavez knew the public supported the farmworkers. So he announced a boycott of California grapes. This meant that no one would buy grapes unless farmers met some of the workers' demands.

Chavez sent workers to different cities all around the United States. They asked store owners not to sell grapes. They asked the public not to buy grapes. Many truck drivers agreed not to haul grapes. The boycott spread. Many grape growers went out of business. But still the strike went on.

REREAD
Why do you think Cesar tried a boycott?

After a few years, some of the strikers began to get tired. They wanted to use more violent methods of getting what they wanted. Riots, dynamite, and shooting were suggested. But Chavez insisted on using only nonviolent tactics. To bring attention to this point, he began a twenty-five-day hunger strike.

tactics
(tăk′ tĭks)
n. methods used to get results

Cesar Chavez: Civil-Rights Champion **65**

Chavez won the support of civil rights groups and churches. Many famous Americans joined *La Causa*. Robert Kennedy was a close friend of Chavez. Dr. Martin Luther King, Jr., supported Chavez. Union leaders and even the pope supported *La Causa*. Money to help the striking workers came too. At last, the grape growers gave in. After five years, the grape
110 boycott was over. So was the strike. Chavez and the farmworkers had won.

THINK IT THROUGH
Why was Cesar's firm position on nonviolence a wise choice in this strike?

FOCUS
Cesar's work continued. Read to find out what other sacrifices he made.

Over the next twenty years, *La Causa* went on. Chavez kept working to help the farmworkers. He demanded an end to the use of dangerous pesticides on crops. He won rest periods for pickers. And the hated short hoe was banned.

> **pesticides**
> (pĕs′ tĭ sīdz′)
> chemicals used
> to kill insects

In the 1970's Chavez led a lettuce boycott and another grape boycott. In a 1972 protest
120 over right-to-work laws he went on a twenty-four-day fast. In 1988 he went on a thirty-six-day fast to protest the use of pesticides in fields. This fast caused much damage to his kidneys.

In 1993 Chavez died at the age of sixty-six. Doctors said his death was caused by fasting and his life of hardship.

Cesar Chavez had devoted his life to *La Causa*. All his life he chose to live penniless. He never owned a

A student at a holiday celebration holds a sign that reads "Long Live Cesar!"

house or a car. He never took enough money to live
130 on, earning only $6,000 his last year. The rest of the
money he raised he poured back into the UFW.
Although his health was failing in his later years, he
never quit working for the union.

Cesar Chavez was one of the truly heroic figures of
the twentieth century. He gave dignity
and hope not only to farmworkers, but
to all Mexican Americans. Cesar Chavez
was a giant in the civil-rights movement
of the United States.

> **REREAD**
> Notice that the
> writer expresses
> opinions about
> Chavez at the
> end.

THINK IT THROUGH

1. What sacrifices did Cesar make for the cause of the farmworkers?
2. What did Cesar achieve for the workers? What methods did he use to achieve them?
3. The author says Cesar Chavez was one of the truly heroic figures. Has she proved her statement? How?

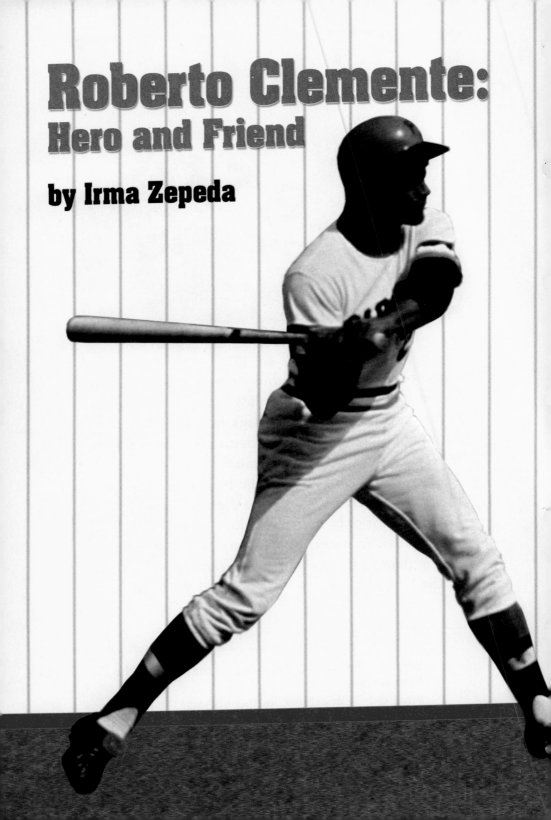

Roberto Clemente:
Hero and Friend

by Irma Zepeda

What makes a hero? Perhaps it is courage and the desire to help others. Find out about the life of a hero.

Connect to Your Life

Who are your heroes? What stories about heroes have your parents shared? With a partner, make a list of heroes. Talk about their qualities and actions.

Key to the Biography

This true account of Clemente's life includes terms and figures about baseball. If necessary, reread those sections to make sure you understand them. Roberto Clemente started out on a team in the *minor leagues* of baseball. There, players develop their skills. If their abilities impress others, they move up to the *major leagues.*

Vocabulary Preview

Words to Know

determined   prejudice
prospects   potential

 Reading Coach CD-ROM selection

Anytime you have an opportunity to make things better and you don't, then you are wasting your time on this Earth.

—Roberto Clemente

FOCUS

Learn about the goal Roberto Clemente sets early in his life.

Roberto Clemente was born on August 18, 1934. He was born on the island of Puerto Rico. Roberto's family lived in a small house in the town of Carolina. Like most families there, the Clementes worked hard to earn a living. Roberto's father worked long days cutting sugar cane. In his spare time, he also sold meat and other foods to earn a few extra dollars. To help the family, the Clemente children held odd jobs. Roberto delivered milk for a 10 few pennies a day.

The Clementes could not buy any luxuries—not even a baseball for Roberto. Instead, Roberto and his friends used sticks to practice batting cans. They had no gloves, pads, or even a real bat. They simply loved the game. To Roberto, baseball players were heroes. He dreamed of becoming a great player someday. Roberto was determined to work hard to make his dream come true.

determined
(dĭ tûr′ mĭnd)
adj. not willing to change one's mind

In high school, Roberto joined the baseball team.
20 Roberto was a top runner, but he knew that speed
was not enough. Baseball players needed strong arms
to throw the ball fast and hit it hard. To strengthen
his arms and legs, Roberto joined the track team. He
threw the javelin and ran in races. The javelin is a
light spear with a pointed edge. It is used in distance-
throwing contests. Roberto once threw the javelin 195
feet. For a high school student, that was an amazing
act. Whenever Roberto had a chance, he squeezed a
rubber ball. This would help strengthen his arm
30 muscles. In time, Roberto became one of the best
players on the team.

THINK IT THROUGH
What steps does Roberto take to become a great baseball
player?

FOCUS
Read to find out how Roberto performs in the minor leagues.

One day as Roberto was playing ball, Pedrín Zorilla
watched him closely. Zorilla was the owner of a local
baseball team. He was also a scout for the Brooklyn
Dodgers. A scout is a person who looks for talented
players. Zorilla asked Roberto to join his team. This
was Roberto's first professional contract. He made little
money, but he knew it would be enough to help his
family. There was one problem. Roberto's
40 parents were unhappy with his decision to
become a baseball player. They wanted him

to go to college. After Roberto pleaded with them, they finally gave in.

The next season, the Dodgers held a clinic in San Juan. A clinic is a group session in which baseball prospects are asked to try out. Al Campanis, the chief scout, did not have high hopes for the prospects. He did not think any player would be good enough for
50 the majors.

However, Roberto proved to be different. Campanis watched Roberto fire fast balls at the catcher. Then Campanis had the boys run the 60-yard dash. Roberto's record was 6.4 seconds. The world record was 6.1 seconds. The final test was batting the ball. So far, Roberto was a terrific discovery. Campanis knew he should not build false hope. Roberto had to hit the ball against one of the Dodgers' minor league pitchers. To everyone's surprise, line drives rocketed off
60 Roberto's bat. He was amazing!

Campanis wanted to sign Roberto at once. However, major league rules did not allow a prospect to be signed before he graduated from high school. In 1954, after his high school graduation, Roberto joined the Dodgers' farm team in Montreal, Canada. Farm teams help young players get ready for the major leagues. At the time, scouts from other teams could watch young players. If the scouts wanted, they could sign a
70 contract with a player.

Even though the Dodgers wanted to sign Roberto, there was still some prejudice in the major leagues. Behind the scenes, major league teams avoided having more than four black players. The Dodgers already

prospects
(prŏs' pĕkts')
n. people with possibilities

line drives
hits that move low and fast, usually in a straight line

prejudice
(prĕj' ə dĭs)
n. unfair treatment, usually based on race or religion

had four black players. They did not want to lose Roberto, so they sent him to Montreal.

The Dodgers kept quiet
80 about Roberto. They did not play him often so that scouts would not notice him. However, their plan failed. Scouts from the Pittsburgh Pirates thought Roberto had the potential to become a great player. They quickly signed a contract with him. At the time, Pittsburgh was last in the National League.
90 When Roberto joined the team in 1955, they had lost more than 100 games. The team had placed last for three years in a row. They needed a powerful player like Roberto.

Roberto Clemente in uniform as a Pittsburgh Pirate

potential
(pǝ tĕn′ shǝl)
n. ability

THINK IT THROUGH
What sets Roberto above the rest of the players?

FOCUS ————
Roberto's career as a Pittsburgh Pirate soars. Read to find out what he achieves.

Roberto played hard that first year. As a right fielder, he caught balls in midair to block home runs. Many times he threw his body against walls or fences to catch the ball. Pain mattered little to him.

As a batter, he swung at almost every ball. This is
100 usually the sign of a young, inexperienced player. Most
players learn to control their swing as they gain
experience. At the end of the year, Roberto's batting
average was .255. A batting average of .300 is better
than most. By the end of his second year, Roberto was
batting at .311.

When Roberto was not playing for the Pirates, he
would return to Puerto Rico. While he was there he
played in the Winter Leagues. Most ball players rest
during the off-season. Roberto continued to play no
110 matter how tired he was. He knew that his people
might never see him play in person. He wanted his
fans to enjoy watching him. In 1966, an article in
Sporting News reported, "Every Puerto Rican is a
Roberto Clemente fan."

Clemente catching a ball in midair

Roberto was a hero. His fans knew Roberto had worked to become a professional baseball player. They also knew how much he cared about them.

In 1960 and 1971, Roberto led the Pirates to the World Series. The Pirates won both times, although the odds were against them. Roberto was chosen the MVP (Most Valuable Player) in the 1971 World Series. He batted .414, hit 2 home runs, and had 12 hits and 4 RBIs. On September 30, 1972, Roberto had his 3000th career hit. At the time, only ten men had achieved this goal.

RBIs
runs batted in; a rating of a player's batting ability

THINK IT THROUGH
What are Roberto's achievements as a player?

FOCUS
With all Roberto's success, he was still setting goals. Discover how Roberto wished to help others.

He was finally the baseball player he had dreamed of becoming. But Roberto had one more dream. It was perhaps his most important dream. With money from governments, businesses, and many other people, he had plans to build Ciudad Deportiva (Sports City). He wanted to give the children of Puerto Rico a place where they could learn about sports. Roberto believed that young children could learn the value of hard work through sports. He wanted to give children something that would be rewarding and helpful. But his dream would have to wait.

On December 23, 1972, an earthquake struck Managua, Nicaragua. Roberto had visited Managua the year before. While he was there, Roberto met a

140 young orphan boy, Julio Parrales. The boy had lost both his legs in a car accident. Thanks to Roberto, Julio would soon have a pair of artificial legs.

When Roberto heard the news of the earthquake, he began to worry about Julio. Right away he signed up to help the victims. He collected money, food, clothes, and medicine. Roberto would not rest until he had enough supplies to fill an airplane. He wanted to make sure that the supplies reached the poorest people.

150 On December 31, 1972, Roberto and four others filled an old plane with the supplies. Before takeoff, the plane had engine problems. Roberto's family and friends begged him not to go. But he insisted that he would deliver the supplies himself. Shortly after takeoff, the plane began to lose speed. It crashed into the sea after going only about a mile.

When news of the accident spread, thousands of people searched the sea for days. They found the remains of the pilot, a sock, and a small suitcase that 160 belonged to Roberto. The searchers finally gave up. They believed that Roberto and the others had drowned. Five days after the crash, Manny Sanguillen, Roberto's old friend and teammate, led his own search. To his disappointment, only fish and sharks roamed the sea. Roberto's body was never found. That New Year's Eve, the country lost a hero.

REREAD
All these people searched. How does that show their love for Roberto?

Today, Roberto is remembered as one of the greatest athletes. In 1973, he was the first 170 Hispanic voted into the Hall of Fame. The Hall of Fame is the highest honor a baseball player can receive. Many schools and parks across the United States and in Puerto Rico are named after Roberto

Clemente. In Carolina, Puerto Rico, visitors are greeted with a twelve-foot statue of Roberto as they enter the Roberto Clemente Sports City—his final dream come true.

THINK IT THROUGH

1. Which of Roberto Clemente's goals was reached after his death?
2. Becoming a Baseball Hall of Fame member shows that Roberto was an outstanding player. Find evidence from the selection that shows him as an outstanding human being.
3. Look over the details about Roberto's disappearance. Use the information to make a time line of the events.

TROMBONES AND COLLEGES

by Walter Dean Myers

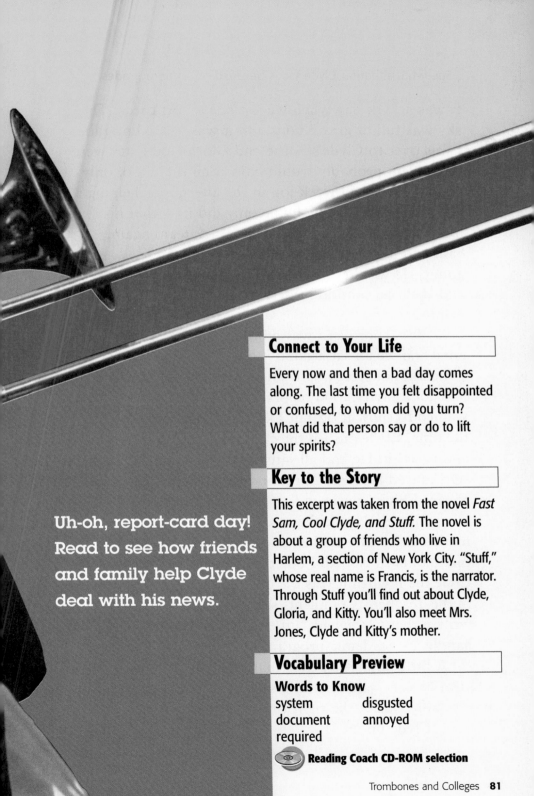

Uh-oh, report-card day!
Read to see how friends
and family help Clyde
deal with his news.

Connect to Your Life

Every now and then a bad day comes along. The last time you felt disappointed or confused, to whom did you turn? What did that person say or do to lift your spirits?

Key to the Story

This excerpt was taken from the novel *Fast Sam, Cool Clyde, and Stuff*. The novel is about a group of friends who live in Harlem, a section of New York City. "Stuff," whose real name is Francis, is the narrator. Through Stuff you'll find out about Clyde, Gloria, and Kitty. You'll also meet Mrs. Jones, Clyde and Kitty's mother.

Vocabulary Preview

Words to Know

system	disgusted
document	annoyed
required	

Reading Coach CD-ROM selection

It was a dark day when we got our report cards. The sky was full of gray clouds and it was sprinkling rain. I was over to Clyde's house and Gloria and Kitty were there. Sam probably would have been there too, only he had got a two-week job in the afternoons helping out at Freddie's. Actually he only did it so that his mother would let him be on the track team again. Sam and his mother had this little **system** going. He would do something good-doing
10 and she'd let him do something that he wanted to.

> **system**
> (sĭs' təm)
> *n.* set way of doing things

Clyde's report card was on the kitchen table and we all sat around it like it was some kind of a big important **document**. I had got a pretty good report card and had wanted to show it off but I knew it wasn't the time. Clyde pushed the card toward me and I read it. He had all satisfactory remarks on the side labeled Personal Traits and Behavior. He had also
20 received B's in music and art appreciation. But everything else was either a C or a D except mathematics. His mathematics mark was a big red F that had been circled. I don't know why they had to circle the F when it was the only red mark on the card. In the Teacher's Comments section someone had written that Clyde had "little ability to handle an **academic program**."

> **document**
> (dŏk' yə mənt)
> *n.* official report

"A little ability is better than none," I said. No one said anything so I figured it
30 probably wasn't the right time to try to cheer Clyde up.

> **academic program**
> classes in subjects that lead to college

I knew all about his switching from a
commercial program to an academic
program, but I really hadn't thought he'd
have any trouble.

"I saw the grade adviser today. He said I
should switch back to the commercial
program." Clyde looked like he'd start crying any
minute. His eyes were red and his voice was shaky.

40 "He said that I had to take mathematics over
and if I failed again or failed another required
subject I couldn't graduate. The way it is
now I'm going to have to finish up in the
summer because I switched over."

commercial program
classes in subjects that lead directly to a job

required
(rĭ kwīrd')
adj. needed

THINK IT THROUGH

What does Clyde have to do in order to stay in an academic program?

FOCUS

Clyde's mother comes home. Read to find out what Clyde decides.

"I think you can pass it if you really want to,"
Kitty said. Clyde's sister was so pretty I couldn't even
look at her. If I did I started feeling funny and
couldn't talk right. Sometimes I daydreamed about
marrying her.

50 Just then Clyde's mother came in and he gave a
quick look at Kitty.

"Hi, young ladies and young gentlemen." Mrs.
Jones was a kind of heavy woman but she was pretty,
too. You could tell she was Kitty's mother if you
looked close. She put her package down and started

taking things out. "I heard you people talking when I first came in. By the way you hushed up I guess you don't want me to hear what you were talking about. I'll be out of your way in a minute, soon as I put the
60 frozen foods in the refrigerator."

"I got my report card today," Clyde said. His mother stopped taking the food out and turned toward us. Clyde pushed the report card about two inches toward her. She really didn't even have to look at the card to know that it was bad. She could have told that just by looking at Clyde. But she picked it up and looked at it a long time. First she looked at one side and then the other and then back at the first side again.

REREAD

What do you think Clyde's mother will say?

70 "What they say around the school?" she asked, still looking at the card.

"They said I should drop the academic course and go back to the other one." I could hardly hear Clyde, he spoke so low.

"Well, what you going to do, young man?" She looked up at Clyde and Clyde looked up at her and there were tears in his eyes and I almost started crying. I can't stand to see my friends cry. "What are you going to do, Mr. Jones?"

80 "I'm—I'm going to keep the academic course," Clyde said.

"You think it's going to be any easier this time?" Mrs. Jones asked.

"No."

THINK IT THROUGH

Which program does Clyde choose? Is this the choice you expected him to make? Give reasons for your answer.

"Things ain't always easy. Lord knows that things ain't always easy." For a minute there was a faraway look in her eyes, but then her face turned into a big smile. "You're just like your father, boy. That man never would give up on anything he really wanted. Did I ever tell you the time he was trying to learn to play the trombone?"

"No." Clyde still had tears in his eyes but he was smiling, too. Suddenly everybody was happy. It was like seeing a rainbow when it was still raining.

REREAD
Why do you think everyone reacts this way?

"Well, we were living over across from St. Nicholas Park in this little rooming house. Your father was working on a job down on Varick Street that made transformers or some such nonsense—anyway, he comes home one day with this long package all wrapped up in brown paper. He walks in and sits it in the corner and doesn't say boo about what's in the bag. So at first I don't say anything either, and then I finally asks him what he's got in the bag, and he says, 'What bag?' Now this thing is about four feet long if it's an inch and he's asking *what* bag." Mrs. Jones wiped the crumbs from Gloria's end of the table with a quick swipe of the dish cloth, leaving a swirling pattern of tiny bubbles. Gloria tore off a paper towel and wiped the area dry.

"Now I look over at him and he's trying to be nonchalant. Sitting there, a grown man, and big as he wants to be and looking for all the world like somebody's misplaced son. So I says, 'The bag in the corner.' And

nonchalant
(nŏn' shə länt')
not seeming to care

he says, 'Oh, that's a trombone I'm taking back to the pawn shop tomorrow.' Well, I naturally ask him what he's doing with it in the first place, and he says he got carried away and bought it but he realized that we really didn't have the thirty-five dollars to spend on foolishness and so he'd take it back the next day. And all the time he's sitting there scratching his chin and rubbing his nose and trying to peek over at me to see how I felt about it. I just told him that I guess he knew what was best. Only the next day he forgot to take it back, and the next day he forgot to take it back, and finally I broke down and told him why didn't he keep it. He said he would if I thought he should.

"So he unwraps this thing and he was just as happy with it as he could be until he tried to get a tune out of it. He couldn't get a sound out of it at first, but then he started oomping and woomping with the thing as best he could. He worked at it and worked at it and you could see he was getting disgusted. I think he was just about to give it up when the lady who lived under us came upstairs and started complaining about the noise. It kept her Napoleon awake, she said. Napoleon was a dog. Little ugly thing, too. She said your father couldn't play, anyway.

disgusted
(dĭs gŭs' tĭd)
adj. irritated and impatient

"Well, what did she say that for? That man played that thing day and night. He worked so hard at that thing that his lips were too sore for him to talk right sometime. But he got the hang of it."

"I never remembered Pop playing a trombone," said Clyde.

"Well, your father had a streak in him that made him stick to a thing," she said, pouring some rice into

150 a colander to wash it off, "but every year his goals got bigger and bigger and he had to put some things down so that he could get to others. That old trombone is still around here some place. Probably in one of them boxes under Kitty's bed. Now, you children, excuse me, young ladies and gentlemen, get on out of here and let me finish supper."

THINK IT THROUGH
Why do you think Mrs. Jones shares this memory about Clyde's father?

We all went into Clyde's living room.

"That was my mom's good-doing speech," Clyde
said. "She gets into talking about what a great guy
160 my father was and how I was like him and whatnot."

"You supposed to be like your father," Sam said.
"He was the one that raised you, right?"

"She wants me to be like him, and I want to be like
him, too, I guess. She wants me to keep on trying
with the academic thing."

"What do you want to do," Sam asked, "give it up?"

"No. Not really. I guess I want people like my
mother to keep on telling me that I ought to do it,
really. Especially when somebody tells me I can't do it."

170 "Boy," Sam said, sticking his thumbs in his belt and
leaning back in the big stuffed chair, "you are just like
your father."

Then we all went into Clyde's room and just sat
around and talked for a while. Mostly about school and
stuff like that, and I wanted to tell Clyde that I thought
I could help him if he wanted me to. I was really getting
good grades in school, but I thought that
Clyde might get annoyed if I mentioned it.
But then Gloria said that we could study
180 together sometime and that was cool too.

annoyed
(ə noid')
adj. bothered

THINK IT THROUGH

1. From Clyde's viewpoint, why does his mother
   share the memory about his father?
2. Mrs. Jones might have reacted differently to Clyde's
   report card. Why do you think she reacts as she
   does?
3. How does Clyde feel about his mom's desire that
   he keep on trying?

In a Neighborhood in Los Angeles

by Francisco X. Alarcón

What puts the grand in grandmother? This poem has some answers.

Connect to Your Life

You may have grandparents in your life. Or you may only know of grandparents through old photographs or your parents' stories. Recall what you know.

Key to the Poem

In a poem, the **speaker** is the voice that talks to the reader. The speaker may even use the word I to express a thought or a feeling. In this poem, the speaker is probably the poet himself talking about his own grandmother. In many other poems, the speaker and the poet may not be the same. A poet sometimes speaks through a character.

| Find out the speaker's relationship with his grandmother.

I learned
Spanish
from my grandma

mijito
5 don't cry
she'd tell me

mijito
(mē hē′ tô)
my son

on the mornings
my parents
would leave

10 to work
at the fish
canneries

my grandma
would chat
15 with chairs

sing them
old
songs

dance
20 waltzes with them
in the kitchen

when she'd say
niño barrigón
she'd laugh

*niño
barrigón*
(nē′ nyô
bä rē gôn′)
big boy

25 with my grandma
   I learned
   to count clouds

   to point out
   in flowerpots
30 mint leaves

   my grandma
   wore moons
   on her dress

   Mexico's mountains
35 deserts
   ocean

   in her eyes
   I'd see them
   in her braids

40 I'd touch them
   in her voice
   smell them

   one day
   I was told:
45 she went far away

but still
I feel her
with me

whispering
50 in my ear
mijito

THINK IT THROUGH

1. How does the speaker feel about his grandmother?
   Find lines in the poem to support your answer.
2. What details from the poem show the
   grandmother's special qualities?
3. In what way do you think the speaker's
   grandmother remains with him?

Mudslinging

by Jennifer Owings Dewey

Some families stick together like glue. Others use mud. This information about one Native American group will give you a new view of marriage.

■ Connect to Your Life

When you think of the word *wedding,* what pictures come to your mind? Jot down a description or make a quick sketch.

■ Key to the Article

A **ritual** is an action or a ceremony. People perform a ritual to celebrate or to recognize a special event. This informative article tells about mudslinging, a ritual of the Hopi people.

■ Vocabulary Preview

Words to Know
custom   hilarity
sacred   disputes
wistful

 Reading Coach CD-ROM selection

Read to discover what happens during the first part of the Mudslinging ritual.

"Here is something hard to believe," a Hopi friend named Dan once told me. "Adult people throwing mud at each other for a reason. It's a Hopi custom we call Mudslinging."

> **custom**
> (kŭs' təm)
> *n.* something done regularly by a group

"Tell me," I urged. I'd never heard of Mudslinging. It sounded like fun to have a reason to throw mud at somebody.

"Marriage is a solemn passage among the Hopi," Dan said. "In our villages the wedding
10 ceremonies go on for a week. The day before the wedding, the groom's father visits the bride's house. He knocks on the door and insists on being let in. With him are other members of the groom's family: aunts and uncles, sisters and brothers.

> **solemn passage**
> serious event

"Those inside the house open the door just a crack and say, 'Who are you? What do you want?' They act like they don't know him. 'War is declared!' the groom's father announces loudly. He pushes the door open, and then the craziness begins."

20 Dan pauses before going on with his story. He grins, his dark eyes shiny with humor.

"The groom and his family have secretly prepared buckets of mud, which they have brought with them. The mud is four different colors, one for each of the four directions: north, south, east, and west. It is sacred mud. These people rush into the bride's house and grab everyone, including the bride, and drag them out into the yard. The groom's family dig into the buckets of
30 mud and begin throwing it, smearing it on every person they can catch. The bride's family dip into the

> **sacred**
> (sā' krĭd)
> *adj.* holy

mud, too. Before long the yard is swarming with people of all ages, from babies to old grandmothers and grandfathers, flinging mud at each other as if they've lost their minds.

"While this goes on, some of the mud throwers yell insults back and forth at each other. It is the aunties of the groom who do this. They say how ugly the bride is, what a terrible cook her mother is, things like that."

THINK IT THROUGH
What happens to the bride's side of the family?

FOCUS
The description of Mudslinging continues. Find out what Dan sees as a possible reason for Mudslinging.

I laughed to hear this. "What happens next?" I asked. Dan was eager to continue his description of the Mudslinging.

"If the bride's people are able to catch the groom's father, they hold him down and give him a haircut. This makes him feel foolish. It's an insult." Dan's grin widened. "The Mudslinging ends peacefully. Once the buckets are emptied and everyone is coated with mud, the participants shake hands and make peace. Food is shared, a feast of corn and mutton, a lot of food."

REREAD
Retell what happens here.

"And the wedding takes place the next day?" I asked.

"Yes," Dan said, a wistful expression appearing on his handsome face. "This is how it was for me when I got married.

wistful
(wĭst′ fəl)
adj. dreamy

There was much hilarity, and sacred rituals, too, and then I became a husband, no longer a single man."

hilarity
(hǐ lǎr′ ǐ tē)
n. fun and laughter

60   "Why do they do the Mudslinging? Was it fun when it happened to you? Or was it horrible?"

"It was a lot of fun. Maybe the reason for it is to get troubles over with in a happy way before the marriage, the mother-in-law problems, the father-in-law problems."

I nodded. It made sense.

"When two families come together and become joined, there are always disputes. It's expected. Mudslinging gets everyone's energy

disputes
(dǐ spyo͞ots′)
n. arguments

70   for arguing out of the way, at least for a while," Dan added. A thoughtful smile came to his face when he was finished with his storytelling.

THINK IT THROUGH

1. What does Dan think is the reason for Mudslinging?
2. How does Dan feel about Mudslinging? How do you know?
3. If you could, would you participate in a Mudslinging? Why or why not?

Another April

by Jesse Stuart

It's finally spring. Grandpa is free to go outdoors. As he enjoys some of his favorite things, discover what matters to his family.

Connect to Your Life

Do you know an elderly person whose health is failing? Do you know how to act toward this person? What feelings have you had when you've been around someone very old? Discuss your feelings with classmates.

Key to the Story

In this short story, the narrator tells about a grandfather who is very old. Grandpa is being watched by his daughter and grandson. Watch for the ways these three family members treat one another.

Vocabulary Preview

Words to Know
coarse	bundled
timber	terrapin

 Reading Coach CD-ROM selection

FOCUS

Grandpa is eager to get outdoors again. Read to find out
what he wants to do.

"Now, Pap, you won't get cold," Mom said as she put
a heavy wool cap over his head.

"Huh, what did ye say?" Grandpa asked, holding
his big hand cupped over his ear to catch the sound.

"Wait until I get your gloves," Mom said, hollering
real loud in Grandpa's ear. Mom had forgotten about
his gloves until he raised his big bare hand above his
ear to catch the sound of Mom's voice.

"Don't get 'em," Grandpa said, "I won't ketch cold."

10 Mom didn't pay any attention to what Grandpa
said. She went on to get the gloves anyway. Grandpa
turned toward me. He saw that I was looking at him.

"Yer Ma's a-puttin' enough clothes on me to kill a
man," Grandpa said; then he laughed a
coarse laugh like March wind among the
pine tops at his own words. I started
laughing but not at Grandpa's words. He
thought I was laughing at them and we
both laughed together. It pleased

20 Grandpa to think that I had
laughed with him over

coarse
(kôrs)
adj. rough

something funny that he had said. But I was laughing at the way he was dressed. He looked like a picture of Santa Claus. But Grandpa's cheeks were not cherry-red like Santa Claus's cheeks. They were covered with white thin beard—and above his eyes were long white eyebrows almost as white as percoon petals and very much longer.

REREAD

Is the grandson laughing with or at Grandpa?

30 Grandpa was wearing a heavy wool suit that hung loosely about his big body but fitted him tightly round the waist where he was as big and as round as a flour barrel. His pant legs were as big 'round his pipestem legs as emptied meal sacks. And his big shoes, with his heavy wool socks dropping down over their tops, looked like sled runners. Grandpa wore a heavy wool shirt and over his wool shirt he wore a heavy wool sweater and then his coat over the 40 top of all this. Over his coat he wore a heavy overcoat and about his neck he wore a wool scarf.

pipestem
(pīp' stĕm')
thin, like the thin end of a pipe

The way Mom had dressed Grandpa you'd think there was a heavy snow on the ground but there wasn't. April was here instead, and the sun was shining on the green hills where the wild plums and the wild crab apples were in bloom enough to make you think there were big snowdrifts sprinkled over the green hills. When I looked at Grandpa and then looked out at the window at the sunshine and the green grass, I laughed 50 more. Grandpa laughed with me.

"I'm a-goin' to see my old friend," Grandpa said just as Mom came down the stairs with his gloves.

"Who is he, Grandpa?" I asked, but Grandpa just looked at my mouth working. He didn't know what I was saying. And he hated to ask me the second time.

Mom put the big wool gloves on Grandpa's hands. He stood there just like I had to do years ago, and let Mom put his gloves on. If Mom didn't get his fingers back in the glove-fingers exactly right, Grandpa 60 quarreled at Mom. And when Mom fixed his fingers exactly right in his gloves the way he wanted them, Grandpa was pleased.

REREAD

Describe how you think Mom is treating Grandpa.

"I'll be a-goin' to see 'im," Grandpa said to Mom. "I know he'll still be there."

THINK IT THROUGH
Where is Grandpa going? Why does getting ready take so long?

FOCUS ——————
Read to discover why Mom is so careful about Grandpa.

Mom opened our front door for Grandpa and he stepped out slowly, supporting himself with his big cane in one hand. With the other hand he held to the door facing. Mom let him out 70 of the house just like she used to let me out in the spring. And when Grandpa left the house, I wanted to go with him, but Mom wouldn't let me go. I wondered if he would get away from the house—get out of Mom's sight—and pull off his shoes and go barefooted and wade the creeks like I used to do when Mom let me out. Since Mom wouldn't let me go with Grandpa, I watched him as he walked slowly down the path in front of our house. Mom stood there watching Grandpa too. I think she was 80 afraid that he would fall. But Mom was fooled;

facing
frame

Grandpa toddled along the path better than my baby brother could.

"He used to be a powerful man," Mom said more to herself than she did to me. "He was a timber cutter. No man could cut more timber than my father; no man in the timber woods could sink an ax deeper into a log than my father. And no man could lift the end of a bigger saw log 90 than Pop could."

timber
(tĭm' bər)
n. tree

REREAD
How does this description of Grandpa compare to how he is now?

"Who is Grandpa goin' to see, Mom?" I asked.

"He's not goin' to see anybody," Mom said.

"I heard 'im say that he was goin' to see an old friend," I told her.

"Oh, he was just a-talkin'," Mom said.

I watched Grandpa stop under the pine tree in our front yard. He set his cane against the pine tree trunk, pulled off his gloves and put them in his pocket. Then 100 Grandpa stooped over slowly, as slowly as the wind bends down a sapling, and picked up a pine cone in his big soft fingers. Grandpa stood fondling the pine cone in his hand. Then, one by one, he pulled the little chips from the pine cone—tearing it to pieces like he was hunting for something in it—and after he had torn it to pieces he threw the pine-cone stem on the ground. Then he pulled pine needles from a low-hanging pine bough, and 110 he felt of each pine needle between his fingers.

bough
(bou)
tree branch

He played with them a long time before he started down the path.

"What's Grandpa doin'?" I asked Mom.

But Mom didn't answer me.

"How long has Grandpa been with us?" I asked Mom.

"Before you's born," she said. "Pap has been with us eleven years. He was eighty when he quit cuttin' timber and farmin'; now he's ninety-one."

I had heard her say that when she was a girl he'd walk out on the snow and ice barefooted and carry wood in the house and put it on the fire. He had shoes but he wouldn't bother to put them on. And I heard her say that he would cut timber on the coldest days without socks on his feet but with his feet stuck down in cold brogan shoes, and he worked stripped above the waist so his arms would have freedom when he swung his double-bitted ax. I had heard her tell how he'd sweat and how the sweat in his beard would be icicles by the time he got home from work on the cold winter days. Now Mom wouldn't let him get out of the house, for she wanted him to live a long time.

REREAD

Why do you think Mom shared these memories about Grandpa?

THINK IT THROUGH

How does Mom feel about the changes in her father?

FOCUS

Grandpa's walk continues. Read to find out a change the narrator notices about his grandfather.

As I watched Grandpa go down the path toward the hog pen, he stopped to examine every little thing

along his path. Once he waved his cane at a
butterfly as it zigzagged over his head, its polka-dot wings fanning the blue April air.

Grandpa would stand when a puff of wind came along, and hold his face against the wind and let the wind play with his white whiskers. I thought maybe his face was hot under his beard and he was letting the wind cool his face. When he reached the hog pen, he called the hogs down to the fence. They came running and grunting to Grandpa just like they were talking to him. I knew that Grandpa couldn't hear them trying to talk to him, but he could see their mouths working and he knew they were trying to say something. He leaned his cane against the hog pen, reached over the fence, and patted the hogs' heads. Grandpa didn't miss patting one of our seven hogs.

REREAD
Picture this scene in your mind.

As he toddled up the little path alongside the hog pen, he stopped under a blooming dogwood. He pulled a white blossom from a bough that swayed over the path above his head, and he leaned his big bundled body against the dogwood while he tore each petal from the blossom and examined it carefully. There wasn't anything his dim blue eyes missed. He stopped under a redbud tree before he reached the garden to break a tiny spray of redbud blossoms. He took each blossom from the spray and examined it carefully.

bundled
(bŭn' dld)
adj. wrapped up

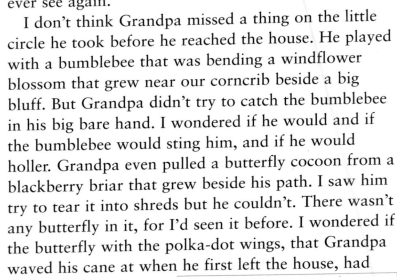

170   "Gee, it's funny to watch Grandpa," I said to Mom; then I laughed.

"Poor Pap," Mom said. "He's seen a lot of Aprils come and go. He's seen more Aprils than he will ever see again."

I don't think Grandpa missed a thing on the little circle he took before he reached the house. He played with a bumblebee that was bending a windflower

180 blossom that grew near our corncrib beside a big bluff. But Grandpa didn't try to catch the bumblebee in his big bare hand. I wondered if he would and if the bumblebee would sting him, and if he would holler. Grandpa even pulled a butterfly cocoon from a blackberry briar that grew beside his path. I saw him try to tear it into shreds but he couldn't. There wasn't any butterfly in it, for I'd seen it before. I wondered if the butterfly with the polka-dot wings, that Grandpa waved his cane at when he first left the house, had

190 come from this cocoon. I laughed when Grandpa couldn't tear the cocoon apart.

"I'll bet I can tear that cocoon apart for Grandpa if you'd let me go help him," I said to Mom.

"You leave your Grandpa alone," Mom said. "Let 'im enjoy April."

> **REREAD**
> Why doesn't the boy seem to take Grandpa's walk seriously?

Then I knew that this was the first time Mom had let Grandpa out of the house all winter. I knew that Grandpa loved the sunshine and the fresh

200 April air that blew from the redbud and dogwood blossoms. He loved the bumblebees, the hogs, the pine cones, and pine needles. Grandpa didn't miss a thing along his walk. And every day from now on

until just before frost Grandpa would take this little walk. He'd stop along and look at everything as he had done summers before. But each year he didn't take as long a walk as he had taken the year before. Now this spring he didn't go down to the lower end of the hog pen as he had done last year. And when I
210 could first remember Grandpa going on his walks, he used to go out of sight. He'd go all over the farm. And he'd come to the house and take me on his knee and tell me about all what he had seen. Now Grandpa wasn't getting out of sight. I could see him from the window along all of his walk.

THINK IT THROUGH

How is the grandson's view of Grandpa changing as he watches him and listens to Mom?

FOCUS ——————

Find out whom Grandpa finally meets.

Grandpa didn't come back into the house at the front door. He toddled around back of the house toward the smokehouse, and I ran through the living room to the dining room so I could
220 look out the window and watch him.

> **smokehouse**
> place where meat is kept

"Where's Grandpa goin'?" I asked Mom.

"Now never mind," Mom said. "Leave Grandpa alone. Don't go out there and disturb him."

"I won't bother 'im, Mom," I said. "I just want to watch 'im."

"All right," Mom said.

> **REREAD**
> Do you believe the boy is taking Grandpa's walk more seriously now? Explain.

But Mom wanted to be sure that I didn't bother him so she followed me into the dining room. Maybe she wanted to see what Grandpa was going to do. She stood by the window, and we watched Grandpa as he walked down beside our smokehouse where a tall sassafras tree's thin leaves fluttered in the blue April wind. Above the smokehouse and the tall sassafras was a blue April sky—so high you couldn't see the sky-roof. It was just blue space and little white clouds floated upon this blue.

When Grandpa reached the smokehouse he leaned his cane against the sassafras tree. He let himself down slowly to his knees as he looked carefully at the ground. Grandpa was looking at something and I wondered what it was. I just didn't think or I would have known.

"There you are, my good old friend," Grandpa said.

"Who is his friend, Mom?" I asked.

Mom didn't say anything. Then I saw.

"He's playin' with that old terrapin, Mom," I said.

terrapin
(tĕr′ ə pĭn)
n. turtle

"I know he is," Mom said.

250 "The terrapin doesn't mind if Grandpa strokes his head with his hand," I said.

"I know it," Mom said.

"But the old terrapin won't let me do it," I said. "Why does he let Grandpa?"

"The terrapin knows your Grandpa."

"He ought to know me," I said, "but when I try to stroke his head with my hand, he closes up in his shell."

Mom didn't say anything. She stood by the window watching Grandpa and listening to Grandpa talk to 260 the terrapin.

"My old friend, how do you like the sunshine?" Grandpa asked the terrapin.

The terrapin turned his fleshless face to one side like a hen does when she looks at you in the sunlight. He was trying to talk to Grandpa; maybe the terrapin could understand what Grandpa was saying.

"Old fellow, it's been a hard winter," Grandpa said. "How have you fared under the smokehouse floor?"

| fared |
| (fârd) |
| been doing |

270 "Does the terrapin know what Grandpa is sayin'?" I asked Mom.

"I don't know," she said.

"I'm awfully glad to see you, old fellow," Grandpa said.

He didn't offer to bite Grandpa's big soft hand as he stroked his head.

"Looks like the terrapin would bite Grandpa," I said.

"That terrapin has spent the winters under that smokehouse for fifteen years," Mom said. "Pap has 280 been acquainted with him for eleven years. He's been talkin' to that terrapin every spring."

"How does Grandpa know the terrapin is old?" I asked Mom.

"It's got 1847 cut on its shell," Mom said. "We know he's ninety-five years old. He's older than that. We don't know how old he was when that date was cut on his back."

"Who cut 1847 on his back, Mom?"

"I don't know, child," she said, "but I'd say
290 whoever cut that date on his back has long been under the ground."

THINK IT THROUGH
In what way does the terrapin respond to Grandpa? How is it different from the way it has behaved with the boy?

FOCUS ———
As you read, notice all the things the terrapin makes the boy think about.

Then I wondered how a terrapin could get that old and what kind of a looking person he was who cut the date on the terrapin's back. I wondered where it happened—if it happened near where our house stood. I wondered who lived here on this land then, what kind of a house they lived in, and if they had a sassafras with tiny thin April leaves on its top growing in their yard, and if the person that cut that
300 date on the terrapin's back was buried at Plum Grove, if he had farmed these hills where we lived today and cut timber like Grandpa had—and if he had seen the Aprils pass like Grandpa had seen them and if he enjoyed them like Grandpa was enjoying this April. I wondered if he had looked at the dogwood blossoms, the redbud blossoms, and talked to this same terrapin.

"Are you well, old fellow?" Grandpa asked the terrapin.

The terrapin just looked at Grandpa.

310   "I'm well as common for a man of my age," Grandpa said.

"Did the terrapin ask Grandpa if he was well?" I asked Mom.

"I don't know," Mom said. "I can't talk to a terrapin."

"But Grandpa can."

"Yes."

"Wait until tomatoes get ripe and we'll go to the garden together," Grandpa said.

320   "Does the terrapin eat tomatoes?" I asked Mom.

"Yes, that terrapin has been eatin' tomatoes from our garden for fifteen years," Mom said. "When Mick was tossin' the terrapins out of the tomato patch, he picked up this one and found the date cut on his back. He put him back in the patch and told him to help himself. He lives from our garden every year. We don't bother him and don't allow anybody else to bother him. He spends his winters under our smokehouse floor buried in the dry ground."

330   "Gee, Grandpa looks like the terrapin," I said.

Mom didn't say anything; tears came to her eyes. She wiped them from her eyes with the corner of her apron.

> **REREAD**
> Why does Mom cry?

"I'll be back to see you," Grandpa said. "I'm a-gettin' a little chilly; I'll be gettin' back to the house."

The terrapin twisted his wrinkled neck without moving his big body, poking his head deeper into the April wind as Grandpa pulled his bundled body up by
340 holding to the sassafras tree trunk.

Who's in Charge?

Drama

Can you control everything that happens to you? Good or bad, some things are beyond our control. The characters in this unit would probably agree. Events often leave them wondering, "Who's in charge?"

When you read the plays, or **dramas,** pay attention to what the characters say to each other. The characters tell the story in a play. You will be reading the **script,** or written form, of each play. Imagine how the actors would say the words you are reading. In fact, the best way to enjoy a play is to see it acted on the stage. Maybe you will act out parts of the play yourself.

The Telephone

by John Murray

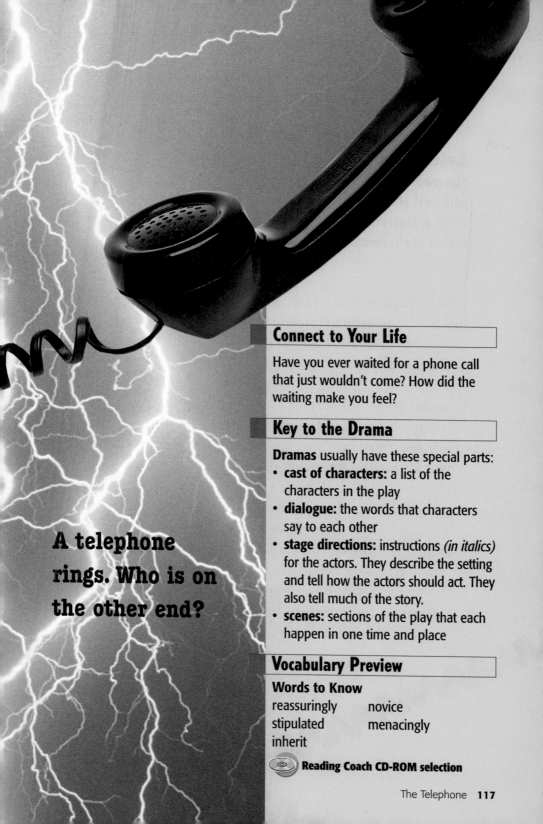

A telephone rings. Who is on the other end?

Connect to Your Life

Have you ever waited for a phone call that just wouldn't come? How did the waiting make you feel?

Key to the Drama

Dramas usually have these special parts:
- **cast of characters:** a list of the characters in the play
- **dialogue:** the words that characters say to each other
- **stage directions:** instructions *(in italics)* for the actors. They describe the setting and tell how the actors should act. They also tell much of the story.
- **scenes:** sections of the play that each happen in one time and place

Vocabulary Preview

Words to Know

reassuringly	novice
stipulated	menacingly
inherit	

Reading Coach CD-ROM selection

Read the cast of characters, the narrator's words, and all the stage directions. Find out what you need to know in order to understand this play.

Cast of Characters

Narrator
Mildred Hathaway, a young woman
Aunt Elizabeth, an elderly woman
Victor Hathaway, Mildred's husband

Before Curtain Rise: *Area before curtain is dimly lighted. If possible, colored spotlights move across curtain to create eerie effect.* Narrator *enters right and addresses audience.*

Narrator (*mysteriously*). Good evening. We are about to visit a haunted house. . . . But we will not see ghosts or specters from another world, for the haunting of Hathaway House is quite a different matter. (*Ring of telephone is heard from behind curtain.*) How often have you heard a telephone ring? (*Telephone rings again.*) Can anyone ever know who—or what—is waiting at the other end of the line? (*Telephone rings again.*) That telephone call might be (*pointing into audience*)— for you! (Narrator *exits*. *Curtains open.*)

> **specters**
> (spĕk′ tərz)
> shadowy forms
> that are not real

> **exits**
> (ĕg′ zĭts)
> leaves the stage

10

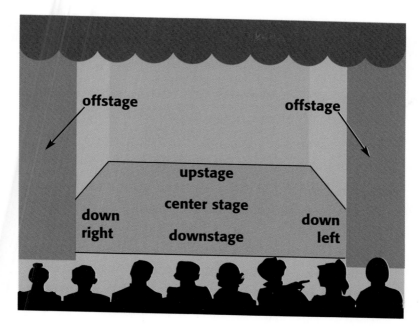

Time: *Late evening.*

Setting: Drawing room *of Hathaway House. Through* French window *, upstage,*
20 *we see occasional flashes of lightning. Sounds of thunder are heard from offstage. There is a sofa down left, and a telephone on a table beside it.*

> **drawing room**
> room used for guests

> **French window**
> window that goes all the way to the floor

At Curtain Rise: Mildred Hathaway *stands near French window, pulling back drapes and staring out at storm.* Aunt Elizabeth, *wearing black shawl, sits on sofa. She touches telephone, then nods to herself. There is a flash of lightning.* Mildred *jumps, then crosses hurriedly to sit beside* Elizabeth.

THINK IT THROUGH

Where does this play take place? Who are the characters?

30 **Elizabeth.** Were you frightened by the lightning, Mildred, my dear? A storm can be frightening.

Mildred (*nervously*). No, no, I'm not afraid. Aunt Elizabeth, won't you let me help you to your room?

Elizabeth. No, Mildred, I must wait a little longer. (*points to telephone*) I must be awake, in case Jonathan calls tonight. (*Crash of thunder is heard. Mildred jumps nervously.*) You're very nervous, my child. Really, you shouldn't be afraid of Hathaway House. It was once a happy place, but now there are

40 only memories. (*suddenly*) I must light the fire in Jonathan's room. (*She stands.*) He always loved to sit and watch the fire. (*She pats Mildred's hand reassuringly.*) We'll have a cup of tea as soon as I get back. (*She exits, smiling to herself. Restlessly, Mildred crosses to French window, pulls back drapes. Sudden flash of lightning reveals a man standing outside. Mildred screams in terror, backs away.*

50 *The man, Victor Hathaway, opens window, steps into room.*)

> **reassuringly**
> (rē' ə shŏŏr' ĭng lē)
> *adv.* in a way that makes one trust

> **REREAD**
> What do this and earlier stage directions tell you about Mildred's state of mind?

Mildred (*in relief, nearly hysterical*). Oh, Victor, it's you! How you frightened me!

Victor (*roughly*). What's the matter with you, Mildred? You can't go to pieces now!

Mildred (*frantically*). Oh, Victor, take me away from this house! I can't stay here another night!

Victor (*sarcastically*). Why? Are you afraid of my Uncle Jonathan?

Mildred. Yes, I am! This house belongs to your Aunt Elizabeth, not to us. Why did you ever bring me here?

Victor (*laughing bitterly*). You're a silly fool!

Mildred (*hysterically*). But, you don't understand! Elizabeth still waits every day for Jonathan to telephone her—and he's been dead for six weeks! (*Sudden crash of thunder is heard. She points to French window. She continues in frenzied tones.*) We all know he's out there in the family

70 vault . We went to the funeral and saw them seal the door of his tomb!

> **vault**
> (vôlt)
> place for burials

THINK IT THROUGH

Who is Jonathan and where is he?

FOCUS

Read on to discover why Victor is so bitter.

Victor. My dear wife, *we* know that Uncle Jonathan is dead, but Aunt Elizabeth can't seem to accept it. You know Uncle Jonathan was always afraid of being buried alive. He stipulated in his will that a telephone should be installed in the vault. So here we have it—a direct line to Jonathan Hathaway's vault. (*points to telephone*)

> **REREAD**
> Why did Jonathan want a telephone in the vault?

> **stipulated**
> (stĭp' yə lā' tĭd)
> *v.* ordered; past tense of *stipulate*

80 **Mildred** (*wringing her hands*). I know all that, but—

Victor (*interrupting*). Jonathan was a wealthy man. When Aunt Elizabeth is gone, my brother Spencer and I will inherit the millions of dollars he left to her. Think of it, Mildred— millions of dollars!

inherit

(ĭn hĕr′ ĭt)

v. receive from one who has died

Mildred (*drawing away, frightened*). I don't want the money, Victor. Please take me away from here!

90 **Victor** (*soothingly*). All in good time, my dear. When Aunt Elizabeth is no longer with us.

Mildred. Don't say such things!

Victor (*abruptly*). Where is Aunt Elizabeth?

Mildred (*pointing to door*). Upstairs—preparing Jonathan's room.

Victor. Good. Nothing must happen to Aunt Elizabeth—not yet. I have other plans for her! I'm going upstairs for a moment myself. (*He exits. From*

REREAD

What do you think Victor's "plans" are?

100 *offstage, clock is heard chiming eleven times. As it chimes,* Mildred *paces floor.*)

THINK IT THROUGH
What is keeping Victor from getting his uncle's money?

FOCUS
Read on to find out *exactly* what Victor plans to do to Aunt Elizabeth.

Mildred. Eleven o'clock. Uncle Jonathan died at eleven o'clock. (*She sits on sofa, stares at phone. Suddenly phone rings.* Mildred *screams, jumps to her feet. Phone rings*

again. Slowly, her hand trembling, she
110 *picks up receiver, speaks into phone.*) Yes?
Yes? . . . who's there? (*shrilly*) Why don't you
answer? Please, answer me! (*Slowly*
she hangs up receiver.) There was no
one on the line! (*Behind her, drapes at*
French window move. She turns and begins to walk
toward window as if sleepwalking, her hand
outstretched, trembling. Suddenly drape is thrown
aside and Victor *strides into room.* Mildred *gasps*
and collapses onto sofa.) Victor, what were you
120 doing out there?

Victor. Just conducting a little experiment.

Mildred (*suddenly remembering*). The telephone! The
telephone rang from Jonathan's vault!

Victor. Relax, my dear. Have you forgotten
that I'm not a novice at working with
telephones? After all, I am an electrical
engineer.

> **novice**
> (nŏv′ ĭs)
> *n.* beginner

Mildred (*horrified*). Did *you* make that phone ring,
Victor?

130 **Victor** (*nodding*). Yes. I spliced the wire and
connected it to a buzzer outside.
(*menacingly*) I don't intend to wait any
longer to inherit the Hathaway fortune.

> **menacingly**
> (mĕn′ ĭ sĭng lē)
> *adv.* in a
> threatening way

Mildred. Don't talk like that, Victor!

Victor. Quiet! When Aunt Elizabeth returns, I'll make
some excuse to leave the room. Then the telephone
will ring again. . . . Perhaps the shock will be too
much for Aunt Elizabeth's heart.

Mildred. I won't let you do this! I'm going to tell her
140 what you're planning!

> **REREAD**
> Who do you
> think called?

Victor (*menacingly*). No, I don't think you'll do that. (*She backs away from him, frightened.*) Cooperate with me, Mildred, and in a little while you'll have the luxuries you've always wanted. (*Aunt Elizabeth enters.*)

THINK IT THROUGH

What is Victor planning to do?

FOCUS

Read on to find out if Mildred goes along with Victor's plan.

Elizabeth. It's so nice and warm in Jonathan's room. Such a bright fire! I know he'll be delighted.

Victor. How about a cup of tea, Aunt Elizabeth?

Mildred (*quickly*). I'll fix it.

150 **Victor.** No, Mildred. (*smiles*) I'll attend to the tea. I'll attend to everything. (*He exits right.*)

Mildred (*desperately*). Wouldn't you like to lie down, Auntie? I'll bring the tea to your room.

Elizabeth (*sadly*). No, I'll wait here a little while longer. The telephone call, you know. (*She sits on sofa.*)

Mildred. But it's so cold in here.

Elizabeth. I don't mind the cold, my dear. You know, I feel so close to Jonathan tonight. Oh, how he loved to sit in this room with me! He never

160 liked being alone. (|gestures| to phone) That's why he wanted the telephone. He was afraid of being left there—alone—in the dark.

> **gestures**
> (jĕs′ chərz)
> points with a hand

Mildred (*nervously*). Please don't talk like that, Aunt Elizabeth.

Elizabeth (*taking her hand*). Don't worry, dear. Someday Jonathan will come back, and I'll never be alone again.

REREAD
What does this tell you about Elizabeth?

(*Telephone rings.* Mildred *jumps and* 170 *stares at* Aunt Elizabeth *in terror.* Aunt Elizabeth *smiles happily.*) It's Jonathan! I knew he'd call. (*She reaches for telephone.* Mildred *grabs her hand.*)

Mildred (*desperately*). Don't answer that phone! Don't you understand? Jonathan is dead! (*Phone rings again.*)

Elizabeth (*with quiet dignity*). Please, Mildred, I must answer. (Mildred *releases her hand, and* Elizabeth *picks up receiver and speaks into it.*) Hello? Hello? Is that you, Jonathan? . . . I can't 180 hear anything. . . . Jonathan? (*Slowly she replaces receiver; to* Mildred) There was no one on the line. Jonathan needed me, and you kept me away from the telephone. (Victor *enters, carrying tray with teapot and cups. He puts tray on coffee table.*)

THINK IT THROUGH

How does Mildred try to protect Aunt Elizabeth from Victor?

Victor. What happened?

Elizabeth (*dejectedly*). Jonathan tried to call me, but Mildred wouldn't let me answer the phone until it was too late. Too late! (*She stares off into space, as if in a trance.* Victor *turns angrily on* Mildred.)

190

| dejectedly |
| (dĭ jĕk′ tĭd lē) |
| sadly |

Victor. I warned you not to interfere!

Mildred (*agitated*). I don't care what happens to me—I can't let you harm Aunt Elizabeth! (*to* Aunt Elizabeth) Aunt Elizabeth, you must realize that Jonathan is dead. The phone call wasn't from him—Victor did something to the phone. I'll—I'll prove it to you. I'll go out to the vault. I'll prove that Jonathan Hathaway is dead!

REREAD
Where is Mildred going? Why?

200 **Elizabeth** (*brightening*). You'll go to the vault? Oh, Mildred, you are so kind! I'll get your coat. (*She exits.*)

Mildred (*calmly*). I know what you're thinking, Victor, but I don't care. I was a fool to listen to you. First thing tomorrow I'm going to call Aunt Elizabeth's lawyer, and tell him everything. (Victor *raises his hand as if to strike her, just as* Aunt Elizabeth *re-enters with raincoat. Quickly* Victor *drops his hand.*)

Elizabeth (*handing raincoat to* Mildred). Go quickly!

210 Jonathan is waiting for you! (Mildred *puts on coat, walks toward French window.*)

Victor (*starting after her*). I'm coming, too, Mildred.

REREAD
Why do you think Victor is going with Mildred?

(*They exit.* Elizabeth *stands looking after them,* *then walks downstage, stands near telephone.* *Suddenly telephone rings. She picks up receiver.*)

Elizabeth (*into phone*). Yes? Yes? . . . Oh, Jonathan, I can hear you perfectly! . . . How long I've waited! . . . Yes, Victor and Mildred will be there in a minute. . . .

220   You'll meet them at the door of the vault? . . . Oh, yes, they'll be very much surprised! . . . Yes, Jonathan, I'll be waiting for you. I'll be waiting. (*Hangs up phone and walks to French window, parts drapes and looks out. Suddenly sound of* Victor *screaming in strangled voice is heard from offstage, followed by sound of* Mildred's *shrill scream. Sound of a squeaking door followed by heavy thud is heard.* Aunt Elizabeth

230   *drops drape, returns to center stage; thoughtfully*) Sounds as if Jonathan was there to meet them, all right! (*laughs in satisfied way as curtain closes*)

> **REREAD**
> What is the meaning of Victor's "strangled" voice? the heavy thud?

THINK IT THROUGH

1. What do you think happens to Victor at the end? What about Mildred?
2. Is Jonathan dead or alive at the end? Use evidence from the play to explain your opinion.
3. Why does Elizabeth laugh at the end?

The Prince and the Pauper

by **Mark Twain**
adapted by **Joellen Bland**

A prince and a poor boy trade places just for fun. But something goes terribly wrong.

Connect to Your Life

Suppose you switched places with a king or a queen for a day. Discuss the kinds of things you would do if you were "in charge" for a full day.

Key to the Drama

This play takes place in England in the 1500s. You will find many old-fashioned words. Read all the side notes. Ask your teacher for help.

Pay close attention to the events in the plot. **Plot** means the events that happen in a story. The plot leads to a **climax,** the most important event in the story. At first, this plot may be confusing. The events switch back and forth between two boys who look alike. You might write down important events to keep track of what is going on.

As the play opens, the young prince and a young pauper trade places. When they put on each other's clothes, people start confusing them with each other. Soon events get out of control. Read the play to find out what happens.

Vocabulary Preview

Words to Know

heir	impostor
affliction	oppress

 Reading Coach CD-ROM selection

Five hundred years ago, England was not an easy place to live, especially if you were poor. The pauper in the title of this play was very poor—a **pauper** is a person who has nothing at all. Paupers made their living by begging in the streets. Even children were sent out to the streets to beg. Keep this in mind as you read *The Prince and the Pauper.*

FOCUS _____

Try to visualize the setting and the stage directions to figure out what is going on at the beginning of the play.

Cast of Characters
Edward, Prince of Wales
Tom Canty, the Pauper
Lord Hertford
Lord St. John
King Henry VIII
Herald
Miles Hendon
John Canty, Tom's father
Hugo, a young thief
Two Women
Justice
Constable (policeman)
Jailer
Sir Hugh Hendon
Two Prisoners
Two Guards
Three Pages
Lords and Ladies
Villagers

All photographs of characters are from the movie version of *The Prince and the Pauper*.

Scene 1

Time: 1547.

Setting: *Westminster Palace, England. Gates leading to courtyard are right. Slightly to left, off courtyard and inside gates, interior of palace* anteroom *is visible. There is couch with rich robe draped on it, screen at rear, bellcord, mirror, chairs, and table holding bowl of nuts and large golden seal. Piece of armor hangs on one wall. Exits rear and downstage.*

> **anteroom**
> (ăn' tē rōōm')
> waiting room

10

At Curtain Rise: Two Guards *stand left and right of gates. Several* Villagers *hover nearby, straining to see into courtyard where* Prince *is playing. Two* Women *enter right.*

1st Woman. I have walked all morning just to have a glimpse of Westminster Palace.

2nd Woman. Maybe if we can get near enough to the gates, we can see the young prince. (*Tom Canty, dirty and ragged, comes out of crowd and steps close to gates.*)

Tom. I have always dreamed of seeing a real prince! (*Excited, he presses his nose against the gates.*)

1st Guard. Mind your manners, you young beggar! (*Seizes Tom by collar and sends him sprawling into crowd. Villagers laugh as Tom slowly gets to his feet.*)

Prince (*rushing to gates*). How dare you treat a poor subject of the King in such a manner! Open the gates and let him in! (*As Villagers see Prince, they remove hats, and bow low.*)

> **subject**
> (sŭb′ jĭkt)
> person under the king's control

Villagers (*shouting together*). Long live the Prince of Wales! (*Guards open gates and Tom slowly passes through, as if in a dream.*)

Prince (*to Tom*). You look tired, and you have been treated cruelly. I am Edward, Prince of Wales. What is your name?

Tom (*in awe*). Tom Canty, Your Highness.

THINK IT THROUGH
How did Tom Canty get into the palace?

Prince. Come into the palace with me, Tom. (*Prince*
40   *leads* Tom *into anteroom. Villagers*
      pantomime *conversation, and all but*
      a few exit.) Where do you live, Tom?

pantomime
(păn′ tə mĭm′)
pretend to talk,
but make no
sound

Tom. In Offal Court, Your Highness.

Prince. Offal Court? That's an odd
      name. Do you have parents?

Tom. Yes, Your Highness.

Prince. How does your father treat you?

Tom. If it please you, Your Highness,
      when I am not able to beg for a penny
50   for our supper, he treats me to
      beatings.

REREAD
What kind of life
does Tom have?

Prince (*shocked*). What! My father is not a calm man,
      but he does not beat me. (*looks at* Tom
      thoughtfully) You speak well and have an easy
      grace. Have you been schooled?

Tom. Very little, Your Highness. A good priest who
      shares our house has taught me from his books.

Prince. Do you have a pleasant life in Offal Court?

Tom. Pleasant enough, Your Highness, save when I am
60   hungry. We have Punch and Judy shows, and
      sometimes we lads have fights in the street.

Prince (*eagerly*). I should like that. Tell me more.

Tom. In summer, we run races and swim in the river,
      and we love to wallow in the mud.

Prince (*wistfully*). If I could wear your clothes and play in the mud just once, with no one to forbid me, I think I could give up the crown!

Tom (*shaking his head*). And if I could wear your fine clothes just once, Your Highness . . .

70 **Prince.** Would you like that? Come then. We shall change places. You can take off your rags and put on my clothes—and I will put on yours. (*He leads* Tom *behind screen, and they return shortly, each wearing the other's clothes.*) Let's look in this mirror. (*leads* Tom *to mirror*)

Tom (*in the* Prince's *clothes*). Oh, Your Highness, it is not proper for me to wear such clothes.

REREAD
Describe the Prince now. Describe Tom.

Prince (*in* Tom's *rags, excitedly*). Heavens,
80   do you not see it? We look like brothers!
We have the same features and | bearing |.
If we went about together, dressed alike,
there is no one who could say which is the
Prince of Wales and which is Tom Canty.

> **bearing**
> (bâr′ ĭng)
> the way a person
> stands, sits, walks,
> or behaves

THINK IT THROUGH
> Why are the Prince and Tom envious of each other's lives?

FOCUS
> Read on to find out how the Prince gets into trouble.

Tom (*drawing back, rubbing hand*). Your Highness, I
am frightened. . . .

Prince. Do not worry. (*seeing* Tom *rub hand*) Is that a
bruise on your hand?

Tom. Yes, but it is a slight thing, Your Highness.

90 **Prince** (*angrily*). It was shameful and cruel of that
guard to strike you. Do not stir a step until I come
back. I command you! (*He picks up
golden seal and carefully puts it into
piece of armor. He then dashes out to
gates.*) Open! Unbar the gates at once!
(2nd Guard *opens gates, and as* Prince
runs out, 1st Guard *seizes him,* | boxes | *him
on the ear, and knocks him to ground.*)

> **REREAD**
> Watch for this
> seal later.

> **boxes**
> (bŏk′ sĭz)
> hits

1st Guard. Take that, you little beggar, for
100   the trouble you have made for me with the Prince.
(Villagers *roar with laughter.*)

Prince (*picking himself up, turning on* Guard
furiously). I am Prince of Wales! You shall hang for
laying your hand on me!

1st Guard (*presenting arms; mockingly*).
I salute Your Gracious Highness!

(*then, angrily shoving* Prince *aside*) Be
off, you mad bag of rags! (Prince *is
surrounded by* Villagers, *who hustle*
110   *him off.*)

REREAD
Why does the
guard treat the
Prince this way?

Villagers (*ad lib, as they exit, shouting*). Make way for
His Royal Highness! Make way for the Prince of
Wales! Hail to the Prince! (*etc.*)

THINK IT THROUGH
What has happened to the Prince?

FOCUS
What is happening at the same time to Tom, the beggar
dressed as the Prince?

Tom (*admiring himself in mirror*). If only the boys in
Offal Court could see me! They will not believe me
when I tell them about this. (*looks around
anxiously*) But where is the Prince? (*looks
cautiously into courtyard*. Two Guards *immediately
snap to attention and salute. He quickly ducks back
120   into anteroom as* Lords St. John *and* Hertford *enter
at rear.*)

Hertford (*going toward* Tom, *then
stopping and bowing low*). My Lord,
you look distressed. What is wrong?

REREAD
Who does
Hertford think
he's talking to?

Tom (*trembling*). Oh, I beg of you, be
merciful. I am no prince, but poor
Tom Canty of Offal Court. Please let
me see the Prince, and he will give my
rags back to me and let me go unhurt.
130   (*kneeling*) Please, be merciful and spare me!

merciful
(mûr′ sĭ fəl)
showing great
kindness

Hertford (*disturbed*). Your Highness, on your knees? To me? (*bows quickly, then, aside to* St. John) The Prince has gone mad! We must inform the King. (*to* Tom) A moment, Your Highness. (Hertford *and* St. John *exit rear.*)

Tom. Oh, there is no hope for me now. They will hang me for certain! (*Hertford and* St. John *reenter, supporting* King. Tom *watches in awe as they help him to couch, where he sinks down wearily.*)

140 **King** (*beckoning* Tom *close to him*). Now, my son, Edward, my prince. What is this? Do you mean to deceive me, the King, your father, who loves you and treats you so kindly?

Tom (*dropping to his knees*). You are the King? Then I have no hope!

> **REREAD**
> Why do you think Tom is scared?

King (*stunned*). My child, you are not well. Do not break your father's old heart. Say you know me.

Tom. Yes, you are my lord the King, whom God
150 preserve.

King. True, that is right. Now, you will not deny that you are Prince of Wales, as they say you did just a while ago?

Tom. Your Grace, believe me, I am the lowest of your subjects, being born a pauper, and it is by great mistake that I am here. I am too young to die. Oh, please, spare me, sire!

King (*amazed*). Die? Do not talk so, my child. You shall not die.

160 **Tom** (*gratefully*). God save you, my king! And now, may I go?

King. Go? Where would you go?

Tom. Back to the alley where I was born and bred to misery.

King. My poor child, rest your head here. (*He holds* Tom's *head and pats his shoulder, then turns to* Hertford *and* St. John.) Alas, I am old and ill, and my son is mad. But this shall pass. Mad or sane, he is my heir and shall rule England. Tomorrow he shall be installed and confirmed in his princely dignity! Bring the Great Seal!

170

> **heir**
> (âr)
> *n.* one who gets a person's money or title after the person dies

Hertford (*bowing low*). Please, Your Majesty, you took the Great Seal from the Chancellor two days ago to give to His Highness the Prince.

King. So I did. (*to* Tom) My child, tell me, where is the Great Seal?

Tom (*trembling*). Indeed, my lord, I do not know.

180

> **REREAD**
> Why doesn't Tom know where the seal is?

King. Ah, your affliction hangs heavily upon you. 'Tis no matter. You will remember later. Listen, carefully! (*gently, but firmly*) I command you to hide your affliction in all ways that be within your power. You shall deny to no one that you are the true prince, and if your memory should fail you upon any occasion of state, you shall be advised by your uncle, the Lord Hertford.

> **affliction**
> (ə flĭk′ shən)
> *n.* cause of pain

190 **Tom** (*resigned*). The King has spoken. The King shall be obeyed.

THINK IT THROUGH
Why does the King think his son is mad?

King. And now, my child, I go to rest. (*He stands weakly, and* Hertford *leads him off, rear.*)

Tom (*wearily, to* St. John). May it please your lordship to let me rest now?

St. John. So it please Your Highness, it is for you to command and us to obey. But it is wise that you
200 rest, for this evening you must attend the Lord Mayor's banquet in your honor. (*He pulls bellcord, and* Three Pages *enter and kneel before* Tom.)

Tom. Banquet? (*Terrified, he sits on couch and reaches for cup of water, but* 1st Page *instantly seizes cup, drops to one knee, and serves it to him.* Tom *starts to take off boots, but* 2nd Page *stops him and does it for him. He tries to remove cape and gloves, and* 3rd Page *does it for him.*) I wonder that you do not try to breathe for me also! (*Lies down cautiously.*
210 Pages *cover him with robe, then back away and exit.*)

St. John (*to* Hertford, *as he enters*). Plainly, what do you think?

plainly
(plān′ lē)
honestly

Hertford. Plainly, this. The King is near death, my nephew the Prince of Wales is clearly mad and will mount the throne mad. God protect England, for she will need it!

St. John. Does it not seem strange that madness could so change his manner from what it used to be? It
220 troubles me, his saying he is not the Prince.

Hertford. Peace, my lord! If he were an impostor and called himself the Prince, that would be natural. But was there ever an impostor, who being called Prince by the King and court, denied it? Never! This is the true Prince gone mad. And tonight all London shall honor him. (*Hertford and* St. John *exit.* Tom *sits up, looks around helplessly, then gets up.*)

230 **Tom.** I should have thought to order something to eat. (*sees bowl of nuts on table*) Ah! Here are some nuts! (*Looks around, sees Great Seal in armor, takes it out, looks at it curiously.*) This will make a good nutcracker. (*He takes bowl of nuts, sits on couch and begins to crack nuts with Great Seal and eat them, as curtain falls.*)

> **impostor**
> (ĭm pŏs′ tər)
> *n.* person who pretends to be someone else

* * * * *

THINK IT THROUGH
Why do people believe that Tom is the Prince, even though he keeps saying that he is not?

FOCUS
Now read on to discover what's happening to the real Prince out on the streets.

Scene 2

Time: *Later that night.*

Setting: *A street in London, near Offal Court. Played before curtain.*

240 **At Curtain Rise:** Prince *limps in, dirty and* tousled. *He looks around wearily. Several* Villagers *pass by, pushing against him.*

> **tousled**
> (tou′ zəld)
> made untidy

Prince (*dressed in rags*). I have never seen this poor section of London. I must be near Offal Court. If only I can find it before I drop! (John Canty *steps out of crowd, seizes* Prince *roughly.*)

250 **Canty.** Out at this time of night, and I warrant you haven't brought a farthing home! If that is the case and I do not break all the bones in your miserable body, then I am not John Canty.

Prince (*eagerly*). Oh, are you his father?

Canty. *His* father? I am *your* father, and—

Prince. Take me to the palace at once, and your son will be returned to you. The King, my father, will make you rich beyond your wildest dreams. Oh, save me, for I am indeed

260 the Prince of Wales.

Canty (*staring in amazement*). Gone stark mad! But mad or not, I'll soon find where the soft places lie in your bones. Come home! (*starts to drag* Prince *off*)

Prince (*struggling*). Let me go! I am the Prince of Wales, and the King shall have your life for this!

Canty (*angrily*). I'll take no more of your madness! (*Raises stick to strike, but* Prince *struggles free and runs off.* Canty *runs after him.*)

* * * * *

THINK IT THROUGH

Why does Tom's father think the Prince is mad?

---

warrant
(wôr′ ənt)
declare

farthing
(fär′ *th*ĭng)
old British coin

REREAD
Who is John Canty and who does he think the Prince is?

Scene 3

270 **Setting:** *Same as Scene 1 (inside Palace), with addition of dining table, set with dishes and goblets, on raised platform. Throne-like chair is at head of table.*

At Curtain Rise: *A banquet is in progress.* Tom, *in royal robes, sits at head of table, with* Hertford *at his right and* St. John *at his left.* Lords *and* Ladies *sit around table, eating and talking softly.*

Tom (*dressed as Prince; to* Hertford). What is this, my Lord? (*holds up plate*)

280 **Hertford.** Lettuce and turnips, Your Highness.

Tom. Lettuce and turnips? I have never seen them before. Am I to eat them?

Hertford (|*discreetly*|). Yes, Your Highness, if you so desire. (Tom *begins to eat food with his fingers. Fanfare of trumpets is heard, and* Herald *enters, carrying scroll. All turn to look.*)

> **discreetly**
> (dĭ skrēt′ lē)
> in a wisely cautious way

Herald (*reading from scroll*). His Majesty, King Henry VIII, is dead! The King is dead! (*All rise and turn to*
290 Tom, *who sits, stunned.*)

All (*together*). The King is dead. Long live the King! Long live Edward, the King of England! (*All bow to* Tom. Herald *bows and exits.*)

Hertford (*to* Tom). Your Majesty, we must call the |council|. Come, St. John. (Hertford *and* St. John *lead* Tom *off at*

> **REREAD**
> Why are they calling Tom the King?

rear. Lords *and* Ladies *follow, talking among themselves. At gates, down right,* Villagers *enter and mill about.* Prince *enters right, pounds on gates and shouts.*)

300

Prince (*still in rags*). Open the gates! I am the Prince of Wales! Open, I say! And though I am friendless with no one to help me, I will not be driven from my ground.

Miles Hendon (*entering through crowd*). Though you be Prince or not, you are indeed a gallant lad and not friendless. Here I stand to prove it, and you might have a worse friend than Miles Hendon.

gallant
(găl′ ənt)
brave

310

1st Villager. 'Tis another prince in disguise. Take the lad and dunk him in the pond! (*He seizes* Prince, *but* Miles *strikes him with flat of his sword. Crowd, now angry, presses forward threateningly, when fanfare of trumpets is heard offstage.* Herald, *carrying scroll, enters up left at gates.*)

Herald. Make way for the King's messenger! (*reading from scroll*) His Majesty, King Henry VIII is dead! The King is dead! (*He exits right, repeating message, and* Villagers *stand in stunned silence.*)

320

Prince (*stunned*). The King is dead!

1st Villager (*shouting*). Long live Edward, King of England!

Villagers (*together*). Long live the King! (*shouting, ad lib*) Long live King Edward! Heaven protect Edward, King of England!

Miles (*taking* Prince *by arm*). Come, lad, before the crowd remembers us. I have a room at the inn, and

330 you can stay there. (*He hurries off with stunned* Prince. Tom, *led by* Hertford, *enters courtyard up rear.* Villagers *see them.*)

REREAD
Why might you call this a "near miss"?

Villagers (*together*). Long live the King! (*They fall to their knees as curtains close.*)

* * * * *

THINK IT THROUGH

How has the King's death affected both Tom and the Prince?

FOCUS

Read Scene 4 to learn what happens when Miles falls asleep.

Scene 4

Setting: Miles's *room at inn. At right is table set with dishes and bowls of food, a chair at each side. At left is bed, with table and chair next to it, and a window. Candle is on table.*

At Curtain Rise: Miles *and* Prince *approach table.*

340 **Miles.** I have had a hot supper prepared. I'll bet you're hungry, lad.

Prince (*dressed in rags*). Yes, I am. It's kind of you to let me stay with you, Miles. I am truly Edward, King of England, and you shall not go unrewarded. (*sits at table*)

Miles (*to himself*). First he called himself Prince, and now King. Well, I will humor him. (*starts to sit*)

Prince (*angrily*). Stop! Would you sit in the presence of the King?

350 **Miles** (*surprised, standing up quickly*). I beg your pardon, Your Majesty. I was not thinking. (*Stares*

uncertainly at Prince, *who sits at table, expectantly.*
Miles *starts to uncover dishes of food, serves* Prince
and fills glasses.)

Prince. Miles, you have a gallant way about you. Are
you nobly born?

Miles. My father is a baronet, Your
Majesty.

> **baronet**
> (băr′ ə nĭt)
> British nobleman

Prince. Then you also must be a baronet.

360 **Miles** (*shaking his head*). My father
banished me from home seven years ago,
so I fought in the wars. I was taken
prisoner, and I have spent the past seven
years in prison. Now I am free, and I am
returning home.

> **banished**
> (băn′ ĭsht)
> forced to leave

Prince. You must have been shamefully wronged! But
I will make things right for you. You have saved me

from injury and possible death. Name your reward
and if it be within the compass of my royal power,
370   it is yours.

Miles (*pausing briefly, then dropping to
his knee*). Since Your Majesty is
pleased to hold my simple duty worthy
of reward, I ask that I and my successors may hold
the privilege of sitting in the presence of the King.

REREAD
Why is Miles
acting like this?

Prince (*taking* Miles's *sword, tapping him lightly on
each shoulder*). Rise and seat yourself. (*returns
sword to* Miles, *then rises and goes over to bed*)

Miles (*rising*). He should have been born a king. He
380   plays the part to a marvel! If I had not thought of
this favor, I might have had to stand for weeks. (*sits
down and begins to eat*)

Prince. Sir Miles, you will stand guard while I sleep. (*lies down and instantly falls asleep*)

Miles. Yes, Your Majesty. (*With a* rueful *look at his uneaten supper, he stands up.*) Poor little chap. I suppose his mind has been disordered with ill usages. (*covers* Prince *with his cape*) Well, I will be his friend and watch over him. (*Blows out candle, then yawns and sits on chair next to bed, and falls asleep. John Canty and* Hugo *appear at window, peer around room, then enter cautiously through window. They lift the sleeping* Prince, *staring nervously at* Miles.)

390

> rueful
> (rōō' fəl)
> unhappy

> **REREAD**
> Does Miles believe the Prince? How do you know?

Canty (*in a loud whisper*). I swore the day he was born he would be a thief and a beggar, and I won't lose him now. Lead the way to the camp, Hugo! (Canty *and* Hugo *carry* Prince *off right, as* Miles *sleeps on and curtain falls.*)

400

* * * * *

THINK IT THROUGH
Why do John Canty and Hugo carry off the Prince?

FOCUS
What will the Prince's life be like with John Canty?

Scene 5
Time: *Two weeks later.*
Setting: *Country village street. May be played before curtain.*
Before Curtain Rise: Villagers *walk about.* Canty, Hugo, *and* Prince *enter.*

Canty. I will go in this direction. Hugo, keep my mad son with you, and see that he does not escape again! (*exits*)

410 **Hugo** (*seizing* Prince *by the arm*). He won't escape! I'll see that he earns his bread today, or else!

Prince (*dressed in rags; pulling away*). I will not beg with you, and I will not steal! I have suffered enough in this miserable company of thieves!

Hugo. You shall suffer more if you do not do as I tell you! (*raises clenched fist at* Prince) Refuse if you dare! (Woman *enters, carrying wrapped bundle in a basket on her arm.*) Wait here until I come back.

420 (Hugo *sneaks along after* Woman, *then snatches her bundle, runs back to* Prince, *and thrusts it into his arms.*) Run after me and call, "Stop, thief!" Be sure you lead her astray! (*Runs off.* Prince *throws down bundle in disgust.*)

> **REREAD**
>
> What does Hugo do to try to trick the woman?

Woman. Help! Thief! Stop, thief! (*rushes at* Prince *and seizes him, just as several* Villagers *enter*) You little thief! What do you mean by robbing a poor woman? Somebody bring the constable! (Miles *enters and watches.*)

430 **1st Villager** (*grabbing* Prince). I'll teach him a lesson, the little villain!

Prince (*struggling*). Unhand me! I did not rob this woman!

Miles (*stepping forth and pushing man back with the flat of his sword*). Let us proceed gently, my friends. This is a matter for the law.

Prince (*springing to* Miles's *side*). You have come just in time, Sir Miles. Carve this rabble to rags!

Miles. Speak softly. Trust in me and all shall go well.
440 (Constable *enters*)

Constable (*reaching for* Prince). Come along, young
rascal!

Miles. Gently, good friend. He shall go peaceably to
the Justice.

Prince. I will not go before a Justice! I did not do this
thing!

Miles (*taking him aside*). Sire, will you
reject the laws of the realm, yet demand
that your subjects respect them?

realm
(rělm)
kingdom

450 **Prince** (*after a pause; calmly*). You are
right, Sir Miles. Whatever the King
requires a subject to suffer under the
law, he will suffer himself while he
holds the station of a subject.
(Constable *leads them off right.*
Villagers *follow.*)

REREAD

How do Miles
and the Prince
feel about obey-
ing the law?

* * * * *

Setting: *Office of the* Justice. *A high bench is at
center.*

At Curtain Rise: Justice *sits behind bench.* Constable
460 *enters with* Miles *and* Prince, *followed by* Villagers.
Woman *carries wrapped bundle.*

Constable (*to* Justice). A young thief, your worship, is
accused of stealing a dressed pig from this poor
woman.

Justice (*looking down at* Prince, *then* Woman). My
good woman, are you absolutely certain this lad
stole your pig?

Woman. It was none other than he, your worship.

Justice. Are there no witnesses to the contrary? (*All shake their heads.*) Then the lad stands convicted. (*to* Woman) What do you hold this property to be worth?

REREAD
What does this tell about how the law treats common people?

Woman. Three shillings and eight pence, your worship.

shillings, pence
British coins

Justice (*leaning down to* Woman). Good woman, do you know that when one steals a thing above the value of thirteen pence, the law says he shall hang for it?

Woman (*upset*). Oh, what have I done? I would not hang the poor boy for the whole world! Save me from this, your worship. What can I do?

Justice (*gravely*). You may revise the value, since it is not yet written in the record.

Woman. Then call the pig eight pence, your worship.

Justice. So be it. You may take your property and go. (Woman *starts off, and is followed by* Constable. Miles *follows them cautiously down right.*)

Constable (*stopping* Woman). Good woman, I will buy your pig from you. (*Takes coins from his pocket.*) Here is eight pence.

Woman. Eight pence! It cost me three shillings and eight pence.

Constable. Indeed! Then come back before his worship and answer for this. The lad must hang!

REREAD
Why does the woman let the constable pay so little for the pig?

Woman. No! No! Say no more. Give me the eight pence and hold your peace.

500 (Constable *hands her coins and takes pig.* Woman
exits, angrily. Miles *returns to bench.*)

Justice. The boy is sentenced to a ⸂fortnight⸃
in the common jail. Take him away,
Constable! (Justice *exits.* Prince *gives*
Miles *a nervous glance.*)

> **fortnight**
> (fôrt′ nīt′)
> two weeks

Miles (*following* Constable). Good sir, turn your back
a moment and let the poor lad escape. He is
innocent.

Constable (*outraged*). What? You say this to me? Sir, I
510 arrest you in—

Miles. Do not be so hasty! (*slyly*) The pig you have
purchased for eight pence may cost you your neck,
man.

Constable (*laughing nervously*). Ah, but I
was merely ⸂jesting⸃ with the woman, sir.

> **jesting**
> (jĕs′ tĭng)
> joking

Miles. Would the Justice think it a jest?

Constable. Good sir! The Justice has no
more sympathy with a jest than a dead corpse!
(*perplexed*) Very well, I will turn my back and see
520 nothing! But go quickly! (*exits*)

Miles (*to* Prince). Come, my ⸂liege⸃. We are
free to go. And that band of thieves
shall not set hands on you again. I
swear it!

> **liege**
> (lēj)
> lord or king

Prince (*wearily*). Can you believe, Sir Miles, that in
the last fortnight, I, the King of England, have
escaped from thieves and begged for
food on the road? I have slept in a
barn with a calf! I have washed dishes
530 in a peasant's kitchen, and narrowly
escaped death. And not once in all my

> **REREAD**
> Compare the
> Prince's experi-
> ence with Tom's.

wanderings did I see a courier searching for me! Is it not matter for commotion and distress that the head of state is gone?

Miles (*sadly, aside*). Still busy with his pathetic dream. (*to* Prince) It is strange indeed, my liege. But come, I will take you to my father's home in Kent. There you may rest in a house with seventy rooms! I am all impatient to be home

540 again!

(*They exit,* Miles *cheerful,* Prince *puzzled, as curtains close.*)

REREAD

How will the setting change?

* * * * *

THINK IT THROUGH
How do you think the Prince's experiences with the law have affected him?

FOCUS
Discover a sudden change in setting in the next scene.

Scene 6
Setting: *Village jail. Bare stage, with barred window on one wall.*

At Curtain Rise: Two Prisoners, *in chains, are onstage.* Jailer *shoves* Miles *and* Prince, *in chains, onstage. They struggle and protest.*

Miles. But I tell you, I *am* Miles Hendon! My brother, Sir Hugh, has stolen my

550 bride and my estate!

assaulting
(ə sôl′ tĭng)
attacking

Jailer. Be silent! Sir Hugh will see that you pay well for claiming to be his dead brother and for assaulting him in his own house! (*exits*)

REREAD

What has happened to Miles?

Miles (*sitting with head in hands*). Oh, my dear Edith . . . now wife to my brother Hugh, against her will, and my poor father . . . dead!

1st Prisoner. At least you have your life, sir. I am to be hanged for killing a deer in the King's park.

560 **2nd Prisoner.** And I must hang for stealing a yard of cloth to dress my children.

Prince (*moved; to* Prisoners). When I mount the throne, you shall be free. And the laws that have dishonored you shall be swept from the books. (*turning away*) Kings should go to school to learn their own laws and be merciful.

1st Prisoner. What does the lad mean? I have heard that the King is mad, but merciful.

2nd Prisoner. He is to be crowned at Westminster
570 tomorrow.

Prince (*violently*). King? What King, good sir?

1st Prisoner. Why, we have only one, his most sacred majesty, King Edward the Sixth.

2nd Prisoner. Whether he be mad or not, his praises are on all men's lips. He has saved many innocent lives, and plans to destroy the cruelest laws that oppress people.

> **oppress**
> (ə prĕs′)
> *v.* rule harshly

Prince (*turning away, shaking his head*). How can this be? Surely it is not that
580 little beggar boy! (Sir Hugh *enters with* Jailer.)

> **REREAD**
> What has the Prince just realized?

Sir Hugh. Seize the impostor! (Jailer *pulls* Miles *to his feet*.)

Miles. Hugh, this has gone far enough!

Sir Hugh. You will sit in the public stocks, and the boy would join you if he were not so young. See to it, jailer, and after two hours, you may release them. Meanwhile, I ride to London for the

590 coronation! (Sir Hugh *exits and* Miles *is hustled out by* Jailer.)

Prince. Coronation! There can be no coronation without me! (*curtain*)

* * * * *

THINK IT THROUGH
What has the Prince learned while in jail?

FOCUS
Learn whether the Prince makes it to the coronation.

stocks
(stŏks)
wooden frame with holes for feet and hands, used to punish

coronation
(kôr′ə nā′ shən)
ceremony for crowning a king

Scene 7

Time: *Coronation Day.*

Setting: *Outside gates of Westminster Abbey, played before curtain. Painted screen or flat at rear represents Abbey. Throne is center. Bench is near it.*

At Curtain Rise: Lords *and* Ladies *crowd Abbey. Outside gates,* Guards *drive back cheering*

600 Villagers, *among them* Miles.

Miles (*distraught*). I've lost him! Poor little chap! He has been swallowed up in the crowd! (*Fanfare of trumpets is heard, then* Hertford, St. John, Lords *and* Ladies *enter slowly, followed by* Pages, *one of whom carries crown on small cushion.* Tom *follows*

procession, looking about nervously. Suddenly,
Prince, *in rags, steps from crowd, his hand raised.*)

Prince. I forbid you to set the crown of England upon that head. I am the King!

610 **Hertford.** Seize the vagabond!

Tom. I forbid it! He *is* the King! (*kneeling before* Prince) Oh, my lord the King, let poor Tom Canty be the first to say, "Put on your crown and enter into your own right again." (Hertford *and several* Lords *look closely at both boys.*)

> **REREAD**
> Read this passage aloud. Take turns acting out the parts.

Hertford. This is strange indeed. (*to* Tom) By your favor, sir, I wish to ask certain questions of this lad.

Prince. I will answer truly whatever you may ask, my
620 lord.

Hertford. But if you have been well trained, you may answer my questions as well as our lord the King. I need definite proof. (*thinks a moment*) Ah! Where lies the Great Seal of England? It has been missing for weeks, and only the true Prince of Wales can say where it lies.

> **REREAD**
> Where did the Prince carefully put the seal at the beginning of the play?

Tom. Wait! Was the seal round and thick, with letters engraved on it? (Hertford *nods.*) I know
630 where it is, but it was not I who put it there. The rightful King shall tell you. (*to* Prince) Think, my King, it was the very last thing you did that day before you rushed out of the palace wearing my rags.

Prince (*pausing*). I recall how we exchanged clothes, but have no recollection of hiding the Great Seal.

Tom (*eagerly*). Remember when you saw the bruise on my hand you ran to the door, but first you hid this thing you call the Seal.

640 **Prince** (*suddenly*). Ah! I remember! (*to* St. John) My good St. John, you shall find the Great Seal in the armor that hangs on the wall in my chamber . (St. John *hesitates, but at a nod from* Tom *hurries off.*)

> **chamber**
> (chām' bər)
> room

Tom (*pleased*). Right, my King! Now the scepter of England is yours again. (St. John *returns in a moment with Great Seal, holds it up for all to see.*)

> **scepter**
> (sĕp' tər)
> special stick that is a symbol of power

All (*shouting*). Long live Edward, King of
650 England! (Tom *takes off cape and throws it over* Prince's *rags. Trumpet fanfare is heard.* St. John *takes crown and places it on* Prince. *All kneel.*)

Hertford. Let the small impostor be flung into the Tower!

Prince (*firmly*). I will not have it so. But for him, I would not have my crown. (*to* Tom) My poor boy, how was it you could remember where I hid the Seal?

660 **Tom** (*embarrassed*). I did not know what it was, my King, and I used it to . . . crack nuts. (*All laugh.* Miles *steps forward, staring in amazement.*)

Miles. Is he really the King, the sovereign of England, and not the poor and friendless Tom o' Bedlam I thought he was? (*sinks down on bench*) I wish I had a bag to hide my head in!

> **sovereign**
> (sŏv' ər ĭn)
> ruler

1st Guard (*rushing up to him*). Stand up, you mannerless clown! How dare you sit in the presence of the King!

Prince. Do not touch him! He is my trusty servant, Miles Hendon, who saved me from shame and possible death. For his service, he owns the right to sit in my presence.

Miles (*bowing, then kneeling*). Your Majesty!

Prince. Rise, Sir Miles. I command that Sir Hugh Hendon, who sits within this hall, be seized and put under lock and key until I have need of him. (*beckons to* Tom) From what I have heard, Tom Canty, you have governed the realm with royal gentleness and mercy in my absence. Henceforth, you shall hold the honorable title of King's Ward! (Tom *kneels and kisses* Prince's *hand.*) And because I have suffered with the poorest of my subjects and felt the cruel force of unjust laws, I pledge myself to a reign of mercy for all! (*All bow low, then rise.*)

All (*shouting*). Long live the King! Long live Edward, King of England!

THINK IT THROUGH

1. Why did the confusion between the Prince and Tom continue throughout the play?
2. How was Miles rewarded for his friendship and loyalty? How was Tom rewarded for his actions?
3. Why did the Prince promise to rule with mercy for all?

Special Places

Unit 5

Poetry

Poets use ideas, images, and feelings. Poets choose words for their sounds and meanings. Some poems create a **mood,** or feeling. Others may have a special **form,** or shape, such as the haiku you will read. The poems in this unit will show you special places.

Poets use many tools to create their poems. Sometimes they use **rhyme,** words that end in the same sound. **Sensory imagery**—words that appeal to the five senses—is also important in poetry. All poems have a **speaker,** the voice that talks to the reader. As you read, let the speakers take you to special places.

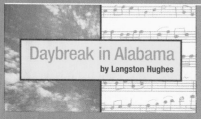

Dust
of Snow

by Robert Frost

Sometimes the smallest thing can change your whole day.

Reading Coach
CD-ROM selection

Connect to Your Life

Have you ever had a bad day? Was *everything* about that day bad? Did the sun shine? Was your lunch okay? Think of one small thing that went *right* on your bad day.

Key to the Poem

Words **rhyme** when the sounds at the ends are repeated. In this poem, *crow* and *snow* end in the same sound. Read the poem aloud; listen for the rhyming words. Also listen for the **speaker,** the voice talking to you.

Vocabulary In line 8, **rued** means "felt sorry about."

Dust of Snow
by Robert Frost

The way a crow
Shook down on me
The dust of snow
From a hemlock tree

5 Has given my heart
A change of mood
And saved some part
Of a day I had rued.

THINK IT THROUGH

1. The speaker is the voice talking to you in every poem. What happens in lines 1–4 that makes the speaker feel better?
2. Do you think the speaker is expecting anything to happen? Why or why not?
3. Which words rhyme in the first half of the poem? In the second half?

Elevator

by Lucille Clifton

How can a book help you escape?

Reading Coach
CD-ROM selection

Connect to Your Life

When do you feel that you want to escape or get away? What makes you feel better?

Key to the Poem

The **form** of a poem is the way the words and lines are arranged on the page. Sometimes a poem can look like what it is about. This tall, narrow poem should remind you of an elevator. What is the speaker doing there?

Vocabulary In line 5, **project** means "public housing."

Elevator

by Lucille Clifton

down
in the corner
my book and i
traveling
5 over the project
walls
so the world
is more than this
elevator
10 stuck between
floors again
and home
is a corner
where i crouch
15 safe
reading waiting
to start moving
up

THINK IT THROUGH

1. What is the speaker doing in the elevator? How does this activity make the speaker feel?
2. What do you think the speaker means in lines 7–9: "so the world is more than this elevator"?
3. What do you think this poet is trying to tell you about life?

Haiku

by Issa

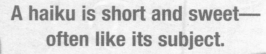

A haiku is short and sweet—
often like its subject.

Connect to Your Life

Do you ever stop to watch
one tiny insect? Or do you
ever look at just one petal
on a flower? What is the
smallest, simplest thing
you have ever stopped
to study?

Key to the Poem

Reading Coach CD-ROM selection

A **haiku** is a short Japanese poem. It usually has
only three lines. Haiku poets often write about
details in nature. In only three lines, the poet
must create a clear picture for the reader. Let
each of these haiku put a picture in your mind.

Haiku

by Issa

Don't worry, spiders,
I keep house
    casually.

        Don't kill that fly!
    Look—it's wringing its hands,
        wringing its feet.

    Under the evening moon
the snail
    is stripped to the waist.

THINK IT THROUGH

1. What small subject does each haiku describe?
2. How are the subjects of these haiku like the subject of "Dust of Snow" on page 161?
3. Make a simple drawing to illustrate one of these haiku.

Happy Thought

by Jesús Papoleto Meléndez

What makes you giggle?

Connect to Your Life

Have you ever gotten the giggles and been unable to stop? Where were you? Why do you think you couldn't stop?

Key to the Poem

The **mood** of a poem is the way it makes you feel. This poem has a mood that you will probably recognize.

**Reading Coach
CD-ROM selection**

Happy Thought

by Jesús Papoleto Meléndez

have you ever been in a
crowded train
& thought
a happy thought
5 & it's slipped
from thought
to smile
& from smile
to giggle?
10   /people stare.

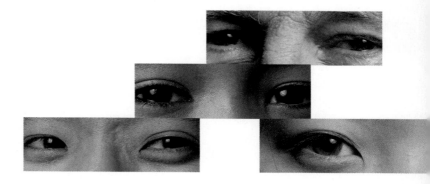

THINK IT THROUGH

1. What happens in the poem?
2. Why do you think people stare? What do you think
   the speaker does when people stare?
3. Describe the mood of this poem. What details
   create that mood?

Daybreak in Alabama

by Langston Hughes

What sights and sounds make up your favorite place?

**Reading Coach
CD-ROM selection**

Connect to Your Life

Think of a place that you like. Draw a picture of three things you like about that place. What colors are they? How do they sound? smell? taste? feel to the touch?

Key to the Poem

Some poems contain **sensory imagery,** or words that help you make pictures in your mind. The words make you use your senses. You can almost see, smell, hear, taste, or touch something. What images in this poem help you imagine daybreak in Alabama?

Daybreak in Alabama

by Langston Hughes

When I get to be a composer
I'm gonna write me some music about
Daybreak in Alabama
And I'm gonna put the purtiest songs in it
5   Rising out of the ground like a swamp mist
And falling out of heaven like soft dew.
I'm gonna put some tall tall trees in it
And the scent of pine needles
And the smell of red clay after rain
10   And long red necks
And poppy colored faces
And big brown arms
And the field daisy eyes
Of black and white black white black people
15   And I'm gonna put white hands
And black hands and brown and yellow hands
And red clay earth hands in it
Touching everybody with kind fingers
And touching each other natural as dew
20   In that dawn of music when I
Get to be a composer
And write about daybreak
In Alabama.

THINK IT THROUGH

1. Find an image in the poem that tells how
   something looks. What colors are mentioned?
2. Now find images that tell how something smells
   and how something feels to the touch.
3. How do those images make you feel about Alabama?
   How does the speaker feel about Alabama?

GRAFFITI

BY JANE YOLEN

A LITTLE GRAFFITI CAN SAY
A LOT ABOUT THE PERSON
WHO WROTE IT.

Connect to Your Life

Where have you seen graffiti? Did you think about the writer? How do you think the writer felt when he or she wrote it?

Key to the Poem

Every poem has a **speaker,** the one who is talking to you when you read the poem. The speaker in this poem has something to say to you about life.

This poem also has a theme. The **theme** is a message that the poet wants you to understand about life. Is that what this speaker is talking about?

Reading Coach CD-ROM selection

GRAFFITI

BY JANE YOLEN

I read a sad poem
on the wall
on my way to school:

SOME DAY SUGAR

5   YOU GONNA FIND

NO ONE IN THE WORLD

GONNA GIVE YOU SWEET

But I thought of Mama
ironing my skirt
10   this morning,
Daddy giving me
a brand new box of crayons,
and all my aunts and uncles
lining up for hugs
15   yesterday,
a whole day
before my birthday.

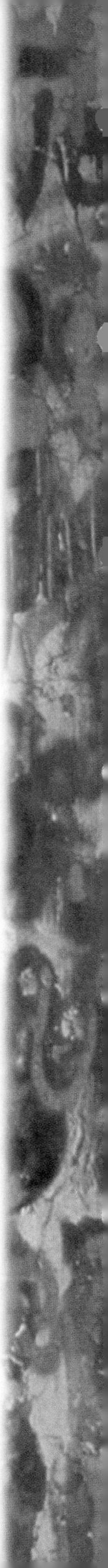

Sweet may not be
a box of candy;
20 sweet may not be
a chocolate birthday cake.
But you can taste it
your whole life long.

Anyway—
25 what does someone know
who has to use a wall
to write a poem?

THINK IT THROUGH

1. What does the message on the wall mean to you?
2. Does the speaker agree or disagree with the message on the wall? How do you know?
3. What is the theme of this poem, or its message about life?

The Battle Is On!

Unit 6

Mixed Genres

In a war, a battle is a kind of test. A battle can be a test of strength. It can be a test of courage or of wisdom. A fighter must be ready for all that a battle might be. Even then, there's no promise of survival.

In this unit, you'll read a **folk tale, historical fiction,** a **true account,** and a **legend.** You'll meet fighters from across time and learn their fighting ways. You'll read about what it's like to win or to lose.

High as Han Hsin

At a time of war, is brain power better than muscle power? See what happens in this tale of a great general.

**translated by
Arthur Bowie Chrisman**

Connect to Your Life

Which is better, physical strength or the ability to think? Share your opinion with another classmate.

Key to the Folk Tale

A **folk tale** is a story that has been passed by word of mouth. Folk tales may be set in the distant past and involve amazing events. This tale about the character Han Hsin (hän' shĭn') takes place long ago in China. As you read, you will come across a few Chinese words. They give the folk tale a flavor of another time and place.

Vocabulary Preview

Words to Know

| imbecile | wits | ambush |
| idiotic | cunning | |

 Reading Coach CD-ROM selection

Han Hsin was not at all high as to stature. He was short, short as a day in the Month of Long Nights. But as a leader of bow-drawing men, his place is high. As inventor of the world's first kite, he rose very high indeed, and that accounts for the saying "High as Han Hsin."

The night that saw Han Hsin's birth was no ordinary night. It was a night of fear and grandeur. The Shen who places the stars in the sky
10 had a shaking hand that eve. His fingers were palsied and could not hold. Star after star dropped down toward earth, and the people prayed and wept, the while they exploded firecrackers. It's a sinister sign when the stars tumble out of the sky. This the people knew. Therefore, they trembled.

Shen
supreme being, like God

sinister
(sĭn' ĭ stər)
evil; warning of trouble

But amid the falling stars was one that rose, as if the Shen had tossed it, as if the Shen had thrown it high. One large star mounted higher and higher the
20 while its companions fell. Wise men, astrologers, they who scan the heavens, said: "The stars that fall are mighty men who die. The star that rises—that is the star of a future great man—born this night."

The wise men of the village kept careful watch over Han Hsin. He had been born on the night of the Rising Star. They thought perhaps he might be the ward of the Star. They watched

ward
(wôrd)
child under protection

closely for signs to strengthen their belief. But for some years Han Hsin disappointed them.

30 He rattled his calabash in an extremely ordinary manner. There was no hint of greatness in the way he bounced a ball. Yet the astrologers held to their faith, and watched—and finally were rewarded.

calabash
(kăl′ ə băsh′)
dried, hollowed-out fruit from a calabash vine

There came a rain, not a hard rain, nevertheless a wetting rain, sufficient to drive the villagers under shelter. But Han Hsin remained in the open where quick drops pelted. A foolish villager noticed him and said, laughing: "Look you at our future great man.

40 He knows not enough to seek cover from the storm. Ho. Ho. Ho. How wise."

An old astrologer said: "Hush, *Chieh Kuo* [Dunce]; do you not see that the youth makes a bridge? Come with me." They went closer to have a more complete view. The flowing water had formed a little island in the street. Upon the island were many ants. As the water rose, the island grew smaller—and the number of ants grew smaller, many being swept away to their death. Han Hsin raised a bridge from island to

50 mainland. The ants quickly discovered his bridge and crossed to safety. "It is a sign," said the old astrologer, "*Chi li* [a good omen]. He has befriended the ants. The ants will remember. Someday they will do him an equal service—helping him to become great."

THINK IT THROUGH
How does Han Hsin help the ants? Why are the wise men pleased with his actions?

FOCUS ———————————————————
Han Hsin's actions continue to confuse others. Keep reading
to find out the unusual thing he does next.

Han Hsin discovered in the King's paved road a
hatchet of better than fair metal. None of the villagers
could prove ownership. Little Han was permitted to
keep his treasure. Quite soon a spirited chopping was
heard—steel ringing upon stone. A foolish villager said:
60 "Look. Han Hsin uses his fine hatchet to chop the old
millstone—thus demonstrating his great genius. Ho.
Ho. Ho. He uses valuable edged steel to chip stone."

The old astrologer said, "Hush, *Sha
Tzu* [Imbecile]; come with me, and
behold." A worn-out millstone lay at
the edge of the road. Through the hole
in its center grew a bamboo tree. The
hole was small. Already it hindered the tree's growth.
Retarded as it was, the bamboo could never reach a
70 full growth. Han Hsin belabored the stone till it split
in two pieces. Then there was plenty of room for the
tree. There was nothing to "pull its elbow."

imbecile
(ĭm' bə sĭl)
n. silly or stupid person

"That is good," asserted the astrologer. "He saves
the bamboo from death. Someday the bamboo will
reward him—help him to become great."

THINK IT THROUGH
How does Han Hsin save a bamboo tree?

FOCUS ———————————————————
Han Hsin meets a prince and faces a challenge. Read to find
out how the prince deals with Han Hsin.

Shortly afterward, the astrologer gave Han Hsin a
note of recommendation to the King. Han went to the
King, seeking employ. He wished a command in the

army. But His Majesty was in a sulky mood and would
not see the boy. Therefore, Han continued his journey
into Chin Chou, a neighboring country. He went to the
ruler, Prince Chin, and exhibited his note. The prince
read—and laughed. "You are too small to serve in my
army. My soldiers are giants, all—very strong. You—are
Ko Tsao [Little hopping insect]. No." Han solemnly
declared that his strength was that of a river in flood,
and begged for a trial. "Well, if you are determined,"
said the prince, "take my spear and raise it
above your head." The prince's spear was
solid iron from point to heel, and longer than
the mast of a sea-venturing junk.
Furthermore, it had been greased with
tiger fat to prevent rust. Han grasped the
spear to raise it. His fingers slipped. Down
crashed the heavy weapon. "Take whips
and lash him out of the city—clumsy knave that he is!"
Prince Chin roared in a great voice—angrily. The spear
had missed His Royal Person by the merest mite.

An old councilor spoke: "Your Highness, surely it
cannot be that you intend to let the rogue live? He will
someday return with an army to take revenge."

"Nonsense," said the prince. "He is no more than an
ant—and idiotic besides. How could such a
fellow secure an army?"

"Nevertheless, I fear the ant will work
your downfall. He must be killed." The
councilor insisted. He argued so strongly for Han's
death that, rather than hear more, the prince consented.
"It is useless. But do as you wish. Send a squad of
horses to overtake him and fetch back his head."

THINK IT THROUGH

Why does the prince give Han Hsin a death sentence?

junk
(jŭngk)
Chinese ship

REREAD
Why does Prince
Chin give Han
this impossible
test?

idiotic
(ĭd′ ē ŏt′ ĭk)
adj. stupid

| Find out how a stick of bamboo helps Han Hsin.

When Han Hsin beheld the soldiers approaching at top speed, there was no doubt in his mind as to what harsh errand brought them. He knew they intended to have his head. But Han, having lived so long with his head, had become fond of it, and preferred to keep it on his shoulders. But how? How could it be saved? There was no escape by running. There was no place to hide. The boy must use his wits.

wits
(wĭts)
n. ability to think fast

120 Hastily tying a cord to his bamboo staff, he threw the staff into a tiny shallow puddle of water that lay beside the road. The soldiers galloped up to find him seated on the bank—fishing—and weeping. "And what ails you, simpleton?" a soldier asked. "Have you lost your nurse?" Between sobs Han answered, "I am hungry and I can't catch any fish." "What a booby!" said another soldier. "He fishes in a puddle no larger than a copper cash." "Look," said yet another, "he throws in the pole, and holds the hook in his hand. What a

130 *chieh kuo;* as foolish as Nu Wa, who melted stones to mend a hole in the sky. Do you suppose this is the creature we were told to kill?" He was answered: "Nonsense. Prince Chin doesn't send his cavalry to kill an ant. Spur your horses."

When the troops returned and reported their lack of success, there was much talk. The councilor raged, offering to resign. He was positive that so long as Han Hsin lived, the government would be in danger. He was bitter because the troops had

140 mistaken Han's cunning for imbecility.

cunning
(kŭn' ĭng)
n. skill in fooling others

Merely to humor the councilor, Prince Chin mounted a horse and galloped away with his troops.

THINK IT THROUGH

Why do the soldiers leave Han Hsin alone?

FOCUS _____

Prince Chin and Han Hsin meet again. Find out how Han Hsin deals with him.

Han Hsin put his best foot foremost, hurrying toward the border. He longed to trudge the turf of his own country once more. It was not that homesickness urged his steps. Han felt reasonably sure that his friends, the soldiers, would shortly take the road again. The next time they might not be so easily deluded . Therefore, he hastened. But

150 it was useless. His own country was still miles distant when he beheld the dust of men who whipped their horses.

> **deluded**
> (dĭ lōō' dĭd)
> fooled

It is not pleasant to have one's head lopped off. At times it is almost annoying. Han thought quickly. Near by was a melon patch. The melons were large in their ripeness. Upon a huge striped *hsi kua* the boy sat him down and wept. The tears coursed down his cheeks, and his body shook with sobbing. Undoubtedly, his sorrow was great.

160 Prince Chin stopped his steed with a jerk. "*Ai chi*—such grief. Are you trying to drown yourself with tears?" "I—I—I am hungry," stammered Han Hsin. "Hungry? Then why don't you eat a melon?" "I would, sire, but I've lost my knife. So I must s-s-starve." The prince was well assured that he had met with the most foolish person in the world. "What?

Starve because you have no knife? . . . Strike the
melon with a stone. . . . Such a dunce. It would never
do for me to behead this fellow. The Shen who
170 watches over imbeciles would be made angry." A
trooper slashed a dozen melons with his sword. Surely
a dozen would save the idiot from starvation. Oh,
what an idiot!

Han Hsin sat on the ground, obscuring
his features in the red heart of a melon as
the prince and his men departed. His lips
moved—but not in eating. His lips moved
in silent laughter.

obscuring
(ŏb skyo͝or′ ĭng)
hiding

THINK IT THROUGH

How does Han Hsin escape punishment from Prince Chin? How
are his actions similar to when he escapes the soldiers?

FOCUS

Find out what steps Han Hsin takes to win an important job.

Han Hsin bothered no more Kings with notes
180 setting forth the argument that he had been born
under a lucky star, and so deserved well. Quite

casually, he fell in with King Kao Lin's army. He received no pay. His name was not on the muster . He hobnobbed with all the soldiers and soon became a favorite. The boy had a remarkable memory. He learned the name of every soldier in the army.

muster
(mŭs' tər)
list of troops

Further, he learned the good and bad traits of each soldier, knew who could be depended upon and who

190 was unreliable. He knew from what village each man came, and he could describe the village with exactness. All from hearing the soldiers talk.

A fire destroyed the army muster roll. Han Hsin quickly wrote a new list, giving the name of each man, his age, his qualities, his parents, and his village. King Kao Lin marveled. Shortly afterward, he added Han's name to the list—a general.

THINK IT THROUGH
How does Han Hsin win the position of general?

FOCUS
Han Hsin is now a general. Find out the surprises he has for two of Prince Chin's armies.

Prince Chin made war upon King Kao Lin. He marched three armies through the kingdom, and where

200 the armies had passed there was desolation , and no two stalks of grain remained in any field. Han Hsin moved against the smallest of the three armies. The enemy waited, well hidden above a mountain pass through which Han must march. It was an excellent ambush — there was no other passage. The mountain was so steep no man could climb it.

desolation
(dĕs' ə lā' shən)
destruction

ambush
(ăm' bŏosh)
n. hiding place for a surprise attack

Han caused his soldiers to remove their jackets and fill them with sand, afterward tying bottom and top

210 securely. The sandbags were placed against a cliff, to form a stairway. Up went Han and his men, to come upon the enemy from behind and capture the whole army— cook and general.

REREAD
How does Han Hsin avoid the ambush?

The second hostile army retreated to the river Lan Shui. It crossed the river, then burned all boats and bridges. So safe from pursuit felt the hostile general, he neglected to post sentries . Instead, he ordered all the men to feast and

220 make pleasure. Han Hsin ordered his men to remove the iron points from their spears. The hollow bamboo shafts of the spears were lashed together, forming rafts. Armed only with light bows, the men quickly crossed Lan Shui River and pounced upon their unready enemy. The feast was eaten by soldiers other than those for whom it had been intended.

sentries
(sĕn′ trēz)
watchmen

THINK IT THROUGH
How does Han Hsin defeat the two armies?

FOCUS
Han Hsin now plans against Prince Chin's largest army. See what idea he discovers along the way.

Prince Chin led the third and largest army. He had far more braves than Han commanded. There could be no whipping him in open battle. In strategy lay the

230 only hope. Han Hsin clothed many thousand scarecrows and placed them in the battle line—a scarecrow, a soldier—another scarecrow, another

scarecrows
(skâr′ krōz′)
fake figures made to look like people

soldier. In that manner, to all appearance, he doubled his army. Forthwith, he wrote a letter demanding surrender—pointing out that since his army was so much larger than Chin Pa's, to fight would be a useless sacrifice.

Prince Chin took long to decide upon his course. So long it took him that Han grew impatient and sat down to write again. While he wrote, a strong wind broke upon the camp. The papers on Han's table were lifted high in air. Higher and higher they swirled, higher than an eagle—for the Shen of Storms to read. Han's golden knife, resting on a paper, was lifted by the wind, transported far over the foeman's camp.

Immediately an idea seethed in the leader's mind. If a small piece of paper could carry a knife, might not a large piece carry the knife's owner? Especially when that owner happened to be not much more weighty than a three-day bean cake? It seemed reasonable.

REREAD

What idea is Han Hsin getting?

Again the little general took spears from his soldiers. The iron points were removed and the long bamboo shafts were bound together in a frame. Over the frame was fastened tough bamboo paper in many sheets. Away from prying enemy eyes, the queer contrivance was sent into the air. It proved skyworthy, lifting its maker to a fearsome height. Thus was the *feng cheng* invented. Thus was the kite, little brother of the airplane, invented by Han Hsin.

contrivance
(kən trī′ vəns)
invention

THINK IT THROUGH
Summarize the two parts of Han Hsin's plan.

Now it's time for Han Hsin to face the largest army. Find out how he uses his brain once again.

The night showed no moon. Not a star had been lighted. The wind blew strong, with an eerie whistling. It was such a night as demons walk about their mischief, and honest men keep under their quilts. Out of the sky above the enemy camp came a great flapping sound. Could it be a dragon? All eyes peered upward through the darkness. . . . Two red eyes appeared. . . .

270 Nothing more could be seen. . . . Only the two evil eyes. A voice came from the sky. "Return to your homes," boomed the voice. "The battle is lost. Return to your homes, ere they too are lost." The men of Chin shook with their fear. The Shen of the Sky had spoken. They had heard his voice. They had heard the flapping of his wings. They had seen his red and terrible eyes. How could the men of Chin know that the words they heard

280 were uttered by Han Hsin? How could they know that the flapping was caused by a man-made thing, later to be named *"feng cheng"* [kite]? And how could they know that the eyes were mere bottles filled with insects called "Bright at night" [Fireflies]? The men of Chin could not know. They loosened the ropes of their tents—and the tents came down.

Prince Chin tried in vain to hold his followers. No longer followers were they. They were fugitives, fleeing to their homes.

290 Only a few hundred remained true to their prince. Doubly armed with the weapons that had been thrown away, they ascended a steep and rocky hill, there to make their last great fight.

> **ere**
> (âr)
> before

> **REREAD**
> What do you think is happening?

> **in vain**
> without success

But Han Hsin had anticipated just such action, and had prepared for it. Unseen, he had slipped through the enemy lines and climbed the hill. With a brush dipped in honey he wrote words upon a stone. As he wrote, came hungry ants. The ants came—to aid—and to feast. Soon the stone was black with a 300 crawling multitude.

Prince Chin scaled the hill to its summit. Ten thousand swords could not dislodge him from those rocks. He would make the enemy pay a red price for success. . . . His gaze fell upon the rock. . . . He saw a host of ants forming characters that read "THE BATTLE IS LOST." His men also beheld, and they said, "The ant is wisest of all animals. Let us crawl in the dust, for we are conquered."

310 So Han Hsin victored over the three hostile armies. His country was invaded no more. In time it became really his country, for he ruled it—as a King—ruled it well. But now his wise rule is forgotten. He is remembered as the man who first made kites.

summit
(sŭm' ĭt)
top

characters
(kăr' ək tərz)
writing

THINK IT THROUGH

1. How does Han Hsin defeat Prince Chin?
2. Early in the tale, Han Hsin helps ants and a bamboo tree. How do they help him later?
3. Think about Han Hsin's actions throughout the tale. In your opinion, why is this little man so successful?

FOR WANT OF A horshoe NAIL

adapted from James Baldwin

They are only two horseshoe nails. Yet they cost a king everything. Discover what happens behind the scenes of a battle.

Connect to Your Life

In the title of the selection, the word *want* means "being without something necessary." When has *not* having something hurt you?

Key to the Story

This story takes place when horses were very important in wartime. Blacksmiths made metal tools for riders and to be used for horses.

Vocabulary Preview

Words to Know
determine   reins
advancing
retreat

Reading Coach CD-ROM selection

A battle is about to begin. Find out about the quick decision that someone makes.

King Richard the Third was preparing for the fight of his life. An army led by Henry, Earl of Richmond, was marching against him. The contest would determine who would rule England.

determine
(dĭ tûr′ mĭn)
v. decide

The morning of the battle, Richard sent a groom to make sure his favorite horse was ready.

"Shoe him quickly," the groom told the blacksmith. "The king wishes to ride at the head of his troops."

10 "You'll have to wait," the blacksmith answered. "I've shoed the king's whole army the last few days, and now I've got to go get more iron."

shoed
(shood)
fitted with a horseshoe

"I can't wait," the groom shouted impatiently. "The king's enemies are advancing right now, and we must meet them on the field. Make do with what you have."

advancing
(ăd văn′ sĭng)
v. moving forward

So the blacksmith bent to his task. From 20 a bar of iron he made four horseshoes. He hammered and shaped and fitted them to the horse's feet. Then he began to nail them on. But after he had fastened three shoes, he found he did not have enough nails for the fourth.

"I need one or two more nails," he said, "and it will take some time to hammer them out."

"I told you I can't wait," the groom said impatiently. "I hear the trumpets now. 30 Can't you just use what you've got?"

"I can put the shoe on, but it won't be as secure as the others."

"Will it hold?" asked the groom.

"It should," answered the blacksmith, "but I can't be certain."

"Well, then, just nail it on," the groom cried. "And hurry, or King Richard will be angry with us both."

THINK IT THROUGH
What does the groom tell the blacksmith to do?

FOCUS
Read on to discover how the groom's decision affects the battle.

The armies clashed, and Richard was in the thick of
40 the battle. He rode up and down the field, cheering his men and fighting his foes. "Press forward! Press forward!" he yelled, urging his troops toward Henry's lines.

Far away, at the other side of the field, he saw some of his men falling back. If others saw them, they too might retreat. So Richard spurred his horse and galloped toward the broken line, calling on his soldiers to turn and fight.

retreat
(rĭ trēt′)
v. withdraw from attack

He was barely halfway across the field
50 when one of the horse's shoes flew off. The horse stumbled and fell, and Richard was thrown to the ground.

Before the king could grab at the reins, the frightened animal rose and galloped away. Richard looked around him. He saw

reins
(rānz)
n. straps used to control a horse

that his soldiers were turning and running, and Henry's troops were closing around him.

He waved his sword in the air. "A horse!" he shouted. "A horse! My kingdom for a horse!"

60 But there was no horse for him. His army had fallen to pieces, and his troops were busy trying to save themselves. A moment later Henry's soldiers were upon Richard, and the battle was over.

And since that time, people have said,

> For want of a nail, a shoe was lost,
> For want of a shoe, a horse was lost,
> For want of a horse, a battle was lost,
> For want of a battle, a kingdom was lost,
> And all for the want of a horseshoe nail.

THINK IT THROUGH

1. Why does King Richard lose the battle?
2. What do you think the king is feeling at the point that he offers to trade his kingdom for a horse?
3. Reread from line 65 to the end. What lesson do you think the writer of the story wants readers to understand?

Shot Down Behind Enemy Lines

by Don L. Wulffson

Captain Roger
Locher parachuted
from a burning
plane. His struggle
for survival had
just begun.

Connect to Your Life

What was the last survival story you read? Was the person trapped in a terrifying situation? Briefly discuss that experience with a classmate.

Key to the True Account

The true story you are about to read happened in 1972. It took place in the last years of the Vietnam War. Vietnam was a very dangerous place for U.S. soldiers. The jungles held many hidden dangers. Enemy soldiers seemed to attack from out of nowhere. U.S. soldiers depended on planes and missiles. Special planes sprayed chemicals that destroyed the thick jungle growth. Still, the threat of danger was always present.

Vocabulary Preview

Words to Know
sprawled   comrades
navigator   contraption
uninhabited

 Reading Coach CD-ROM selection

Below sprawled the jungles of North Vietnam. As he drifted down in his parachute, Captain Roger Locher's only thought was, *This can't be!* Getting shot down was something that happened to others. Like all fliers, he had never believed it could happen to him. But it had. Unreal as it seemed, it had happened to him!

sprawled
(sprôld)
v. spread out; past tense of *sprawl*

10 Locher had taken off that morning from the airbase on his 407th mission. In the rear of the two-man F-4 Phantom jet, he was the navigator and weapons-systems operator. With air-to-air missiles, he had already knocked out three MiG-21s.

navigator
(năv′ ĭ gā′ tər)
n. one who tells a pilot where to go

MiG-21s
(mĭg′ twĕn′tē wŭnz′)
enemy fighter planes

Suddenly he felt a numbing explosion. "We're hit!" yelled the pilot. The ship flipped over in a ball of flame. It tumbled out of control through space as smoke filled the cockpit.

20 "I'm going to have to eject," Locher shouted. He pulled hard on the ejection lever. He heard a blast as he was shot earthward. Then there was another blast, a great explosion as the plane disintegrated, taking with it the life of the pilot. An instant later Locher's parachute opened. He blacked out.

disintegrated
(dĭs ĭn′ tĭ grā′ tĭd)
broke apart

THINK IT THROUGH
What serious trouble was Locher in?

FOCUS

Discover the dangers Locher faced.

He regained consciousness just before he hit the trees. A canopy of green reached up at him. He smashed through huge leafy branches. He felt a bone-
30 jarring tug as his chute was snagged by a tree. For a moment he swung back and forth in the air. Then he unharnessed himself and dropped to the ground.

There was no way he could untangle the chute from the tree. He knew that the MiGs had already spotted him and had probably radioed his position. There was no time to lose. He scrambled up the side of a small mountain, careful not to leave any trail.

In ten minutes he was gasping for breath. He felt dizzy and his legs were getting rubbery. He crawled into
40 thick jungle growth and lay down to get his strength back. Lying there, he began to realize the predicament he was in. He had no food. He was ninety miles from the nearest pickup area where he could use his radio to contact a rescue team. He was in strange terrain . The enemy was everywhere.

terrain
(tə rān')
countryside

REREAD

Summarize Locher's situation.

Crash Diet

With a compass and a map to guide him, Locher carefully set out southwest. Each step had to be checked for boot prints, broken twigs, or other signs that could give him away.

At noon he suddenly froze. He heard excited yelling coming straight at him. It was a search party of Vietnamese soldiers! He crawled into some thick brush. He lay still as the enemy came into view. He could see their faces. He could see their guns and sharp bayonets . Locher held his breath as the soldiers walked by within a few feet of his hiding place.

> **bayonets**
> (bā' ə nĭts)
> blades on the ends of rifles

The next day it happened again. He heard screams, shouts, rifle fire. *They're trying to scare me, flush me out like a game bird,* he thought. *Stay put. They've practically got to step on you to find you.*

70

Hunger was beginning to take its toll on Locher. All he could find to eat were a few pieces of unripe jungle fruit. Water was no problem. It rained almost every night. But in the mornings he had to dry out, being careful not to let his boots and socks rot.

Mosquitoes and other insects tormented him endlessly. His skin was covered with red welts and stinging bites. Too, leeches crawled up inside his clothing. Time and

80 again he would pull up his pants to find his legs covered with the ugly things. Their

> **leeches**
> (lē' chĭz)
> worms that suck people's blood

slimy black bodies were bloated with his blood. With disgust, he tore them from his flesh and crushed them.

THINK IT THROUGH

What were some of the dangers Locher had to deal with during two days in the jungle?

FOCUS —————

Locher's struggle continued. Read about new problems he faced.

One nightmarish day passed into the next. Locher grew steadily weaker. He stumbled on through the jungle, not always sure of where he was going. Razor-sharp elephant grass slashed him. Dense brush often blocked his way. Sometimes he pushed through miles of jungle in order to make only a few yards of
90 headway. On the twelfth day he found a wide, well-worn path leading south. With newfound spirit he headed down it. It was a real relief from pushing through jungle brush.

The path led down into a narrow valley. It seemed uninhabited. But suddenly Locher saw two children coming right at him. They were herding water buffalo to pasture. He dove into some bushes. For the rest of the day he lay there in hiding, not daring to
100 move. In the evening, the children began herding the buffalo home. One of the beasts passed within a few feet of Locher. It stepped on a sapling, whacking it down on his ankles. He opened his mouth in pain but stifled any sound.

> **uninhabited**
> (ŭn' ĭn hăb' ĭ tĭd)
> *adj.* without people

> **sapling**
> (săp' lĭng)
> young tree

After dark he wormed his way up the side of a mountain which overlooked a village. Hiding there, he spent a miserable night.

When morning finally came, he pulled a damp, crumbling map from his pocket. With difficulty, he
110 studied it. He found that in twelve days he had gone only seven miles! Ahead of him lay the Red River plain. It was nearly twenty miles wide and filled with small villages. He knew he could never cross it without being captured.

REREAD
How long might it have taken Locher to cross the valley?

Very weak, and not knowing what else to do, Locher remained in his hiding place. One day fused with another. On the twentieth day he knew he was wasting away. He squeezed skinny arms and legs.
120 He rubbed his buttocks and found only skin and bone. Slowly, the jungle was doing what the enemy could not. It was killing him.

THINK IT THROUGH
Why did Locher get discouraged? In what ways was the jungle killing Locher?

FOCUS
Read to find out what finally happened to Locher.

He drifted in and out of sleep. One afternoon he suddenly awoke to the flashes of surface-to-air missiles. They were being fired from the village below at U.S. aircraft. Even if it meant giving his position away to the enemy, he had to let his comrades know he was still alive. He pressed the transmitter button on his radio.
130 Both frightened and excited, he spoke into

comrades
(kom′ rădz′)
n. persons sharing an activity

the radio: "Any U.S. aircraft that reads Oyster One Bravo, please come in."

He switched to receive and heard, "Go ahead, Oyster One Bravo."

The voice startled him. For a long moment Locher did not know what to say. He laughed. "Hey, I'm still down here after twenty-two days!" said Locher. "Relay that I'm okay."

REREAD
What do you think happened next?

He switched back to receive. The radio
140 remained silent. He repeated his message. Again there was no reply. His heart sank. No one had heard him. For a long while he hung his head. Then suddenly he was startled to hear another voice on the radio. It was saying, "We've got your position, buddy. Rescue forces on the way. Hold on. We're coming in."

Magically, helicopters appeared on the horizon. They came in high, then swooped down toward where Locher stood. He signalled the choppers by flashing a mirror. He was sure he was only moments away from
150 being rescued. But in the next instant MiGs appeared, their cannons blazing at the helicopters. Then, from the village, antiaircraft weapons joined the battle. In disbelief, Locher watched as the helicopters swooped down low to escape the deadly fire. They slipped over a ridge, then were gone.

REREAD
Is this what you thought would happen? Why?

It's all over, Locher told himself. He thought sadly of the loved ones he would never see. He thought of the pilots who had risked their lives for him. Sick and near
160 death, he sat down. He rolled onto his side in the jungle muck, waiting to die. He drowsed fitfully the rest of the afternoon and through the night.

THINK IT THROUGH
Why did Locher lose hope here?

In his sleep Locher heard the steady beat of
helicopter rotors. He opened his eyes. It
was morning. Another pair of choppers
was headed toward him! He thought he
was dreaming. He blinked. The choppers
were real. One slid in toward him. The other held
back, ready to act in an emergency.

> **rotors**
> (rō′ tərz)
> spinning parts
> of machines

170   The lead helicopter hovered fifty feet above him. It
began lowering a penetrator, a torpedo-shaped device
with enough weight to break through the thick jungle
growth.

Automatic rifle fire broke out from the village. The
second chopper went into action. It swept down and
sideways. Rockets hissed, snaked toward the enemy.
Explosions of red and orange billowed skyward,
swept back over the village. Mini-guns blazed at the
hidden foe.

180   The penetrator smashed through the overhanging
trees. Broken leaves floated down with it like huge
green birds. Locher grabbed the
contraption . Trying to hold it steady, he
pulled down the seat. He struggled to get
into the seat. He slipped and fell. He
grabbed the seat again, swivelled sideways
into it. Then he felt himself floating, being lifted
skyward. The jungle faded below. He looked up. He
watched himself being reeled into the chopper.

> **contraption**
> (kən trăp′ shən)
> *n.* mechanical
> device

190   "Brother, do you look awful!" laughed one man as
another pulled him on board. Locher did not know
what to say. He was too weak—and too happy—to
say anything.

The ride home was the most beautiful journey of his life. The whole way he kept smiling. He looked at the crew and wanted somehow to say thank you. *But how* 200 *do you thank people for saving your life?* he wondered. There was nothing he could do but look at them with a big loving grin and let the tears roll down through his beard.

Captain Roger Locher smiles a short time after his rescue.

THINK IT THROUGH

1. How did the pilots rescue Locher?
2. What part of Locher's time in the jungle seemed the most dangerous? Give a reason for your opinion.

Fa Mulan

by Robert D. San Souci

To keep her family safe, a girl becomes a warrior. See what happens as Fa Mulan learns the art of war.

Connect to Your Life

Talk about the warriors you've seen in movies, comic books, and video games. What do they usually look like? What are they able to do?

Key to the Legend

A **legend** is a story passed down over time. It is about a person who may or may not have really lived. Often the main character of a legend is a brave hero. The first stories about a character called the Maiden of Yueh come from ancient China. She was described as a female warrior. After a thousand years of retelling, that warrior may have become the character Fa Mulan.

Vocabulary Preview

Words to Know

scrolls	veterans	daring
stallion	fatal	

 Reading Coach CD-ROM selection

Fa Mulan **205**

"Fa Mulan! Stop!" Elder Sister ordered as the two walked from the family farm to the market. But Mulan sliced the air with a bamboo stake . "I am a swordswoman like the Maiden of Yueh!" she cried.

stake
(stāk)
stick with a point at one end

"Proper young women do not play with swords!" scolded Elder Sister. "They do not go to war!"

"War may come to me," Mulan said. "The Tartars have crossed the northern border and are burning many
10 towns." While Elder Sister shopped, Mulan crossed the market to where an anxious crowd studied twelve scrolls pasted to a wall.

scrolls
(skrōlz)
n. rolls of paper, usually with writing on them

"What are these?" Mulan asked.

"They list the men who must serve in the Khan's army," a woman answered.

Mulan gasped when she recognized one name. "My father!" she cried. "But he is too old and weak to fight."

"If a man does not report to the Khan's army," the
20 woman said, "he and his family will be punished."

The next day as Mulan sat at her loom, she formed a brave plan. At last she went to her parents. They saw her troubled look and heard her anxious sigh. "What is on our daughter's mind?" they asked gently. "What is in her heart?"

REREAD
What do you think Mulan will do?

"The Khan is drafting many men, and Father's name is on the list," Mulan explained.

"Little Brother is too young. I am strong.
30 Elder Sister says I act like a man. Let me serve in Father's name."

REREAD
Does Mulan do what you thought she would do?

"It is too dangerous!" her father protested. "And the Khan does not let women serve as soldiers."

In the end her parents agreed, because Mulan's plan was the only way to save the family.

Mulan went back to the market, where she bought a spirited stallion. She also bought a saddle, bridle, and long whip.

40   At dawn she cut her hair short, put on her father's armor, and fastened his weapons to the horse's saddle.

stallion
(stăl′ yən)
n. adult male horse

Bidding farewell to her sorrowful family, she set out bravely for the Yellow River, where the Khan's army was camped.

THINK IT THROUGH
What steps does Mulan take to solve her family's problem?

FOCUS
Discover what happens when Mulan joins the army.

"What is your name?" a soldier with a scroll demanded.

Deepening her voice, Mulan gave her father's name.

50　　　The man nodded, marked his list, and waved her away.

Leading her stallion to the water, Mulan whispered, "I am afraid, but also excited." She pointed her sword at the setting sun.

"I will be like the Maiden of Yueh, the greatest swordswoman."

Before sunrise, the army marched to Black Mountain. In that lonely place, the only sound was the cry of birds and the whicker of wild horses. But as 60 the troops marched north across the grasslands beyond, to join with other armies that the Khan had raised, Mulan heard a new sound: the jangle of Tartar bridles and armor.

Soon the Tartars swept over the plain. Spotting the Khan's forces, the enemy halted. The two armies faced each other.

Shouting orders, the Chinese generals positioned their troops. Mulan and other new soldiers were placed beside veterans. Then the
70 sudden pounding of drums filled the air—the signal to attack! With a shout, Mulan urged her steed at the enemy. An armored Tartar rider raced to meet her. The shock of their clashing spears nearly unseated Mulan. But she imagined how the Maiden of Yueh would react. She struck the Tartar's shield and helmet. Her mount suddenly lurched sideways, forcing the enemy's horse to buck and rear, unsettling his rider. Taking this advantage, Mulan delivered a fatal
80 thrust, and the man tumbled into the dust.
Soon after this, the Khan's forces broke the Tartar line. As the Chinese surged forward, Mulan helped drive the enemy back.

veterans
(vĕt′ ər ənz)
n. soldiers with long experience

fatal
(fāt′ l)
adj. deadly

THINK IT THROUGH
What helps Mulan to survive her first battle?

FOCUS
Mulan gains more experience in war. Find out how she wins the respect of her fellow warriors.

In the months that followed, Mulan increased her strength and improved her swordplay. "You excel because you balance female and male energies," one veteran told her. "A good swordsman should appear as calm as a fine lady, but he must be capable of quick action like a surprised tiger."
90 Mulan studied the art of war to learn how great generals planned and carried out battles. Her courage

and skill with a sword were praised by soldiers, officers, and even officials sent by the Khan.

Mulan missed her family. She kept apart from the soldiers of her squad, her "fire companions," because of her secret. But sometimes one or another of the brave, handsome young men would touch her heart. She would dream of leaving the battlefield for the fields of home, of becoming a bride, a wife, a
100 mother. However, duty to family and country, and her sense of honor, pushed all these dreams aside.

REREAD
What other kind of life has Mulan put aside?

Each time the Khan's armies met the Tartars, Mulan was in the thick of battle, encouraging her fellow warriors, setting a brave example, and driving back the enemy.

Valor and ability won her the command of a company, then of a small troop that made surprise raids on the Tartars. Mulan
110 rose in rank until she became a general, commanding one of three armies preparing for what promised to be the deciding battle of the twelve-year war.

valor
(văl' ər)
courage

THINK IT THROUGH
How does Mulan become a general?

FOCUS —————
The general prepares her warriors for battle. Find out the news she learns afterwards.

Meeting with the other generals, Mulan outlined a plan that the others quickly approved. "We will follow the classic wisdom that says, 'Act like a shy maiden to make the enemy think you are no threat.

Then surprise them like a hare just let loose, and catch them off guard.'"

hare
(hâr)
animal similar to a rabbit

The Khan's army separated, one group
120 heading east, the other west. Mulan's troops marched north toward the Tartar force. She ordered her soldiers to march ragtag so they looked like a mob, not a real army.

When the two armies faced off, the Tartars laughed to see Mulan's troops looking so disorganized. They thundered across the plain like hounds after a hare. But the hare had a surprise waiting. At Mulan's command, her foot soldiers formed crisp battle lines. Then her cavalry galloped to meet the enemy, who
130 were caught off guard. The Tartars, reeling from Mulan's attack, were crushed in the jaws of her deadly trap, as the Khan's other troops charged in from the east and west.

REREAD
How did Mulan fool the enemy in this battle?

At the height of the victory celebration, messengers arrived and informed Mulan that she must appear before the Khan in the royal
140 city of Loyang.

She feared that the Khan might have discovered that one of his generals was a woman. If so, he might punish her and her family for her daring .

daring
(dâr′ ĭng)
n. boldness

THINK IT THROUGH
Why does Mulan feel both pride and fear?

FOCUS ————————————————————
Read to see how the Khan reacts to Mulan.

When she reached the royal city, Mulan was immediately brought to the palace. She bowed before the Khan's throne. "General," the Khan began, "you have served me well and have brought honor to your
150 family. Your deeds are enough to fill twelve books. I give you a thousand strings of copper coins as a reward. What else do you wish?"

"Now that the kingdom is safe," Mulan answered, "I ask only to return home and take up my old life. And I request the loan of your swiftest mount to carry me there."

A small honor guard of her fire companions accompanied Mulan home. What excitement there was at her arrival! Father, Mother, Elder Sister, and
160 Little Brother—how grown he was!—showered her with tears and smiles.

In her room, Mulan changed her armor and boots for a silk robe and brocade slippers. She powdered her face and arranged her hair like a soft cloud.

At last Mulan stepped into the room where her fire companions and family waited. Her comrades were amazed and confused.

"Our general is a woman!" cried one.

Smiling, Mulan said, "When the male rabbit 170 bounds across the meadow, and the female runs beside him, no one can tell which is which. So it is when soldiers fight side by side."

The companion who had spoken—the one Mulan felt closest to—returned her smile, saying, "In the field, what is the need of telling he-rabbit from she-rabbit? But when they return to their burrow, the rabbits know which partner is husband and which is wife. So they build a life together."

REREAD

What does Mulan's closest companion really mean?

180 To Mulan, his words hinted at a bright, shared tomorrow. Then each of her fire companions bowed to her, acknowledging all she had achieved and their loyalty to their former general. Mulan bowed to them in turn.

Finally Father said, "We have all heard of famous warrior women, like the Maiden of Yueh. But my daughter's fame will outshine and outlive them all."

THINK IT THROUGH

1. What is Mulan's reward?
2. How do Mulan's fire companions react to her as a female?
3. Mulan is a woman warrior. If she had been a man in this war, would she have been as successful in this war? Explain your opinion.

Decisions Don't Come Easily

Unit 7

Fiction

Ketchup or mustard? Paper or plastic? These are small decisions. Some decisions in life are tough. They may mean the difference between winning and losing—or between life and death.

In this unit, you'll read three selections. One of them is an allegory. An **allegory** is a story in which the characters and setting stand for something else. Often they stand for real people at a certain time in history.

Meet a few characters who are forced to make tough decisions.

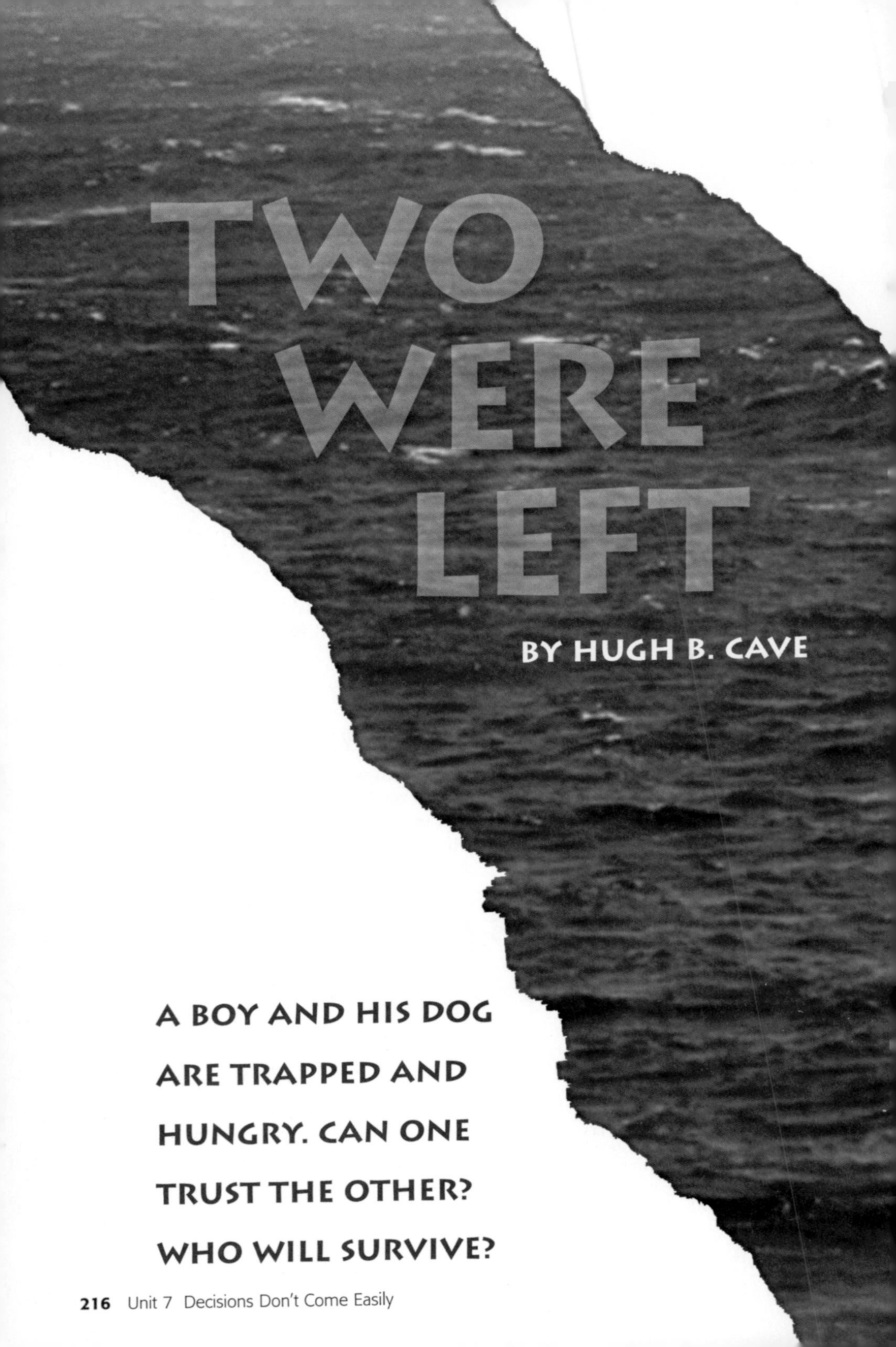

TWO WERE LEFT

BY HUGH B. CAVE

A BOY AND HIS DOG
ARE TRAPPED AND
HUNGRY. CAN ONE
TRUST THE OTHER?
WHO WILL SURVIVE?

Connect to Your Life

Have you ever been very, very cold?
Have you ever been in danger because
of the cold? Where were you at the time?
Share your experience with a classmate.

Key to the Story

In this short story, a boy is on an
ice floe, a huge block of ice. A *husky,*
a large dog with thick fur, is with him.
They are *marooned*—stuck and alone.
Hope is fading.

Vocabulary Preview

Words to Know

essential	ominously
fashioned	descended
suspiciously	

💿 **Reading Coach CD-ROM selection**

FOCUS ——————————

Noni and Nimuk are in great danger. Find out the awful decision that Noni faces.

On the third night of hunger Noni thought of the dog. Nothing of flesh and blood lived upon the floating ice island except those two.

In the breakup of the iceberg, Noni had lost his sled, his food, his fur, even his knife. He had saved only Nimuk, his devoted husky. And now the two marooned on the ice eyed each other warily—each keeping his distance.

10 Noni's love for Nimuk was real, very real—as real as the hunger and cold nights and the gnawing pain of his injured leg in its homemade brace. But the men of his village killed their dogs when food was scarce, didn't they? And without thinking twice about it.

And Nimuk, he told himself, when hungry enough, would seek food. One of us will soon be eating the other, Noni thought. So . . .

> **REREAD**
> What problem is upsetting Noni?

He could not kill the dog with his bare hands. Nimuk was powerful and much fresher

20 than he. A weapon, then, was essential.

> **essential**
> (ĭ sĕn′ shəl)
> *adj.* necessary

Removing his mittens, he unstrapped the brace from his leg. When he had hurt his leg a few weeks before, he had fashioned the brace from bits of harness and two thin strips of iron.

> **fashioned**
> (făsh′ ənd)
> *v.* shaped or formed; past tense of *fashion*

Kneeling now, he wedged one of the iron strips into a crack in the ice and began to rub the other against it with firm, slow strokes.

Nimuk watched him intently, and it seemed to Noni

30 that the dog's eyes glowed more brightly as night waned.

He worked on, trying not to remember why. The slab of iron had an edge now. It had begun to take shape. Daylight found his task completed.

THINK IT THROUGH
What has Noni decided to do? Why?

FOCUS
Read to find out who survives.

Noni pulled the finished knife from the ice and thumbed its edge. The sun's glare, reflected from it, stabbed at his eyes and momentarily blinded him.

Noni steeled himself.

40   "Here, Nimuk!" he called softly.

The dog watched him suspiciously.

"Come here," Noni called.

Nimuk came closer. Noni read fear in the animal's gaze. He read hunger and suffering in the dog's labored breathing and awkward, dragging crouch. His heart wept. He hated himself and fought against it.

> **steeled**
> (stēld)
> prepared to do something hard

> **suspiciously**
> (sə spĭsh' əs lē)
> *adv.* without trust

Closer Nimuk came, wary of his intentions. Now Noni felt a thickening in his throat. He
50   saw the dog's eyes and they were wells of suffering.

Now! Now was the time to strike!

> **REREAD**
> What do you think Noni will do next?

A great sob shook Noni's kneeling body. He cursed the knife. He swayed blindly; flung the weapon far from him. With empty hands outstretched he stumbled toward the dog, and fell.

The dog growled ominously as he warily circled the boy's body. And Noni was sick with fear.

60 In flinging away his knife he had left himself defenseless. He was too weak to crawl after it now. He was at Nimuk's mercy, and Nimuk was hungry.

The dog circled him and was creeping up from behind. Noni shut his eyes, praying that the attack might be swift. He felt the dog's feet against his leg, the hot rush of Nimuk's breath against his neck. A scream gathered in the boy's throat.

Then he felt the dog's hot tongue caressing his face.

70 Noni's eyes opened, staring incredulously. Crying softly, he thrust out an arm and drew the dog's head down against his own. . . .

The plane came out of the south an hour later. Its pilot looked down and saw the large, floating floe. And he saw something flashing.

It was the sun gleaming on something shiny which moved. His curiosity aroused, the pilot banked his ship and descended, circling

80 the floe. Now he saw a dark, still shape that appeared to be human. Or were there two shapes?

descended
(dĭ sĕn' dĭd)
v. moved from a higher to a lower place; past tense of *descend*

He set his ship down in a water lane and investigated. There were two shapes, boy and dog. The boy was unconscious but alive. The dog whined feebly but was too weak to move.

The gleaming object which had trapped the pilot's attention was a crudely fashioned knife stuck into the ice a little distance away and quivering in the wind.

THINK IT THROUGH

1. Do you think the decisions both the boy and dog make are believable? Why or why not?
2. How do you think *you* would act if you were Noni?

Terrible Things

An Allegory of the Holocaust

by Eve Bunting

Each time the Terrible Things come, an awful change happens. Learn a lesson about the damage done by doing nothing.

Connect to Your Life

What do you know about Nazi Germany of the 1930s and 1940s? What group of people did not fit the Nazi view of a "master race"? What terrible things did the Nazis do to those who didn't fit in? In small groups, discuss what you know about this period of history.

Key to the Story

"Terrible Things" is an allegory. In an **allegory,** the characters and events stand for something else. Often they stand for *real* people at a certain time in history.

"Terrible Things" features animal characters in a forest. As you read the story, think about the Nazis and the terror they once caused. Think about the Holocaust, the deliberate killing of millions of people. The main targets were the Jewish people, yet there were other groups of victims, too. Think about what fear causes people to do—or not do.

Vocabulary Preview

Words to Know

clearing	quills
content	bristled
shimmering	

Read to find out what happens when the Terrible Things first appear in a quiet forest clearing.

The clearing in the woods was home to the small forest creatures. The birds and squirrels shared the trees. The rabbits and porcupines shared the shade beneath the trees and the frogs and fish shared the cool brown waters of the forest pond. They were content.

clearing
(klîr′ ĭng)
n. land from which trees have been removed

content
(kən tĕnt′)
adj. satisfied

Until the day the Terrible Things came.

Little Rabbit saw their terrible shadows
10 before he saw them. They stopped at the edge of the clearing and their shadows blotted out the sun.

"We have come for every creature with feathers on its back," the Terrible Things thundered.

"We don't have feathers," the frogs said.

"Nor we," said the squirrels.

"Nor we," said the porcupines.

"Nor we," said the rabbits.

The little fish leaped from the water to show the shine of their scales, but the birds twittered nervously
20 in the tops of the trees. Feathers! They rose in the air, then screamed away into the blue of the sky.

But the Terrible Things had brought their terrible nets and they flung them high and caught the birds and carried them away.

The other forest creatures talked nervously among themselves.

"Those birds were always too noisy," Old Porcupine said. "Good riddance, I say."

30 "There's more room in the trees now," the squirrels said.

REREAD
Is this the reaction you expected? Explain.

"Why did the Terrible Things want the birds?"
Little Rabbit asked. "What's wrong with feathers?"

"We mustn't ask," Big Rabbit said. "The Terrible
Things don't need a reason. Just be glad it wasn't us
they wanted."

THINK IT THROUGH

What do the Terrible Things want? Why are they able to get
what they want?

FOCUS ——————————————

The Terrible Things return. Find out how Big Rabbit reacts.

Now there were no birds to sing in the clearing. But
life went on almost as before. Until the day the
Terrible Things came back.

40   Little Rabbit heard the thump of their terrible feet
before they came into sight.

"We have come for every bushy-tailed creature who
lives in the clearing," the Terrible Things thundered.

"We have no tails," the frogs said.

"Nor do we. Not real tails," the porcupines said.

The little fish leaped from the water to show the
smooth shine of their finned tails and the rabbits
turned their rumps so the Terrible Things could see
for themselves.

50   "Our tails are round and furry," they said. "By no
means are they bushy."

The squirrels chittered their fear and ran high into the
treetops. But the Terrible Things swung their terrible

nets higher than the squirrels could run and wider than the squirrels could leap and they caught them all and carried them away.

"Those squirrels were greedy," Big Rabbit said. "Always storing away things for themselves. Never sharing."

REREAD
What attitude does Big Rabbit show here?

60   "But why did the Terrible Things take them away?" Little Rabbit asked. "Do the Terrible Things want the clearing for themselves?"

"No. They have their own place," Big Rabbit said. "But the Terrible Things don't need a reason. Just mind your own business, Little Rabbit. We don't want them to get mad at us."

THINK IT THROUGH
What advice does Big Rabbit give Little Rabbit? Why?

FOCUS
Discover why Big Rabbit feels safe from the visits of the Terrible Things.

Now there were no birds to sing or squirrels to chitter in the trees. But life in the clearing went on almost as before. Until the day the Terrible Things
70 came again.

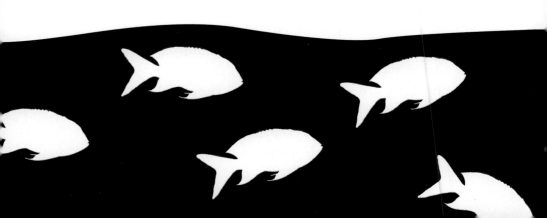

Little Rabbit heard the rumble of their terrible voices.

"We have come for every creature that swims," the Terrible Things thundered.

"Oh, we can't swim," the rabbits said quickly.

"And we can't swim," the porcupines said.

The frogs dived deep in the forest pool and ripples spiraled like corkscrews on the dark, brown water. The little fish darted this way
80 and that in streaks of silver. But the Terrible Things threw their terrible nets down into the depths and they dragged up the dripping frogs and the shimmering fish and carried them away.

"Why did the Terrible Things take them?" Little Rabbit asked. "What did the frogs and the fish do to them?"

"Probably nothing," Big Rabbit said. "But the Terrible Things don't need a reason. Many creatures
90 dislike frogs. Lumpy, slimy things. And fish are so cold and unfriendly. They never talk to any of us."

Now there were no birds to sing, no squirrels to chitter, no frogs to croak, no fish to play in the forest pool. A nervous silence filled the clearing. But life went on almost as usual. Until the day the Terrible Things came back.

spiraled
(spī′ rəld)
moved in circles
or coils

shimmering
(shĭm′ ər ĭng)
adj. shining with
a flickering light

REREAD
Try to picture this
scene in your
mind. How does
it compare to the
opening scene of
the story?

Little Rabbit smelled their terrible smell before they came into sight. The rabbits and the porcupines

100 looked everywhere, except at each other.

"We have come for every creature that sprouts quills," the Terrible Things thundered.

The rabbits stopped quivering. "We don't have quills," they said, fluffing their soft, white fur.

The porcupines bristled with all their strength. But the Terrible Things covered them with the curl of their terrible nets

110 and the porcupines hung in them like flies in a spider's web as the Terrible Things carried them away.

"Those porcupines always were bad tempered," Big Rabbit said shakily. "Prickly, stickly things!"

quills

(kwĭlz)
n. sharp, hollow spines, like pointed needles

bristled

(brĭs' əld)
v. stiffened; past tense of *bristle*

This time Little Rabbit didn't ask why. By now he knew that the Terrible Things didn't need a reason. The smell still filled the clearing, though the Terrible Things had gone.

"I liked it better when there were all kinds of
120 creatures in our clearing," he said. "And I think we should move. What if the Terrible Things come back?"

"Nonsense," Big Rabbit said. "Why should we move? This has always been our home. And the Terrible Things won't come back. We are the White Rabbits. It couldn't happen to us."

THINK IT THROUGH

Big Rabbit thinks he knows the Terrible Things. Do you think he knows as much as he thinks he does? Use evidence from this part of the story to support your view.

FOCUS

The Terrible Things return. Read to discover what Little Rabbit learns.

As day followed peaceful day Little Rabbit thought Big Rabbit must be right. Until the day the Terrible Things came back.

Little Rabbit saw the terrible gleam of their terrible
130 eyes through the forest darkness. And he smelled again the terrible smell.

"We have come for any creature that is white," the Terrible Things thundered.

"There are no white creatures here but us," Big Rabbit said.

"We have come for you," the Terrible Things said.

The rabbits scampered in every direction. "Help!" they screamed. "Somebody help!" But there was no

one left to help. And the big, circling nets dropped
140   over them and the Terrible Things carried them away.

All but Little Rabbit, who was little enough to hide
in a pile of rocks by the pond and smart enough to
stay so still that the Terrible Things thought he was a
rock himself.

When they had all gone Little Rabbit crept into the
middle of the empty clearing. I should have tried to
help the other rabbits, he thought. If only we
creatures had stuck together, it could have been
different.

150   Sadly, Little Rabbit left the clearing. He'd go tell
other forest creatures about the Terrible Things. He
hoped someone would listen.

THINK IT THROUGH

1. Little Rabbit thinks it could have been different.
   Why didn't the animals stick together? Review the
   story for evidence to support your answer.
2. The writer of this tale bases it on the time when
   the Nazis caused terror. The Nazis sent groups of
   people to death camps. What do you think is this
   tale's theme or message?
3. Why do you think the writer tells a fictional story
   with animal characters instead of describing the
   real events?

Speech by Parson Martin Niemöller

The Nazis came first for the Communists.
But I wasn't a Communist,
so I didn't speak up.
Then they came for the Jews,
5 but I wasn't a Jew,
so I didn't speak up.
Then they came for the trade unionists,
but I wasn't a trade unionist
so I didn't speak up.
10 Then they came for the Catholics,
but I was a Protestant
so I didn't speak up.
Then they came for me.
By that time there was no one left.

THE LADY
OR
THE TIGER?

by Frank L. Stockton, retold by Sue Baugh

A beautiful woman

    waits behind one door.

A deadly tiger

    waits behind another.

Will the servant

    choose love or doom?

The Lady or the Tiger? **233**

> A king has complete control of his kingdom. Find out how he deals with those who break his rules.

In the days of old there lived a king and his beautiful daughter. The king admired his neighbors, who lived in the Roman Empire, and even copied some of their ways. But his ancestors had been barbarians. They rode where they wanted. They took what they wanted and answered to no one but themselves. The king had settled down, but he still had the blood of his ancestors in his veins.

barbarians
(bär bâr′ ē ənz) *n.* brutal people

10　He would think of the wildest schemes and ideas for his kingdom. Then, with his power and wealth, he would make them happen. The king was known for getting whatever he wanted.

He also watched over his kingdom with a sharp eye. When his household and government worked smoothly, the king smiled. And when something went wrong, he smiled even more. Nothing made him happier than to crush a mistake or to bring a criminal to justice.

REREAD
What kind of man is the king?

20　The king loved arenas and had one built in his own kingdom. His people came from miles around to watch brave gladiators wage war in the arena. They cheered as wild beasts fought to the death. But he didn't just copy other people's arenas. He added something of his own to improve the minds of his people.

gladiators
(glăd′ ē ā′ tərz) *n.* men who fought each other as a public show

On the inside of the arena, he had two
30　doors built. They looked alike and stood side by side. Behind one was a savage,

savage
(săv′ ĭj) *adj.* fiercely wild

hungry tiger. Behind the other waited a beautiful lady. The inside of each door was covered in thick curtains. That way, no sound of the lady or tiger could reach the outside.

You might ask why the king did this.

He believed that people accused of a crime should choose their own punishment or reward. Luck would decide if the person was guilty or innocent. The
40 people watching would see justice done. What could be more fair?

THINK IT THROUGH
How has the king made his arena different?

FOCUS
Find out how the king decides legal cases.

Not every crime caught the king's interest. But when one did, the king would set a trial day. The royal jailers would bring the accused person to the arena. Hundreds of people would fill the seats to see this trial. High above the arena, the king sat on his throne, with the princess and all his royal followers around him. At the king's signal, a door far below the throne opened. The accused person stepped out into
50 the harsh light of the arena.

He would see the two doors waiting for him. It was his duty and honor to walk right up to these doors and open one of them. If he chose the door with the tiger, that proved he was guilty. The tiger would spring out and tear him apart. At his death, iron bells would ring, and the people would wail and cry. Why

did one so young and fair, or one so old and
respected, have to die like that?

If he chose the door with the lady, that proved he
60 was innocent. The man and woman would be
married right then and there. The king always chose
a lady of the right age and social rank for the man.
What joy! Brass bells rang out the news. The
people shouted and laughed! As the man led his new
wife home, children threw rose petals
along their path. It didn't matter if the
man loved someone else or if he was
already married. The king's word was
law.

REREAD
Why might the choice of the lady be an unhappy one?

70 Think of it! No judge, no jury, no trial,
no lawyers. Just one person choosing life or death.
And it all depended on luck or chance! The accused
person could not know which door hid the tiger or
the lady. In this arena, the king believed, everyone got
what he deserved.

The whole kingdom looked forward
to the king's trial days. When people
came to the arena, they never knew what
would happen. Would they see a bloody
80 death or a joyful wedding?

REREAD
What does this tell you about the people in the kingdom?

The king felt no one could find anything wrong
with this system. After all, the accused person had his
life in his own hands, didn't he? The king was very
pleased with himself for thinking up this idea.

Now, remember the king had a daughter. The
princess was so beautiful that people turned and
stared at her wherever she went. She was
also as strong and willful as her father.
The king loved her more than anyone or
90 anything in his kingdom.

willful
(wĭl' fəl)
adj. always wanting to get one's own way

Among the king's royal servants was a young man so handsome and brave that he had no equal. The daughter fell in love with him—how could she help herself? They kept their love secret for many months. The royal daughter wasn't supposed to be seeing a lowly servant. Then one day the king found out about them.

Oh, the cries of rage and doom! The king threw the young man into prison and set a day for his trial in the arena. Of course, this was a special event. Never before had a lowly subject of the king dared to love his daughter. Everyone talked about the case for days, wondering how it would all turn out.

subject
(sŭb' jĭkt)
one who is under the rule of another

The king ordered his servants to search for the most savage tiger in the kingdom. He also ordered them to search for the most beautiful woman they could find. His servants obeyed and brought both to the king's arena. At last, everything was ready.

THINK IT THROUGH

For this trial, why do you think the king wants the *most* beautiful woman and the *most* savage tiger?

The Lady or the Tiger? **237**

The day of the trial, people came from every part of the kingdom to watch. They pushed their way into the arena and filled the seats. When there were no seats left, people stood outside the walls and listened eagerly for the trial to begin. The king and his court took their places. Across the arena stood the two doors with their awful secret.

Then the people fell silent. Every eye was fixed on the king. He raised his hand and gave the signal. Beneath the royal throne, a door opened, and the young man stepped into the dusty circle. People saw how handsome he was. No wonder the princess loved him. What a terrible thing for him to be there!

The young man walked to the center of the arena. He turned and bowed to the king. But his eyes were on the princess. He thought, "She must know which door hides the tiger and which one hides the lady."

He was right. As soon as the king had set the trial day, the princess had worked day and night to find out. She knew the men who were in charge of the doors. But which one would tell her what she wanted to know? She promised them gold and other fine things. Day after day the princess came. Finally, one of the men told her the secret.

At last she knew behind which door lay the tiger and which one stood the lady, waiting to be chosen. She learned that the tiger was bigger and stronger than any tiger in the arena before. His claws could tear through armor, and his teeth could stab like knives.

The princess also knew who the beautiful lady was
140 and hated her. The lady was from the royal court.
Often the princess had seen this lady—or thought she
had seen her—looking at the young man. Sometimes
she thought her young man even returned the look.
Now and then the princess had seen them talking
together. It was only for a minute or two, but much
can be said in a minute or two. Maybe they were
talking about the weather. Maybe they were agreeing
to meet later. How could the princess know?

Now she sat in the arena beside the king. Her lover
150 turned and looked up at her. He knew her strong
nature. She would never rest until the
secret, hidden even from the king, was
hers.

His eyes asked, "Which door should I
choose?"

REREAD
What do you
think the princess
is feeling?

The question was as plain as if he had shouted it
from where he stood. There was no time to lose. She
must answer quickly.

Her right arm lay on a soft cushion in front of her.
160 She raised her hand and made a slight, quick motion
to the right. No one but the young man saw it.
Everyone else was looking at him.

He turned and walked quickly across the empty
arena. Every heart stopped beating, every breath was
held, every eye was fixed on his handsome face.
Without a thought, he went to the door on the right
and opened it.

Now, the point of the story is this: Did the tiger
come out of that door, or did the lady?

THINK IT THROUGH

The young man follows the motion the princess makes
without a thought. What does this show about him?

170   The more we think about this question, the harder
it is to answer. We have to search deep into the
human heart, which is not easy. Put yourself in the
place of the princess. She is torn between
love and jealousy. She has lost him, but
who should have him? She has an awful
choice to make.

> **jealousy**
> (jĕl′ ə sē)
> *n.* fear of losing
> one's love to
> another person

Oh, many times she had dreamed of that
tiger! In her nightmares she saw her lover
opening the door. She heard the tiger's roar and saw
180 its powerful body leap on the man. She cried out in
terror as the tiger sank its teeth into her lover's neck.

But she had dreamed of the other door more often.
She saw the look of delight on his face when he
opened it, and the beautiful lady was waiting for him.
The princess felt jealousy burn like fire in her body.
She saw him rush to meet the woman, and she felt
hatred twist inside as the woman smiled in victory.
How could the princess stand to see them married
right before her eyes? How could she stand to hear
190 the joyful shouts from the crowd? The brass bells
would ring out. The crowd would cheer madly. She
would watch the happy couple walking on the rose
petals as they went to their home. The noise would
drown out her own scream of rage and loss.

Wouldn't it be better for him to die at once? Then
he and the princess would be together after death.

And yet, that awful tiger, those screams, that blood!

She had spent days and nights trying to decide
which door he should open. She had known he would
200 ask. Finally, the princess knew how she would answer.
That was why she moved her hand to the right.

Her choice is not one to be taken lightly. As the author, I'm really not the one to answer such a hard question. So I leave it with all of you:

Which came out of the opened door—the lady, or the tiger?

THINK IT THROUGH

1. What do you think came out of the opened door? Use evidence from the story to support your answer.
2. What is your reaction to the ending? Explain.
3. Review the actions of the princess. What do you think she should have done? Give a reason for your answer.

Hard to Believe

Unit 8

Nonfiction

Are there alligators in our subways? Are there squirrels that can fly? Clear thinking or science can explain some things. The truth behind other strange things is still unknown.

In this unit, you'll read about some hard-to-believe events. Look for what's fact and what might be opinion.

As you read, feel free to form your own opinions. Ask questions. Seeing isn't always believing.

243

Ships That Could Think

by Edward F. Dolan

*People tell many
tales about ships
and sea adventures.
Few are as strange
as these.*

Connect to Your Life

Who sails ships? What parts of a ship can
you name? With a classmate, fill out a
word web about ships and sailing. Add as
much information to your web as you can.

Key to the Article

This article includes terms that are
related to types of ships and sailing.
Whaling ships hunt for whales. *Merchant
ships* carry products that are intended for
sale. The products are called *cargo.* A
freighter is a special cargo ship that
carries such things as chemicals or
machines.

Vocabulary Preview

Words to Know

vessel   horizon   emerged
course   drifted

 Reading Coach CD-ROM selection

Sailors have always looked on ships as being alive. This is because ships seem to act like human beings. For instance, they often move through the sea with such womanly grace that sailors have come to think of them as women. Whenever seamen talk about a ship, they use the words "she" and "her." You'll hear these words even when the vessel bears a man's name.

vessel
(vĕs′ əl)
n. boat

Further, like some humans, many ships
10 seem to get along well with the people around them. They cooperate with their crews and are a joy to sail. Others prove hard to handle at all times. Some seem to live happy lives. Others seem forever dogged by bad luck.

Some ships even seem to have minds of their own. They have been the cause of some very odd happenings. A perfect example here is the three-masted whaling ship, *Canton*.

three-masted
having three poles that support the sails

A Strange Three Days

Built in 1835, the *Canton* was an
20 American ship. She was known as a vessel that handled easily. She always answered quickly to any turn of the wheel. But, for three days in 1867, while sailing the South Atlantic, she refused to obey her captain. The whaler set her own course and went where she wanted to go.

course
(kôrs)
n. route

It happened as the ship was traveling to the island of St. Helena after capturing several whales. Once there, she was to take on food and water. But, suddenly, the *Canton* seemed
30 dead against going to the island. She veered off to the

side and headed in another direction. The captain brought her back on course. Then a puzzled look crossed his face. Though he was gripping the wheel tightly, the *Canton* swung to the side once more.

Again, the captain brought her back on course. Again, the ship defied him. Off she went in her own direction. She continued to do so, no matter how often he turned the wheel back to the original heading.

40 The captain was a deeply religious man. A thought struck him. Perhaps God, for some reason, wanted the ship to travel in the new direction. If so, the captain was not about to argue. He decided to let the *Canton* go where she wished.

REREAD
How do the captain's actions change? Why?

For the next three days, he allowed the *Canton* to pursue her own course. Then his men sighted a cluster of black dots on the horizon . The *Canton* sped to them. They turned out to be lifeboats. They were 50 crowded with half-starved seamen.

horizon
(hə rī′ zən)
n. line where the earth seems to meet the sky

On being taken aboard, the men explained that they were from a merchant ship. They had been sailing near Africa when their vessel had caught fire days ago. No sooner had they taken to the lifeboats than the blazing ship went to the bottom. The captain estimated that they had drifted more than 150 miles before he came to their rescue.

drifted
(drĭf′ tĭd)
v. wandered; past tense of *drift*

No. *He* hadn't rescued them. His *ship* 60 had. The *Canton* had sought out the exact spot where they were floating in the vast Atlantic. Perhaps God had guided her to that spot. Or perhaps she herself had somehow known where it was. The captain was never able to tell.

Once the men were saved, the *Canton* gave her skipper no more trouble. She obediently followed the course that he set for St. Helena.

THINK IT THROUGH
Where does the *Canton* finally lead the captain? What can't anyone explain about what happened?

FOCUS ⎯⎯⎯⎯⎯⎯⎯⎯
Notice how a French freighter acts differently from the *Canton*.

Looking for Revenge

The *Canton* helped a group of sailors. The French steamer, *Frigorifique,* did exactly the opposite. She
70 terrified the men on a British freighter one March day in 1884. Their ship had accidentally wounded her and she seemed to be looking for revenge.

The *Frigorifique* was heading home along the French coast with a cargo from Spain that March day. She was moving slowly through a heavy fog. Suddenly, the men on deck heard a ship's whistle echoing across the water. Then there was the throbbing sound of approaching engines. And then they saw a ship stumble blindly
80 out of the mist. It was the British coal freighter, *Rumney.* It was coming straight at them.

REREAD
What do you think will happen next?

Up on the bridge, the French captain yelled for the steersman to change course. The sailor spun the wheel hard. The *Frigorifique* began swinging away to safety. But it was too late. With a grinding crash, the *Rumney* steamed into the *Frigorifique's* side.

The French ship reeled to a halt. The *Rumney* was undamaged and backed off. The

90 *Frigorifique* was left with a jagged rip in her ⎡hull⎤. Seawater rushed into the holds. The *Frigorifique* began to ⎡list⎤ and sink. The captain knew immediately that his ship would go to the bottom in minutes. He and his men put lifeboats over the side. They rowed to the *Rumney.*

| **hull** |
| lower body of a ship |

| **list** |
| tilt to one side |

Once safely on board, the French sailors looked back at their stricken ship. Standing with the English crew, they watched the *Frigorifique* struggle back into

100 the fog. Her engines were still running because there hadn't been time to shut them down. They would carry her on for a mile or so before she finally sank. All the men knew that they would never see the ship again.

How wrong they were! The *Rumney* began inching her way through the mist. She had gone but two miles when there were gasps all along the deck. For out of the mist burst a ship. It was the *Frigorifique.* Smoke poured from her stack. She came directly at the

110 *Rumney.* She looked like a charging warrior.

The *Rumney* escaped to the side. The French vessel steamed past, missing a collision by just a few yards. Back into the fog she disappeared.

| **REREAD** |
| Retell what happens in your own words. |

The frightened British and French crewmen stared at each other. The *Frigorifique* should have gone to the bottom. by now.

120 But she was still afloat and steaming hard. She had looked as if she were trying to attack the ship that had harmed her. She had *actually* looked that way! Was it possible that she had been seeking revenge?

It was a question that made the men nervous for the next two miles. Then there were fresh cries of alarm. Once again, the *Frigorifique* broke out of the fog. Again, she came charging at the *Rumney*. Again, the Britisher tried to swing away—but failed this time. The *Frigorifique* smashed into her and tore a gaping 130 hole in her side.

THINK IT THROUGH

What was frightening about the actions of the *Frigorifique?*

FOCUS ——————————

Discover a possible explanation for the *Frigorifique's* actions.

The *Rumney* was now as badly wounded as her attacker. The French and English crews took to the lifeboats as she quickly sank beneath the waves. As for the *Frigorifique*, she continued on her way. She faded back into the fog, leaving a doomed ship behind. Did she have a look of satisfaction about her as she disappeared? The sailors wondered.

The lifeboats set out for the nearby French coast. Fifteen minutes later, they emerged into 140 sunlight—only to see the *Frigorifique* come sailing out of the fog after them. She did not, however, aim for the boats. Rather, she passed close-by along a circling route.

> **emerged**
> (ĭ mûrjd´)
> *v.* came into view; past tense of *emerge*

Both the British and French captains decided to board the ship. They wanted to know why she was still afloat. And, if possible, they wanted to learn why she had twice sought out the *Rumney* as if on a mission of revenge .

150 They found the answers soon after they brought the lifeboats alongside and climbed aboard. There was a simple reason why the *Frigorifique* had not yet sunk. The seawater was pouring in more slowly than was first thought. But, with each passing minute, it was coming faster. The ship did not have long to live.

And why had she twice attacked the *Rumney?* The captains discovered the answer on the bridge. After the *Frigorifique* had been hit, the steersman had found her too hard to handle. He had
160 pulled the wheel over and had lashed it down. This had caused the vessel to sail in a wide circle—a circle that had twice brought her to the *Rumney.*

The captains returned to the lifeboats. They rowed to a safe distance and watched the *Frigorifique* plunge beneath the sea. Then they told their crews about the lashed wheel. The doomed ship hadn't attacked the *Rumney* after all. She hadn't been angrily looking for revenge.

170 But was this the truth of the matter? Many of the nervous sailors were never sure.

THINK IT THROUGH

1. What answers did the two captains find on the *Frigorifique?*
2. Both stories tell of ships that seemed to think. In your opinion, is this possible? Use details from the selection to support your opinion.

Earthquakes

by Franklyn M. Branley

We all live on the earth's crust. It is always moving. Find out how to live with this shaky situation.

Connect to Your Life

Recall the last earthquake report you heard. Where did it happen and how strong was it? What damage did it cause?

Key to the Article

This science article is similar to what you'd find in an earth science textbook. As you read facts about earthquakes, look for special terms in bold type. Pay close attention to the diagrams. The terms and diagrams explain how earthquakes form and how their strength is measured.

Vocabulary Preview

Words to Know

continent	erupt
buckles	satellites
topple	

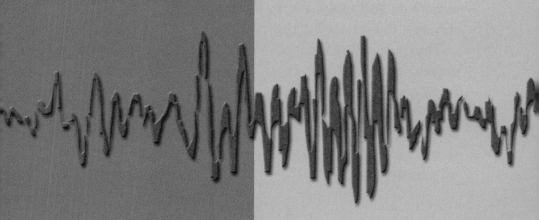

Parts of the Earth are always moving. That's hard to believe, but they are. The movements are so small and so slow, we usually cannot feel them.

Whole mountains move. Big sections of a **continent** like North America can move. Even whole continents move. Right now North America and Europe are moving apart. They move slowly, only as fast as your fingernails grow. So we don't feel the motion.

10 When parts of the Earth move quickly, there may be an earthquake. Every day there are at least a thousand earthquakes on our planet. Most are small, but each year there are a few earthquakes large enough to knock down buildings.

> **continent**
> (kŏn′ tə nənt)
> *n.* one of the seven large land areas on earth

The strength of an earthquake can be measured. We use something called the Richter scale, named after C. F. Richter, an American scientist. Anything that measures less than 2 is a small quake, and 8 or higher is a
20 very big one.

> **REREAD**
> What is the main idea of this paragraph?

Every earthquake has a center. That's where it all begins. Parts of the Earth move up and down or go sideways, and make waves that spread out and go through the whole Earth.

They are called **seismic waves.** The word comes from *seismos,* a Greek word meaning to shake. Scientists all over the
30 world measure the waves on **seismometers.**

Scientists read information from seismometers like this one.

We live on the outer part of Earth. It is called Earth's **crust.** In some places the crust is 30 or 40 miles thick. If Earth were an apple, the crust would be only as thick as the skin of the apple. Most earthquakes occur in the crust.

Large sections of the Earth's crust are always moving. Sometimes two sections push against each other. The place where they meet is called a **fault.** When the sections cannot pass, the Earth bends and buckles. Suddenly the bend releases, and a whole section may move four or five feet at once. That's what happened twelve miles below the surface in Mexico in 1985. The seismic waves from the earthquake's center were strong enough to topple buildings in Mexico City, 220 miles away, and kill several thousand people. The quake measured 8.1 on the Richter scale.

Cutaway Image of the Earth

outer core   mantle   crust

inner core

LOOK CLOSELY Notice how thin the earth's crust is compared to the other sections.

buckles
(bŭk' əlz)
v. crumples

topple
(tŏp' əl)
v. push over

THINK IT THROUGH

Why do earthquakes happen? What do seismic waves show?

FOCUS

What results of earthquakes also cause deaths?

Sometimes two sections of the crust scrape alongside each other. That makes a fault too. The San Andreas Fault is a crack in the Earth that runs north and south for hundreds of miles in California.

In 1906 there was an earthquake along a section of the San Andreas Fault. In seconds, the crust on the west side of the fault moved twenty feet. San Francisco and the area around the city shook and trembled. Fires started, and most of the city burned down.

Most earthquakes occur along the shores of the Pacific Ocean, where the crust moves a lot. Japan has about 7,000 quakes a year. Luckily, most are small.

The San Andreas Fault extends from north of San Francisco to southern California.

There are volcanoes in this part of the world too. Earthquakes often occur in places where there are volcanoes. Melted rock deep under the Earth pushes upward, making the area shake and rumble. These are warnings that a volcano may erupt or that there may be a big earthquake.

erupt
(ĭ rŭpt′)
v. explode

In southern Europe there are several volcanoes. There are also many earthquakes. In Pozzuoli, Italy, a small town not far from Mount Vesuvius, there were 4,000 quakes in one year. Mount Vesuvius is a volcano that has erupted from time to time for several thousand years.

In 1939 a big fault opened up in the bottom of the sea, causing an earthquake just off the coast of Chile in South America. Water rushed into the opening. After it was filled, water kept rushing toward the fault. The water piled high, making a huge wave that traveled toward the shore. The wave was a wall of water called a *tsunami,* a Japanese word. People ran to the hills to escape, but a landslide caused by the quake swept them back into the sea. This was a big undersea earthquake.

THINK IT THROUGH

| What two other natural forces can be connected to a quake?

FOCUS

| What steps can people take to protect lives and property?
| Read to find out.

In a small quake, dishes rattle. Ceiling lights swing. The ground jiggles a bit as if a big truck were going by. It's all over in a few seconds.

During a big earthquake, many buildings fall down. There are also fires. Pipes that carry gas to homes are broken. A spark may set the gas afire. Sometimes firefighters can't fight the flames because water pipes have broken.

During an earthquake, dams may break too. Rivers may be blocked by landslides. So there is often flooding in the area of an earthquake.

In many parts of the world where there are big earthquakes, new buildings are made of steel instead of wood. They are built where the ground is solid so seismic waves will not knock them down. Old bridges and dams are made stronger with extra steel and concrete.

In 1989, there was a serious earthquake near San Francisco. It was the worst in the area since 1906. Sixty-seven people were killed. Bridges and roadways were damaged, and many buildings were destroyed. Because of the way it was built, the famous Golden Gate Bridge swayed in the quake, but it did not collapse.

REREAD

How does this 1989 San Francisco quake compare to the one in 1906?

The Golden Gate Bridge wasn't damaged in the 1989 earthquake. However, the Bay Bridge was. This bridge connects the city of Oakland to San Francisco.

Earthquakes happen without any warning. However, scientists are working to find ways to predict quakes. They use <u>satellites</u> to measure even the smallest motion along faults. These small motions can often become larger.

130

satellites
(săt′ l ĭts′)
n. man-made objects that orbit the Earth

The crust of our planet is always moving, so we will continue to have earthquakes. Most of them, fortunately, will be small ones.

THINK IT THROUGH

1. Name at least three things you can do to try to survive an earthquake.
2. Make a cause-and-effect chart to show what happened in the 1939 earthquake described at the top of page 257.
3. This article shows many dangers that happen because of earthquakes. Name several effects that are damaging or deadly.

Sparky

by Earl Nightingale

> No one thought Sparky was special. Yet he became world famous just by being himself. Discover how.

For Sparky, school was all but impossible. He failed every subject in the eighth grade. He flunked physics in high school, getting a grade of zero. Sparky also flunked Latin, algebra and English. He didn't do much better in sports. Although he did manage to make the school's golf team, he promptly lost the only important match of the season. There was a consolation match; he lost that, too.

10 Throughout his youth Sparky was awkward socially. He was not actually disliked by the other students; no one cared that much. He was astonished if a classmate ever said hello to him outside of school hours. There's no way to tell how he might have done at dating. Sparky never once asked a girl to go out in high school. He was too afraid of being turned down.

Sparky was a loser. He, his classmates . . . everyone knew it. So he rolled with it. Sparky had made up his mind early in life that if things were meant to

20 work out, they would. Otherwise he would content himself with what appeared to be his inevitable mediocrity.

> **consolation match**
> contest for those who lose the first prize

> **inevitable mediocrity**
> average ability that can't be avoided

THINK IT THROUGH

Why did everyone consider Sparky a loser?

Even though Sparky was labeled a loser, he had his own future plan. Discover where his plan one day led him.

However, one thing was important to Sparky—drawing. He was proud of his artwork. Of course, no one else appreciated it. In his senior year of high school, he **submitted** some cartoons to the editors of the yearbook. The cartoons were turned down. Despite this particular **rejection**, Sparky was so
30 convinced of his ability that he decided to become a professional artist.

After completing high school, he wrote a letter to Walt Disney Studios. He was told to send some samples of his artwork, and the subject for a cartoon was suggested. Sparky drew

submitted

(səb mĭt' ĭd)
v. presented for approval; past tense of *submit*

rejection

(rĭ jĕk' shən)
n. act of being refused

"Sparky" at his drawing board

the proposed cartoon. He spent a great deal of time on it and on all the other drawings he submitted.

Finally, the reply came from Disney Studios. He had been rejected once again. Another loss for the loser.

40 So Sparky decided to write his own autobiography in cartoons. He described his childhood self—a little boy loser and chronic underachiever. The cartoon character would soon become famous worldwide. For Sparky, the boy who had such lack of success in school and whose work was rejected again and again, was Charles Schulz. He created the "Peanuts" comic strip and the little cartoon character whose kite would never fly and who never succeeded in kicking a

50 football, Charlie Brown.

> **chronic underachiever**
> one who has performed poorly for a long time

THINK IT THROUGH

1. By what name did the world come to know Sparky?
2. What do you think was the key to Sparky's success? Find details in the essay to support your answer.
3. This essay once appeared in the book *Chicken Soup for the Teenaged Soul.* What message do you think the writer wants to send in telling Sparky's story?

by Phillip Brooks

The Roswell Incident

Have flying saucers crashed on Earth?
Are aliens among us? Strange events that
happened in 1947 may make you wonder.

**Reading Coach
CD-ROM selection**

▪ Connect to Your Life

When you hear the words
flying saucer, what images
come to your mind?
Briefly discuss why people
are so interested in the
idea of visitors from other
planets.

▪ Key to the Article

When the topic is flying
saucers, it's often hard to
find solid facts. Read this
selection carefully. Notice
how the writer presents
the information. Judge the
facts and evidence.

▪ Vocabulary Preview

Words to Know
authorities
spindly
bizarre
procedure
rumor

In 1947, Mac Brazel made an amazing discovery. Read on for the details.

Date: July 3, 1947
Place: Roswell, New Mexico

William "Mac" Brazel rode his horse across the dry desert land of his ranch. He thought about the explosion he had heard last night during a storm. Now he wanted to find out what had caused it.

Something silver glinted in the sunlight, catching Mac's eye. The ground around him was littered with shiny metal pieces. He stopped to pick one up.

10　The fragment was extremely lightweight but unbendable. And it was covered with hieroglyphs.

Mac felt uneasy. The metal looked like nothing on earth. He telephoned the air force base at nearby Roswell.

hieroglyphs
(hī' ər ə glĭfs')
picture symbols
used for writing

Staff from the Roswell base arrived at Mac's ranch. They posted guards around the area where the metal was found.

On July 8, the air force base issued an amazing
20　news statement—they said that the wreckage was from a flying saucer!

Later that day, the base released a second statement. It said that the first story was a mistake. The crashed object was in fact a weather balloon. But was it? Were the authorities covering something up?

authorities
(ə thôr' ĭ tēz)
n. persons who
have power

THINK IT THROUGH

From the information you've read so far, which statement do you think is true? Explain.

Grady Barnett found something very strange 100 miles from Roswell. Read to discover how the Roswell legend grew.

Soon there were stories of a second crash site about 100 miles west of Roswell.

30 An engineer named Grady Barnett said he was working in the desert when he saw a large metal disk on the ground. Scattered around the crumpled disk were five small, gray bodies. They appeared to be dead.

As Grady stood staring, a military vehicle drove up. An officer jumped out. He told Grady to leave at once and, more importantly, never speak about what he had seen.

As he was hustled away, Grady glanced over his shoulder. One of the creatures 40 seemed to open an eye and look back at him.

REREAD
What questions do you have about this event?

Grady Barnett said later that the bodies were "like humans, but they were not humans." They were small, with spindly arms and legs. Their heads were large, with sunken eyes and no teeth.

spindly
(spĭnd′ lē)
adj. slender and long

In the fifty years since the actual event, various witnesses have come forward with bizarre stories about the aliens. Some 50 claim the alien bodies were taken to the Roswell Air Force Base.

bizarre
(bĭ zär′)
adj. strange

One story told how doctors at the Roswell Army Hospital had been ordered on duty at short notice. The shocked doctors were told to cut open and examine the bodies of the dead aliens in a procedure called an autopsy.

procedure
(prə sē′ jər)
n. way of doing something

This is the front page of a Roswell newspaper that appeared in 1947. The major headline describes the actions of the Roswell Army Air Force (RAAF).

When the bodies were cut open, a terrible smell filled the room. Several doctors became too sick to
60 carry on.

The story took another twist in the 1990s, when a video tape was released. The film was supposed to date from 1947 and show the alien autopsy. But many people believe that the film is a fake and the autopsy never happened.

The Roswell legend has continued to grow. New details have been added, including a rumor that the alien bodies were frozen in ice and kept at a top-secret air force base
70 called Area 51.

It seems certain that something did crash at Roswell in 1947. Does the air force know more than it is telling? Were the stories fake? We may never know.

> **rumor**
>
> (rōō′ mər)
> *n.* unproved information spread by word of mouth

THINK IT THROUGH

1. Do you think aliens came to earth in 1947? Use evidence from the selection to support your opinion.
2. The writer supports his story with many facts and details. Why do you think he does this?
3. Why do you think the Roswell incident has been talked about for so many years?

Making Adjustments

Mixed Genres

Adjustments are changes designed to make something work or fit. Think of adjustments as improvements. That's why there is a volume control on a TV and movable straps on a backpack. You can also adjust your own attitude. This kind of adjustment can help you look at problems differently.

In this unit, you'll be reading a **play**, a **short story**, an **informative article**, and a **biography.** The people who make adjustments come from very different places and time periods. Each one makes an adjustment and discovers a new way of "seeing."

THE JADE STONE

by Caryn Yacowitz, adapted by Aaron Shepard

An emperor demands a carving of "a dragon of wind and fire." Find out what the stone carver creates instead.

Connect to Your Life

Think about a time you saw a painting or statue that you thought was a work of art. What do you think caused the artist to create that work?

Key to the Play

Of course, you can read this play silently. However, it was meant to be read aloud. This special kind of drama is called **Readers Theater.** To perform the play, actors simply read it while sitting on chairs or standing. Ordinary plays usually have no narrator and lots of stage directions. Here, four narrators describe most of the settings and actions.

Vocabulary Preview

Words to Know
apprentice
entangled
defy

 Reading Coach CD-ROM selection

Cast of Characters

Narrator 1   Stone
Narrator 2   Apprentice
Narrator 3   Adviser 1
Narrator 4   Adviser 2
Chan Lo   Adviser 3
Emperor

FOCUS

An emperor has special orders for a stone carver. Find out the stone carver's unusual way of beginning a carving.

Narrator 1. Long ago in China there lived a stone carver named

Chan Lo (*bowing*). Chan Lo.

> **REREAD**
> Notice how two characters share one sentence in the dialogue.

Narrator 4. Chan Lo spent his days carving birds and deer and water buffalo from the colored stones he found near the river.

Narrator 2. His young apprentice asked,

Apprentice. How do you know what to carve?

> **apprentice**
> (ə prĕn′ tĭs)
> *n.* one who is learning a job

10 **Chan Lo.** I always listen to the stone.

Narrator 3. . . . replied Chan Lo.

Chan Lo. The stone tells me what it wants to be.

Narrator 1. People came from near and far to buy Chan Lo's carvings.

Narrator 4. So it happened that when the Great Emperor of All China was given a perfect piece of green-and-white jade stone, one of the advisers in the Celestial Palace thought of

> **jade**
> (jād)
> green or white precious stone

20 **Adviser 1.** Chan Lo!

Narrator 2. The humble stone carver was brought before the Great Emperor of All China. Chan Lo bowed deeply.

Emperor. I want you to carve a dragon.

Narrator 3. . . . the emperor commanded.

Emperor. A dragon of wind and fire.

Chan Lo. I will do my best to please you.

Narrator 1. The emperor's men carried the precious stone to Chan Lo's garden.

30 **Narrator 4.** Chan Lo had never seen such a perfect piece of jade. The green-and-white of the stone was like moss-entangled-in-snow.

> **entangled**
> (ĕn tăng' gəld)
> *adj.* twisted together

Narrator 2. The great emperor had commanded, "a dragon of wind and fire." Chan Lo wondered if that was what the stone wanted to be. He spoke to it.

> **Chan Lo.**
> Here I stand, O Noble Stone,
> to carve a creature of your own.
> 40 Whisper signs and sounds from rock
> that I, your servant, may unlock.

> **REREAD**
> What does Chan Lo want to know?

Narrator 3. Chan Lo bent down and put his ear to the stone. From deep inside came a gentle sound.

Stone (*softly*). Pah-tah. Pah-tah. Pah-*tah*.

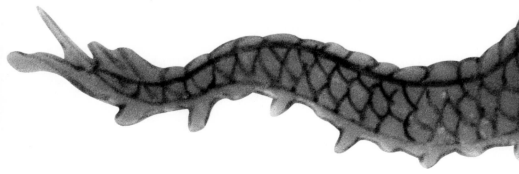

Chan Lo. Do dragons make that sound?

Narrator 1. . . . Chan Lo wondered.

Chan Lo. Perhaps the dragon's tail splashing in the ocean says "Pah-tah, pah-*tah*."

Narrator 4. But he was not sure.

THINK IT THROUGH
How does Chan Lo usually decide what to carve? What is different this time?

FOCUS ———
The stone carver examines the jade stone again. Read to find out what he hears.

50 **Narrator 2.** That evening, Chan Lo thought about dragons.

Narrator 3. But late at night, in his dreams, he heard,

Stone. Pah-tah. Pah-tah.

Stone and Chan Lo. Pah-*tah*.

Narrator 1. The next morning, Chan Lo went to the garden.

Narrator 4. The stone was spring-water-green in the morning light.

Chan Lo.

60   Here I stand, O Noble Stone,
        to carve a creature of your own.
        Whisper signs and sounds from
        rock that I, your
        servant, may
        unlock.

Narrator 2. Chan Lo put his ear to the green-and-white jade and listened.

Narrator 3. Softly the sounds came.

Stone (*softly*). Bub-bub-bubble. Bub-bub-bubble.

70 **Chan Lo.** Do dragons make that sound?

Narrator 1. . . . Chan Lo asked himself.

Chan Lo. Perhaps a dragon rising from the wild waves blows bubbles through his nostrils.

Narrator 4. But these were not mighty dragon bubbles that were coming from the rock. They were gentle, lazy, playful sounds.

REREAD

What other creatures might make such sounds?

Narrator 2. That evening, Chan Lo tried again to think about dragons.

80 **Narrator 3.** But when he went to bed, he heard in his dreams the sound of

Stone. Bub-bub-bubble. Bub-bub-bubble.

Stone and Chan Lo. Bub-bub-bubble.

Narrator 1. In the middle of the night, Chan Lo awoke. He walked into the moonlit garden.

Narrator 4. The stone shone silvery-green in the moonlight.

Chan Lo.
Here I stand, O Noble Stone,
90   to carve a creature of your own.
Whisper signs and sounds from rock
that I, your servant, may unlock.

Narrator 2. He put his ear to the stone. Silence.

Narrator 3. Chan Lo ran his hands over the jade. His fingers felt tiny ridges, and the ridges made a sound.

Stone (*softly*). S-s-s-ah, S-s-s-s-s-ah, S-s-s-s-s-s-s-ah.

Chan Lo. Do dragons have ridges?

Narrator 1. . . . . Chan Lo pondered .

Chan Lo. Yes. They have scales. Scales on
100   their tails and bodies. And their scales
might say, "S-s-s-ah, S-s-s-s-s-ah, S-s-s-s-s-s-s-ah," if one dared to touch them.

Narrator 4. But Chan Lo knew these small, delicate
ridges were *not* dragon scales.

Narrator 2. Chan Lo could not carve what he did not
hear, but he was afraid to disobey the emperor.

Narrator 3. His fear weighed in him like a great stone
as he picked up his tools and began to carve.

THINK IT THROUGH
What do you think Chan Lo will carve? Use lines from the
play to support your opinion.

FOCUS ───────
What does the stone carver make from the jade stone?

Narrator 1. Chan Lo worked slowly and carefully for a
110   year and a day.

Narrator 4. Finally, the carving was complete.

Narrator 2. Early in the morning, before the birds were
awake, Chan Lo and his apprentice wrapped the jade
carving in a cloth and set out for the Celestial Palace.

Narrator 3. Chan Lo entered the Great Hall, where the
three advisers sat waiting for the Great Emperor of
All China. He placed the jade stone on the table in
the center of the room.

Narrator 1. Soon the emperor's advisers grew curious.
120   They scurried to the jade stone and peeked under the cloth.

scurried
(skûr′ ēd)
went with
running steps

Adviser 1 (*surprised*). No dragon!

Adviser 2 (*louder*). *No dragon!*

Adviser 3 (*loudest*). NO DRAGON!

Narrator 4. At that moment, the emperor himself entered the Great Hall.

Emperor. Show me my dragon of wind and fire!

Narrator 2. The advisers whisked the cloth away.

Emperor (*thundering*). *This* is not my dragon!

130 **Adviser 1** (*pointing at Chan Lo*). Punish him!

Adviser 2. *Punish him!*

Adviser 3. PUNISH HIM!

Narrator 3. Chan Lo's knees shook like ginkgo leaves in the wind.

ginkgo leaves
(gǐng′ kō lēvz′)
fan-shaped
leaves of a tree
native to China

Chan Lo. O mighty emperor, there *is* no dragon of wind and fire. I did not *hear* it! I heard these three carp fish swimming playfully in the reeds in the pool of the Celestial Palace.

140 **Emperor.** *Hear* them? You did not *hear* them!

Adviser 1. Chop off his head!

Adviser 2. *Boil him in oil!*

Adviser 3. CUT HIM IN A THOUSAND PIECES!

Narrator 1. But the emperor was so angry, he could not decide which punishment to choose.

THINK IT THROUGH

Why is the emperor angry? What does he plan to do about it?

Emperor. I will let my *dreams* decide his punishment. Now, take him away! And remove that stone from the Celestial Palace!

Narrator 4. Chan Lo was dragged down many flights of stairs and thrown into a black prison cell. The carving was placed outside, near the reeds of the reflecting pool.

Narrator 2. That evening, the emperor thought about dragons.

Narrator 3. But late that night, in his sleep, the emperor dreamed of fish playfully slapping their tails in green water.

Stone. Pah-tah. Pah-tah.

Stone and Emperor. Pah-*tah*.

Narrator 1. In the morning, the emperor's advisers asked,

Adviser 1. What punishment have you chosen?

Narrator 4. But the emperor said,

Emperor. My dreams have not yet decided.

Narrator 2. That evening, the emperor again tried to think about dragons.

Narrator 3. But when he went to bed, the emperor dreamed of fish gliding smoothly through deep, clear water.

Stone. Bub-bub-bubble. Bub-bub-bubble.

Stone and Emperor. Bub-bub-bubble.

Narrator 1. In the morning, the emperor's advisers again asked him,

Adviser 2. What punishment have your dreams chosen?

Narrator 4. But the emperor told them,

Emperor. My dreams have still not decided.

THINK IT THROUGH
How is the emperor now like Chan Lo?

FOCUS ———————

The emperor has again delayed Chan Lo's punishment. Read to find out what he finally decides.

Narrator 2. On the third night, the emperor groaned and tossed in his sleep, but he did not dream.

Narrator 3. He awoke in the darkest hour of the night. A strange sound filled the room.

180 **Stone.** S-s-s-ah, S-s-s-s-s-ah, S-s-s-s-s-s-s-ah.

Narrator 1. The emperor got out of bed and went toward the sound. He hurried down the corridors, through the Great Hall, and out into the moonlit garden.

Narrator 4. There by the reflecting pool was the jade stone. Next to it stood the apprentice, running his fingers down the scales of the three carp fish.

Stone. S-s-s-ah, S-s-s-s-s-ah, S-s-s-s-s-s-s-ah.

Narrator 2. When the apprentice had gone,
190 the emperor sat near the pool and gazed at the jade stone. The shining scales of the jade carp glowed in the moonlight. The fishes' slippery bodies were reflected in the pool. They seemed ready to flick their tails and swim among the reeds.

REREAD
What do you think the emperor is thinking?

Narrator 3. The emperor remained by the pool until his advisers found him at sunrise.

Adviser 3. What punishment have your dreams chosen?

200 **Emperor** (*smiling*). Bring Chan Lo before me.

Narrator 1. Chan Lo bowed deeply before the Great Emperor of All China, ready to receive his terrible punishment.

Emperor. You have disobeyed me, Chan Lo, but you are a brave man to defy the Great Emperor of All China. You have carved the creatures that were in the stone. I, too, have heard them. These three carp fish are dearer to me than any dragon of wind and
210 fire. What reward would you have?

> **defy**
> (dĭ fī′)
> *v.* resist with boldness

Chan Lo (*grateful and relieved, bowing even lower*). Great Emperor, your happiness with my work is my reward. I wish only to return to my village and carve what I hear.

Emperor. You *will* carve what you hear. And you will return to your village in great honor—as befits the Master Carver to the Great Emperor of All China!

Stone. Pah-*tah!*

THINK IT THROUGH

1. The emperor tells Chan Lo, "You *will* carve what you hear." What lesson about artists do you think the emperor has learned?
2. At first the emperor wants a dragon of wind and fire. Why do you think he realizes that the fish are better?
3. Why do you think Chan Lo does not ask for a big reward?

by Lucille Clifton

the carver
for fred

sees the man
in the wood and
calls his name and
the man in the wood
5 breaks through the bark and
the nations of wood call
the carver
Brother

CAN SOMEONE STEAL YOUR HAPPINESS?

ROSAURA IS ABOUT TO FIND OUT.

I told them not to give me a doll, Sonya Fe.

The
STOLEN
PARTY

by Liliana Heker
translated by Alberto Manguel

Connect to Your Life

Has someone ever believed something about you because of how you dressed or where you were born? What did he or she think? How did you feel about it?

Key to the Story

This story takes place in Argentina. In the past there were only two classes of people in that country—the rich and the poor. Poor people often worked as servants for the rich. The rich did not mix with the poor. The two groups lived very separate lives. In "The Stolen Party," a poor girl, Rosaura, believes that she and a girl from a rich family are friends.

Vocabulary Preview

Words to Know

approve   employee
offended   compliment
boisterous

 Reading Coach CD-ROM selection

Rosaura goes to a birthday party and remembers a fight she had earlier with her mother.

As soon as she arrived she went straight to the kitchen to see if the monkey was there. It was: what a relief! She wouldn't have liked to admit that her mother had been right. *Monkeys at a birthday?* her mother had sneered. *Get away with you, believing any nonsense you're told!* She was cross , but not because of the monkey, the girl thought; it's just because of the party.

> cross
> (krôs)
> angry

"I don't like you going," she told her.

10 "It's a rich people's party."

"Rich people go to Heaven too," said the girl, who studied religion at school.

"Get away with Heaven," said the mother. . . .

The girl didn't approve of the way her mother spoke. She was barely nine, and one of the best in her class.

> approve
> (ə prōōv′)
> v. think to be right or good

"I'm going because I've been invited," she said. "And I've been invited because Luciana is my friend. So there."

20 "Ah yes, your friend," her mother grumbled. She paused. "Listen, Rosaura," she said at last. "That one's not your friend. You know what you are to them? The maid's daughter, that's what."

> **REREAD**
> Why does Rosaura's mother believe that Luciana is not Rosaura's friend?

Rosaura blinked hard: she wasn't going to cry. Then she yelled: "Shut up! You know nothing about being friends!"

THINK IT THROUGH

What do Rosaura and her mother fight about? How does Rosaura stand up for herself?

Read to learn why Rosaura believes she and Luciana are friends.

Every afternoon she used to go to Luciana's house
30 and they would both finish their homework while Rosaura's mother did the cleaning. They had their tea in the kitchen and they told each other secrets. Rosaura loved everything in the big house, and she also loved the people who lived there.

"I'm going because it will be the most lovely party in the whole world, Luciana told me it would. There will be a magician, and he will bring a monkey and everything."

The mother swung around to take a
40 good look at her child, and pompously put her hands on her hips.

> **pompously**
> (pŏm′ pəs lē)
> with too much pride

"Monkeys at a birthday?" she said. "Get away with you, believing any nonsense you're told!"

Rosaura was deeply offended . She thought it unfair of her mother to accuse other people of being liars simply because they were rich. Rosaura too wanted to be rich, of course. If one day
50 she managed to live in a beautiful palace, would her mother stop loving her? She felt very sad. She wanted to go to that party more than anything else in the world.

> **offended**
> (ə fĕn′ dĭd)
> v. hurt; past tense of offend

> **REREAD**
> What conflict is going on inside Rosaura?

"I'll die if I don't go," she whispered, almost without moving her lips.

And she wasn't sure whether she had been heard, but on the morning of the party she discovered that her mother had starched her Christmas dress. And in the afternoon, after washing her hair, her mother

I told them not to give me a doll, Sonya Fe.

60 rinsed it in apple vinegar so that it would be all nice and shiny. Before going out, Rosaura admired herself in the mirror, with her white dress and glossy hair, and thought she looked terribly pretty.

THINK IT THROUGH
How does Rosaura feel about Luciana and her family? about other rich people?

FOCUS
Read to learn how Luciana's family treats Rosaura at the party.

Señora Ines also seemed to notice. As soon as she saw her, she said:

> **Señora Ines**
> (sĕ nyô′ rä ē nĕs′)
> Mrs. Ines,
> Luciana's mother

"How lovely you look today, Rosaura."

Rosaura gave her starched skirt a slight toss with her hands and walked into the party with a firm step. She said hello to Luciana and asked about

70 the monkey. Luciana put on a secretive look and whispered into Rosaura's ear: "He's in the kitchen. But don't tell anyone, because it's a surprise."

> **secretive**
> (sē′ krĭ tĭv)
> not open; as if
> keeping a secret

Rosaura wanted to make sure. Carefully she entered the kitchen and there she saw it: deep in thought, inside its cage. It looked so funny that the girl stood there for a while, watching it, and later, every so often, she would slip out of the party unseen and go and admire it. Rosaura was the only one allowed into

80 the kitchen. Señora Ines had said: "You yes, but not the others, they're much too boisterous, they might break something." Rosaura had never broken anything. She even managed the jug of orange juice, carrying it from the kitchen into the dining-room. She held it carefully and didn't spill a single drop. And Señora Ines had said: "Are you sure you can manage a jug as big as that?" Of course she could manage. She wasn't a butterfingers, like the others. Like that

90 blonde girl with the bow in her hair. As soon as she saw Rosaura, the girl with the bow had said:

boisterous	
(boi' stər əs)	
adj. active and noisy	

butterfingers	
(bŭt' ər fĭng' gərz)	
person who drops things	

"And you? Who are you?"

"I'm a friend of Luciana," said Rosaura.

"No," said the girl with the bow, "you are not a friend of Luciana because I'm her cousin and I know all her friends. And I don't know you."

THINK IT THROUGH
How does Señora Ines treat Rosaura?

FOCUS
Read to find out how Rosaura responds to Luciana's cousin.

"So what," said Rosaura. "I come here every afternoon with my mother and we do our homework together."

100 "You and your mother do your homework together?" asked the girl, laughing.

"I and Luciana do our homework together," said Rosaura, very seriously.

The girl with the bow shrugged her shoulders.

"That's not being friends," she said. "Do you go to school together?"

"No."

"So where do you know her from?" said the girl, getting impatient.

110 Rosaura remembered her mother's words perfectly. She took a deep breath.

"I'm the daughter of the employee," she said.

Her mother had said very clearly: "If someone asks, you say you're the daughter of the employee; that's all." She also told her to add: "And proud of it." But Rosaura thought that never in her life would she dare say something of the sort.

120 "What employee?" said the girl with the bow. "Employee in a shop?"

"No," said Rosaura angrily. "My mother doesn't sell anything in any shop, so there."

"So how come she's an employee?" said the girl with the bow.

Just then Señora Ines arrived saying *shh shh*, and asked Rosaura if she wouldn't mind helping serve out the hot-dogs, as she knew the house so much better than the others.

130 "See?" said Rosaura to the girl with the bow, and when no one was looking she kicked her in the shin.

THINK IT THROUGH
What reasons does Rosaura give to show that she and Luciana are friends? Why doesn't the cousin believe her?

Read to find out why Rosaura enjoys the party.

Apart from the girl with the bow, all the others were delightful. The one she liked best was Luciana, with her golden birthday crown; and then the boys. Rosaura won the sack race, and nobody managed to catch her when they played tag. When they split into two teams to play charades, all the boys wanted her for their side. Rosaura felt she had never been so happy in all her life.

> **charades**
> (shə rādz')
> a game in which people act out words or phrases and others try to guess them

140   But the best was still to come. The best came after Luciana blew out the candles. First the cake. Señora Ines had asked her to help pass the cake around, and Rosaura had enjoyed the task immensely, because everyone called out to her, shouting "Me, me!" Rosaura remembered a story in which there was a queen who had the power of life or death over her subjects. She had always loved that, having the power of life or death. To Luciana and the boys she gave the largest pieces, and to the

150   girl with the bow she gave a slice so thin one could see through it.

> **REREAD**
> What do you think Rosaura likes about serving the cake?

After the cake came the magician, tall and bony, with a fine red cape. A true magician: he could untie handkerchiefs by blowing on them and make a chain with links that had no openings. He could guess what cards were pulled out from a pack, and the monkey was his assistant. He called the monkey "partner." "Let's see here, partner," he would say, "Turn over a card." And, "Don't run away,

160   partner: time to work now."

The final trick was wonderful. One of the children had to hold the monkey in his arms and the magician said he would make him disappear.

"What, the boy?" they
all shouted.

"No, the monkey!"
shouted back the
magician.

Rosaura thought that
170 this was truly the most
amusing party in the
whole world.

The magician asked a
small fat boy to come and
help, but the small fat boy
got frightened almost at
once and dropped the
monkey on the floor. The
magician picked him up carefully, whispered
180 something in his ear, and the monkey nodded almost
as if he understood.

"You mustn't be so unmanly, my friend," the
magician said to the fat boy.

"What's unmanly?" said the fat boy.

The magician turned around as if to look for spies.

"A sissy," said the magician. "Go sit down."

Then he stared at all the faces, one by one. Rosaura
felt her heart tremble.

"You, with the Spanish eyes," said the magician.
190 And everyone saw that he was pointing at her.

I told them not to give me a doll, Sonya Fe.

THINK IT THROUGH

What happens to make Rosaura feel she is special?

She wasn't afraid. Neither holding the monkey, nor when the magician made him vanish; not even when, at the end, the magician flung his red cape over Rosaura's head and uttered a few magic words . . . and the monkey reappeared, chattering happily, in her arms. The children clapped furiously. And before Rosaura returned to her seat, the magician said:

"Thank you very much, my little countess."

She was so pleased with the compliment

200 that a while later, when her mother came to fetch her, that was the first thing she told her.

"I helped the magician and he said to me, 'Thank you very much, my little countess.'"

It was strange because up to then Rosaura had thought that she was angry with her mother. All along Rosaura had imagined that she would say to her: "See that the monkey wasn't a lie?" But instead she was so thrilled that she told her mother all about the wonderful magician.

210 Her mother tapped her on the head and said: "So now we're a countess!"

But one could see that she was beaming.

And now they both stood in the entrance, because a moment ago Señora Ines, smiling, had said: "Please wait here a second."

Her mother suddenly seemed worried.

"What is it?" she asked Rosaura.

"What is what?" said Rosaura. "It's nothing; she just wants to get the presents for those who are leaving, see?"

countess
(koun' tĭs)
woman of noble rank

compliment
(kŏm' plə mənt)
n. words of praise

THINK IT THROUGH

How does Rosaura feel toward her mother now? How does her mother react?

220   She pointed at the fat boy and at a girl with pigtails who were also waiting there, next to their mothers. And she explained about the presents. She knew, because she had been watching those who left before her. When one of the girls was about to leave, Señora Ines would give her a bracelet. When a boy left, Señora Ines gave him a yo-yo. Rosaura preferred the yo-yo because it sparkled, but she didn't mention that to her mother. Her mother might have said: "So why don't you ask for one, you blockhead?" That's

230 what her mother was like. Rosaura didn't feel like explaining that she'd be horribly ashamed to be the
odd one out . Instead she said:

| odd one out |
| person who is |
| different from |
| others in a group |

   "I was the best-behaved at the party."
   And she said no more because Señora Ines came out into the hall with two bags, one pink and one blue.
   First she went up to the fat boy, gave him a yo-yo out of the blue bag, and the fat boy left with his mother. Then she went up to the girl and gave her a

240 bracelet out of the pink bag, and the girl with the pigtails left as well.
   Finally she came up to Rosaura and her mother. She had a big smile on her face and Rosaura liked that. Señora Ines looked down at her, then looked up at her mother, and then said something that made Rosaura proud:
   "What a marvelous daughter you have, Herminia."

| marvelous |
| (mär′ və ləs) |
| wonderful |

   For an instant, Rosaura thought that

250 she'd give her two presents: the bracelet and the yo-yo. Señora Ines bent down as if about to look for

something. Rosaura also leaned forward, stretching out her arm. But she never completed the movement.

Señora Ines didn't look in the pink bag. Nor did she look in the blue bag. Instead she rummaged in her purse. In her hand appeared two bills.

"You really and truly earned this," she said handing them over. "Thank you for all your help, my pet."

REREAD

What is Señora Ines paying Rosaura for?

260   Rosaura felt her arms stiffen, stick close to her body, and then she noticed her mother's hand on her shoulder. Instinctively she pressed herself against her mother's body. That was all. Except her eyes. Rosaura's eyes had a cold, clear look that fixed itself on Señora Ines's face.

Señora Ines, motionless, stood there with her hand outstretched. As if she didn't dare draw it back. As if the slightest change might shatter an infinitely delicate balance.

infinitely delicate balance something that can easily be disturbed

THINK IT THROUGH

1. What does Rosaura expect to get? How does she feel about being offered money?
2. How do you think Rosaura happened to come to the party in the first place?
3. In what ways do you think this party changes Rosaura?

ACCEPTANCE

BY J. A. SENN

"I think I expected to be torn to pieces," Jane Goodall once said. This animal watcher has faced dangers. Discover why she took such risks.

Connect to Your Life

Have you ever had a strange animal treat you in a friendly way? What did the animal do? What did the experience teach you about how animals behave?

Key to the Article

This article is about a famous scientist who studies animal behavior. Jane Goodall spent years watching chimpanzees in the wild. Dr. Louis S. B. Leakey, a scientist, often gave her advice. At that time, not much was known about the habits of chimps. Jane hoped to learn a lot by living with them.

Vocabulary Preview

Words to Know

glaring   aggressive   compassion
brutal   instinctively

Reading Coach CD-ROM selection

Jane Goodall gets ready to watch chimps in the wild. Find out what happens.

For nearly two months, Jane observed chimps from the mountain peak. Then she slowly and cautiously moved down the mountain to be closer to them. Soon she noticed that the chimps were more curious about her than they were afraid. But that curiosity quickly turned to unmistakable boldness. Instead of running away like before, they would climb into the trees, rock the branches, and stare at her in silence. This went on for several months.

The Excitement of Danger

10   At one time during those months, Jane decided to follow a group of chimpanzees through a thick part of the forest. As she stopped to get her bearings, she heard a branch snap right beside her. As she swung around, she saw a young chimp sitting in a tree almost directly over her head. Then she saw two females nearby. Suddenly she realized that chimps were all around her—she was surrounded!

> **REREAD**
> How do you think Jane feels during this first meeting?

Jane sat down and tried to remain still.
20 Then she heard a low "huh" sound in the thick vegetation to her right. Soon another "huh" came from behind her, and another from in front of her. These nervous chimpanzee calls continued for approximately 10 minutes. But Jane would only occasionally catch a glimpse of a large hand or a pair of glaring eyes.

> **vegetation**
> (věj′ ĭ tā′ shən)
> plant growth

> **glaring**
> (glâr′ ĭng)
> *adj.* staring in anger

Suddenly the calls grew louder, until the chimps were almost screaming. Then six

30 large males rushed out of their hiding places. As each
chimp became excited, he shook nearby tree branches
and snapped off twigs. One chimp, named Goliath for
his great size and strength, even climbed on a bush near
Jane. She could see his hair standing on
end as he wildly swayed back and forth.
At one point, she thought he was going to
land on top of her. Jane later confessed, "I
think I expected to be torn to pieces."

REREAD
Try to picture what is happening to Jane.

Then, just as quickly as this display of
40 anger had begun, it ended. Quietly, the males joined
the females and their young and left. Years later, Jane
wrote, "My knees were shaking when I got up. But
there was the sense of excitement that comes when
danger has come and left one unharmed. And the
chimpanzees were surely less afraid of me now."

THINK IT THROUGH
What could have happened to Jane?

"I THINK I EXPECTED
TO BE TORN TO
PIECES."
-JANE GOODALL

FOCUS

Jane Goodall continues her work. Read about another experience that holds danger for her.

Another Frightening Experience

Another time, however, Jane was not so lucky. She was waiting for some chimps to pass by a ripe fruit tree when she heard footsteps in the leaves behind her. Trying not to scare the chimps, she lay down on the 50 ground. When the footsteps got closer, they stopped. Then Jane heard a worried "Hoo! Hoo!" from one of the chimps.

Like a flash of lightning, a large male jumped into the tree directly over her. Soon the chimp started to show his rage by hitting the tree's trunk and shaking its branches wildly. His hoots became louder, until he was uttering high-pitched screams of anger. Overcome by fear, Jane remained motionless.

All at once the angry chimp seemed to disappear into 60 the thick vegetation. After a moment of silence, however, he rushed toward Jane and let out a horrifying and brutal scream. She suddenly felt his hand slam down on the back of her head. Though dazed and fearful, she slowly sat up and looked around. When the chimp saw her move, he quickly ran off.

brutal

(broot′ l)
adj. extremely rough

Later she guessed that he must not have recognized her, because she was lying down. The plastic sheet she was wearing to protect herself against the rain 70 also could have confused him. When she discussed this incident with Dr. Leakey, he said, "If you had waved your arms, shouted, or shown anger in any way, you might have been killed. He was merely testing to find out if you were an enemy or not."

REREAD

How does Jane's reaction to danger help her?

This is one of the many chimps Jane Goodall studied.

Dr. Leakey must have been right, because gradually over the next several months, the apes became less aggressive. In fact, Jane was eventually greeted almost as if she were a 80 chimpanzee herself. Sometimes the chimps would show excitement by hooting and shaking the branches. At other times, they showed no interest in her at all.

aggressive
(ə grĕs′ ĭv)
adj. forceful

THINK IT THROUGH

How does the chimps' attitude toward Jane change over time?

Physical Contact

Although the chimps no longer seemed to be afraid of Jane, she was still not able to establish any personal relationships with them. That changed, however, one day about a year after her arrival in Gombe. On that day, Jane was sitting near David Graybeard by a tiny stream in the forest. On the ground she saw a ripe red palm nut. Slowly she picked it up and held it out to him on her open palm. At first he turned his head away. But Jane moved a little closer to him. Once again she held out her hand. This time he looked at the fruit, at Jane, and then back at the fruit. He reached out his hand and held her hand firmly but gently. After a moment, he released her hand and watched the nut drop to the ground.

90

REREAD

Try to picture this scene in your mind. What might the chimp be trying to "say" to Jane?

Jane Goodall and a friend

100   "At that moment I didn't need a scientist to explain what had happened," Jane later wrote in her notes. "David Graybeard had communicated with me. It was as if he had said, 'Everything is going to be okay.' And for those few seconds, the wall between human and chimpanzee was broken down. It was a reward far beyond my greatest hopes." David had become the first chimpanzee to fully accept Jane. . . .

THINK IT THROUGH

Why is this moment with David Graybeard important to Jane?

FOCUS

Read to find out how Jane's purpose changes.

Championing the Rights of Chimps

    After her husband's death, Jane realized that she needed to broaden her work with
110 the chimpanzees. "For years I was selfishly concerned only with the Gombe chimps," she once said. "Now, I'm worried about the treatment and survival of chimps everywhere."

> **championing**
> (chăm′ pē ə nĭng)
> strongly defending

    As a result, she founded the Jane Goodall Institute in Tucson, Arizona, in 1977. The purpose of the institute is to help save the world's dwindling chimpanzee population. Poaching, hunting, and the destruction of chimpanzee habitats have caused the
120 world population of chimps to drop to 175,000. Since 1977, Jane has been lecturing one month a year at the institute. She also spends much of her time raising money throughout the world for her cause. . . .

> **poaching**
> (pō′ chĭng)
> hunting animals where it is forbidden to do so

At the end of many of her lectures and talks, Jane usually tells the story about an eight-year-old chimp named Old Man. At the zoo, he was placed on a human-made island with three females. After he had been there for several years, a young man named
130 Marc Cusano was hired to feed the chimps. He was warned at the time not to go near them. "Those brutes are vicious," he was told. "They'll kill you."

Although he was cautious at first, Marc soon started going closer and closer to the chimps. One day, while he was sitting in his boat, Old Man reached out and gently took a banana from Marc's hand. At that moment Marc and Old Man began a very special friendship that just kept growing. Eventually, Marc even groomed and played with
140 Old Man.

One day when Marc slipped and fell, he startled an infant chimp. Screaming, the infant ran to its mother. To protect her baby, the mother instinctively leaped on Marc and bit his neck. As he lay there, the other two females rushed up and joined in the attack. Then, just when Marc thought he was going to die, Old Man charged toward the three females. He pushed them away and stayed close to
150 Marc. With Old Man's help, Marc was finally able to get into his boat and row away to safety. There is no question in Marc's mind that Old Man saved his life.

Jane Goodall concludes the story with the following challenge. "If a chimpanzee—one, moreover, who has been abused by humans—can reach out across the species barrier to help a human friend in need,

> **instinctively**
> (ĭn stĭngk' tĭv lē)
> *adv.* by natural action; without thinking

> **REREAD**
> How do you think Old Man feels about Marc?

> **species**
> (spē' shēz)
> particular kind of animal

then surely we, with our deeper capacity for
160 compassion and understanding, can
reach out to help the chimpanzees who
need us, so desperately, today. Can't we?"

> **compassion**
> (kəm pǎsh′ ən)
> *n.* concern for
> the suffering of
> others

THINK IT THROUGH

1. What has become Jane's new purpose? How is her telling of Marc's story related to that purpose?
2. Reread the last paragraph. What does Jane think we can learn from chimps?
3. Review the article. What are the dangers of working with wild animals? What are the rewards?
4. Tell three facts you learned about chimps.

Growing Up in a World of Darkness

by James Haskins

A child who is blind learns all about sounds. Then sounds lead him to explore making music. Discover how Stevie Wonder became a wonder of the world.

"See, about sound . . . ," Stevie Wonder says, "there's one thing you gotta remember about sound—sound happens all the time, *all* the time. If you put your hands right up to your ears, if you close your eyes and move your hands back and forth, you can hear the sound getting closer and farther away. . . . Sound bounces off everything, there's always something happening."

Stevie Wonder was born Steveland Morris on May 13, 1950, in Saginaw, Michigan. He was the third boy in a family that would eventually include five boys and one girl. All except Stevie were born without handicaps. He was born prematurely, and his early birth led to his total blindness.

> **handicaps**
> (hăn′ dē kăps′)
> *n.* physical disabilities

"I guess that I first became aware that I was blind," Stevie recalls, "—and I just vaguely remember this—when I'd be wallowing around in the grass back of the house, and I'd get myself and my clothes soiled. My mother would get on me about that. She explained that I couldn't move about so much, that I'd have to try and stay in one place.

"When I was young," he says, "my mother taught me never to feel sorry for myself, because handicaps are really things to be used, another way to benefit yourself and others in the long run."

> **REREAD**
> What attitude is Stevie's mother giving him?

This was the best possible advice Stevie's mother could have given. He learned to regard his blindness in more than one way. It could be a hindrance, but it could also

> **hindrance**
> (hĭn′ drəns)
> something that prevents progress

be a special gift. He was able to accept this idea, sometimes better than his mother could.

"I know it used to worry my mother," Stevie recalls, "and I know she prayed for me to have sight someday, and so finally I just told her that I was *happy* being blind, and I thought it was a gift from God, and I think she felt better after that."

THINK IT THROUGH
What does the author think about Stevie and his mother?

FOCUS _____
Stevie continues to learn ways of dealing with blindness. Read to find out more about his discoveries.

Stevie was a lucky child in many
40 ways. He was lucky to have two brothers close enough to him in age not to understand at first about his blindness and to expect him to do many of the things they did. He was also lucky to have a mother and a father, and occasionally an uncle, who understood how important sound was to him, and how important it was for him to learn to identify things he
50 could not see by their sound. He recalls:

"I remember people dropping money on the table and saying, 'What's that, Steve?' That's a dime—buh-duh-duh-da; that's a quarter—buh-duh-duh-duh-da; that's a nickel. I could almost always get it right except a penny and a nickel confused me.

"I don't really feel my hearing is any better than yours," Stevie says now; "we all have the same

abilities, you know. The only difference is
how much you use it." Encouraged by his

60 family, Stevie used his hearing more and
more as he grew older. He learned how to
tell birds apart by their calls, and to tell
trees apart by the sound their leaves made as they
rustled in the wind. He learned to tell when people
were tired or annoyed or pleased by listening to the
tone of their voices. His world of sound grew larger
and larger, and the most frightening experience for
him was silence. He depended so on sound that
silence, for him, was like total darkness for deaf

70 children. It is hard for sighted and
hearing people to understand this.
Perhaps the best way to understand is to
imagine being shut up in a dark,
soundproof box. People need to feel that
they are part of the world around them. It is hard
enough to do so when one cannot see, or when one
cannot hear; but it is doubly hard for a blind
person in a silent room or a deaf person in
total darkness.

80 He also spent a lot of time beating on
things, to make sounds and to make music.
Although his mother was a gospel singer,
the family was not especially
musical. But Stevie had
shown musical interest and
ability very young. By the
time he was two years old his
favorite toys were two spoons,
with which he would beat

90 rhythmically on pans and
tabletops and anything else his

> **encouraged**
> (ĕn kûr′ ĭjd)
> *adj.* given a
> sense of hope

> **REREAD**
> Can you imagine
> what it would be
> like in a dark,
> soundproof box?

mother would let him beat
on. When she began to worry
about her furniture, she bought
him cardboard drums from the dime
store. None of them lasted very long.
"I'd beat 'em to death," Stevie says with a
chuckle. But there would always be a new
drum, and there were other toy instruments as
100 well.

"One day someone gave me a harmonica to put on
my key chain, a little four-hole harmonica," Stevie
recalls. He managed to get a remarkable range of
sounds from that toy instrument.

"Then one day my mother took me to a picnic and
someone sat me behind my first set of drums. They
put my foot on the pedal and I played. They gave me
a quarter. I liked the sound of quarters."

At a very early age, too, Stevie began to sing. All
110 voices were very important to him, for they brought
him closer to the world around him, a
world he could not see. As he grew older,
his own voice became particularly
important to him, especially at night
when the rest of the house was silent.
He learned the endless possibilities of the
human voice by experimenting with his
own, and by mimicking others'.

> **REREAD**
> Why do you think Stevie uses his voice when his house is still?

> **mimicking**
> (mĭm' ĭ kĭng)
> *n.* imitating

Music itself, not necessarily made by
120 him, became very important to him. He
loved to listen to the radio; his earliest
memory is of hearing Johnny Ace singing "Pledging
My Love" on the radio. Shortly before he entered
school he was given a small transistor radio for his
very own. From then on, that radio was his constant

companion. He even slept with it under his pillow at night. It played softly, providing sounds for him in an otherwise silent apartment. When he started school, he insisted on taking it to school with him.

THINK IT THROUGH

Why does music become important to Stevie? Use examples from this section to explain.

FOCUS

The radio plays an important part in Stevie's life. Read to find out how it helps him.

130 Stevie was enrolled in special classes for the blind in the Detroit public school system. A special bus picked him up every morning and brought him back every afternoon. Stevie wished he could walk to school as his brothers did, and go to their neighborhood school. But he was learning to adjust to the fact that he must lead a different life, and in his special classes he was taught many things that would help him lead as normal a life as possible.

Sighted children attended the same school, and they 140 often whispered about "the blind kids" as they passed by. Adults did the same thing. Somehow, normal people have the idea that blind people cannot hear them. It was hard to deal in an honest way with sighted people or even with his partially sighted classmates.

Being blind is to be exposed to constant
frustrations . Dropping something, especially something small, means having to grope about with little chance of finding 150 it. Some blind children won't even bother looking for an object they have dropped

frustrations
(frŭ strā′ shənz)
feelings of hopelessness at not being able to do what one wants

because they are embarrassed to be seen groping about for it.

Stevie had an additional problem in getting along with other children. Not only was he blind; he was also black. At first it might seem that the idea of skin color should not be very important to a child who has never seen color. But blackness is not just skin color; it is a culture, a way of looking at things. People divide themselves into "Us" and "Them" because of skin color, but that is not the only division. We also divide ourselves because of religion, education, economic class. If everyone in the entire world were blind, people would still divide themselves into "Us" and "Them"; it just would not be on the basis of appearance.

REREAD

This is the author's opinion. Do you agree?

At home, Stevie heard his brothers and their friends talk about the white kids they knew. Before long, even though Stevie could not himself see color, he was very aware of skin color, and in addition to being self-conscious because of his blindness he was a little bit ashamed of being black.

self-conscious
(sĕlf' kŏn' shəs)
adj. very aware of one's own actions and appearance

"I remember when I was little," says Stevie, "I used to listen to this black radio station in Detroit on my way to school. Like I was the only black kid on the bus, and I would always turn the radio down, because I felt ashamed to let them hear me listening to B.B. King. But I *loved* B.B. King. Yet I felt ashamed because—because I was

different enough to want to hear him and because I had never heard him anywhere else."

Stevie was not about to stop listening to B.B. King; he simply played his radio softly in situations where he felt uncomfortable. That radio meant more to him than just about anything else in the world.

190   "I spent a lot of time listening to the radio," Stevie recalls, "and I was able to relate to the different instruments and know what they were. I began to know them by name. I used to listen to this program on station WCHB . . . called 'Sundown.' The disc jockey was named Larry Dixon and he always played a lot of old songs. There was one thing he played, it was his theme song . . . da da duh duh *dommm* da duh . . . da da da da *dommm dommm* da da duh. . . . Oh, it's really a bad tune, really a beautiful song—

200   can't think of the name right now, but I could never forget that tune."

He would sing the words of the songs quietly to himself. He would hum the tunes. He would tap out the beats on his toy drums and try to play the melodies on his four-note harmonica. It frustrated him not to have real,

210   grown-up instruments to play on, and it was hard for him to accept the fact that his mother just did not have enough money to buy real instruments for him. But luck soon proved to be with Stevie.

Young Stevie Wonder with his harmonica

Within the space of about a year and a half, he managed to acquire not one but *three* real
220 instruments.

THINK IT THROUGH

How does the radio help Stevie to develop an interest in music?

FOCUS ___

Discover the changes in Stevie's life when he receives three special gifts.

Every year the Detroit Lions Club gave a Christmas party for blind children, and at Christmastime during his first-grade year at school Stevie went to one. Each child received a gift, and someone must have told the Detroit Lions Club about Stevie's interest in music, for his gift—he could hardly believe it—was a set of real drums! Stevie sat down and began to pound on them right then and there.

Later a neighborhood barber gave Stevie a
230 harmonica—a real one. He practiced and practiced until he had mastered that.

Then, when he was seven, Stevie became the proud owner of a real piano. A neighbor was moving out of the housing project, and she really did not want to take her piano. Knowing how much Stevie loved music, she decided to give it to him. Stevie remembers, "I kept asking, 'When they gonna bring the piano over, Mamma?' I never realized how important that was going to be to me." When the

240 piano finally arrived, it was like all the birthdays Stevie could remember all rolled into one. He ran his hands along the smooth wooden top, down the sides and around the back, down the slim legs, around to the cold metal of the pedals, and back up to the keys, some flat, some raised. He asked his mother to open the top of the piano, so he could feel the strings inside. He asked her what color they were.

> **REREAD**
> What do you think Stevie is trying to do here?

They were kind of gold, and the small

250 wooden blocks between them were light brown. What color was the piano? A dark brown. From that moment on, dark brown, although he had not ever seen it and would never see it, meant something nice to Stevie. And since, he had been told, his skin was a sort of dark brown, too, he began to feel much better about his skin color.

THINK IT THROUGH
Why are the three musical gifts important to Stevie's life?

FOCUS
Read to find out where Stevie's love of music leads him.

By the time he was nine or ten Stevie was a very popular member of the neighborhood. He was certainly the most gifted musically, and he spent many

260 Saturdays and after-school hours on the front porches of neighbors' houses on Horton Street. By this time Stevie had a set of bongo drums, which he had

mastered as he had every other instrument to which he had been exposed. Often he would play his bongos; sometimes it would be the harmonica. Everyone would join in the singing, but Stevie's clear, strong voice always took the lead. Without exception the music was rhythm and blues, the kind the people listened to on WCHB.

270   One of his favorite singing partners was a boy about his age named John Glover. John Glover had a grown-up cousin named Ronnie White, who lived in another part of the city. Ronnie White was a member of the singing group the Miracles, which had enjoyed great success recording with a company named Hitsville USA. Of course, John Glover was very proud to have a cousin like Ronnie White, and he often boasted about him. John Glover was also proud to have a friend like Stevie. "You oughta hear my friend
280 Stevie," he kept telling his cousin. But naturally White was busy, and he didn't really believe this kid Stevie was anything special. Then, one day in 1960, he happened to drop by to visit his relatives on Horton Street, and Stevie just happened to be having one of his front-porch sessions at the time. White did not

The adult Stevie Wonder performs at a Grammy Awards show.

have to listen very long to realize that his little cousin
was right. This kid was something!

White arranged with the president of Hitsville USA,
Berry Gordy, to take Stevie to the company's
290 recording studio and to give him an
audition , and one exciting afternoon
Stevie was taken to the place that would be
like a second home to him for the next ten
years.

audition
(ô dĭsh′ ən)
n. performance to show a skill

Stevie will never forget that afternoon. White took
him around the studio, helping him to the different
instruments and sound equipment, letting him touch
them. It seemed to Stevie that every wonderful
instrument in the world was right there in that sound

300 studio, and he never wanted to leave it. Then he was introduced to Berry Gordy. Gordy listened to him sing, and play the harmonica and drums, and hired him on the spot, which says a lot for Gordy. Few, if any, other record-company owners would have taken such a chance back in 1960. But then, few, if any, other record companies had or would have the history of Gordy's. No other black-owned label would prevail as his would, and perhaps this was because once they were established,
310 those other labels were too busy holding on to their position to take any risk or to try anything new.

prevail
(prĭ vāl′)
succeed

Anyway, signing an artist brought in by a performer already with the company has become a common, and famous, practice of Gordy's. The Supremes were discovered by the Temptations. Diana Ross discovered the Jackson Five.

Of course, Stevie's mother actually signed Stevie's contract with Hitsville, for he was underage. There
320 was little talk of money or other conditions. Stevie's family was so excited, so grateful for this opportunity for him, that they would have agreed to anything!

THINK IT THROUGH

1. Why was Berry Gordy taking a chance when he signed Stevie Wonder?
2. How did Stevie's family and community help make him a star? Think of several ways.
3. Do you think Stevie Wonder would have become a musician if he had been able to see? Use evidence from the biography to support your opinion.

Appearances Can Fool You

Poetry

Many things and people are not what they seem. You cannot judge them by how they look. The poems in this unit invite you to look at familiar things in different ways.

Some of the poets use rhyme and rhythm to give a musical sound to their poems. One uses **free verse,** poetry without rhyme and rhythm. All the poems have a **speaker,** the voice that talks to the reader. Sometimes the voice uses **humor** to make you laugh. Sometimes the voice gives an important message about life, called a **theme.** Take a new look at some familiar things.

Almost Human

by Pat Moon

Can dolphins talk?
To find out, why not
just ask them?

Connect to Your Life

If you have a pet, does your pet almost seem as though it can talk to you? How does it speak with you? With its eyes? With sounds? How does it know what you want?

Key to the Poem

The key to this poem is to know who is talking. The **speaker,** or the voice talking, may not be the poet. You have to read a while to figure out who is talking as well as whom they're talking about.

Vocabulary In line 9, **communicate** means "to give information to another." In line 11, **respond** means "to act in return."

Almost Human

by Pat Moon

Come and see the people dear.
Oh, look how they sit!
Aren't they sweet
The way they laugh?
5 I really must admit
That they seem quite intelligent.
Just hear the sound they make;
You could almost believe
They're trying to communicate.

10 They're very easily trained
And respond to simple rules.
Just watch how they point and wave
As we swim around the pool.
See how they stand and clap
15 When we dive through the hoop?
And the noise they make
When we walk on our tails
Or leap the bar in one swoop!

Just watch how they jump and shout
20 In my favorite part of the shows
When we dive and splash the water
All over the front few rows.

It's time to leave them now, dear,
They've had enough for one day.
25   It's quite amazing what people can do
If you treat them in the right way.

THINK IT THROUGH

1. Who is speaking in the poem? Whom is the speaker talking about?
2. What does the speaker think of people? Give examples to explain your opinion.
3. What would the speaker probably say about the intelligence of animals and people?

POINT OF VIEW

BY SHEL SILVERSTEIN

Everyone loves a holiday meal! Well, maybe not everyone. . . .

Connect to Your Life

Sometimes you see things one way and a friend sees them another way. When is it okay for friends to have different opinions about the same thing?

Key to the Poem

Notice that the title of this poem is "Point of View." **Point of view** means the way someone sees something. Two people can have two different ways of thinking about the same thing. Imagine how different the points of view of an animal and a person would be. This poem contrasts two very different points of view, indeed.

POINT OF VIEW

BY SHEL SILVERSTEIN

Thanksgiving dinner's sad and thankless
Christmas dinner's dark and blue
When you stop and try to see it
From the turkey's point of view.

5 Sunday dinner isn't sunny
Easter feasts are just bad luck
When you see it from the viewpoint
Of a chicken or a duck.

Oh how I once loved tuna salad
10 Pork and lobsters, lamb chops too
Till I stopped and looked at dinner
From the dinner's point of view.

THINK IT THROUGH

1. How does line 4 make the reader laugh?
2. How is the speaker's point of view different from the animals' points of view?
3. Why does the speaker stop enjoying dinners?

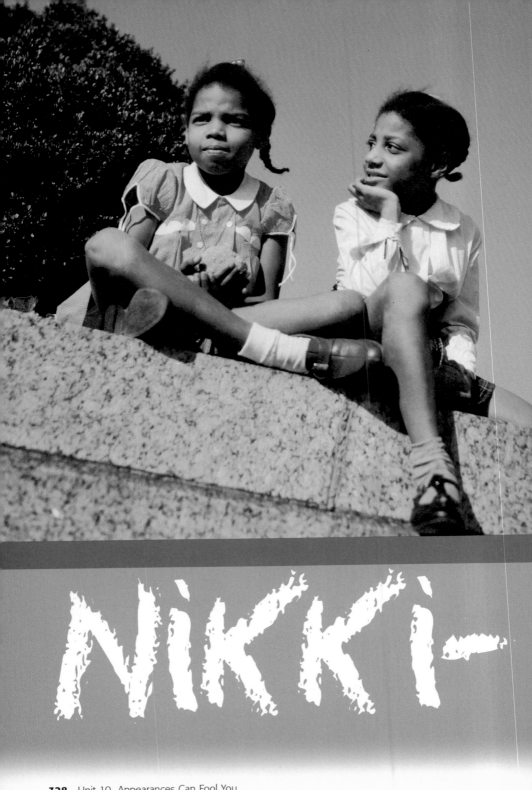

Nikki-

We all have

childhood memories.

What feelings go

along with those

memories?

Connect to Your Life

Do other people see you the way you see yourself? How is their view different from yours?

Key to the Poem

In **free verse,** the poet does not have to use rhyming words or a strong rhythm. This poet expresses thoughts freely, without rhyme or a beat. Notice that the lines are different lengths, depending on what is said. They take the shape of the writer's feelings as they flow onto the paper.

In "Nikki-Rosa" free verse is used to express feelings. Look for the speaker's feelings about childhood.

Vocabulary In line 17, **biographers** means "people who write the life stories of famous people." In line 20, **poverty** means "the state of being poor."

 Reading Coach CD-ROM selection

BY NIKKI GIOVANNI

NIKKI-ROSA

BY NIKKI GIOVANNI

childhood remembrances are always a drag
if you're Black
you always remember things like living in Woodlawn
with no inside toilet
5 and if you become famous or something
they never talk about how happy you were to have
your mother
all to yourself and
how good the water felt when you got your bath
10 from one of those
big tubs that folk in chicago barbecue in
and somehow when you talk about home
it never gets across how much you
understood their feelings
15 as the whole family attended meetings about
   Hollydale
and even though you remember
your biographers never understand
your father's pain as he sells his stock
and another dream goes

20 And though you're poor it isn't poverty that
concerns you
and though they fought a lot
it isn't your father's drinking that makes any difference
but only that everybody is together and you
25 and your sister have happy birthdays and very good
Christmases
and I really hope no white person ever has cause
to write about me
because they never understand
30 Black love is Black wealth and they'll
probably talk about my hard childhood
and never understand that
all the while I was quite happy

THINK IT THROUGH

1. In what ways might the speaker's childhood seem hard?
2. How does the speaker really feel about her childhood?
3. What message, or theme, does the speaker give about her childhood?

Bridges to History

Mixed Genres

Think of the history of the United States as a patchwork quilt. There are patches for all the people and events. The brightest patches are for the dreams that came true.

History is made up of stories, and stories are told in many different ways. In this unit you'll read **historical fiction** as well as **informative articles.** You'll also read a **ballad**—a story in the form of a poem that was sung aloud. Finally you'll read a **folk tale** that someone recorded. As you read all of these pieces, you need to separate fact from fiction.

The Invaders

by Jack Ritchie

The invaders have returned. Is escape possible this time?

Connect to Your Life

What images does the word *invader* bring to your mind? In your opinion, does the word suggest a friendly or unfriendly meeting? Share your opinion with a classmate.

Key to the Story

Expect the unexpected in this story. Its setting and happenings are not as they seem. As you read, look for clues that will help you understand the time and place in which this story happens. Pay close attention to the details the narrator shares.

Vocabulary Preview

Words to Know

craft	captive
seized	savage
exhibited	

 Reading Coach CD-ROM selection

None of them left the ship on the first day of its arrival, but I knew that they would be watching carefully for signs of human life.

The skies were dark with scudding clouds, and the cold wind moved high in the trees. Thin snow drifted slowly to the ground.

From the cover of the forest, I now watched as a small, heavily armed group of them left the large craft . When they reached the edge of 10 the woods, they hesitated for a few moments and then moved cautiously forward.

craft
(krăft)
n. ship

I had seen them before and I knew that in appearance, at least, they were not monsters. They looked very much like us. There were some differences, of course, but all in all, we were really quite similar to them.

REREAD
Make predictions: Who are *they*? Who are *we*?

I met them first when I was almost a boy and I had been without caution. I 20 approached them and they seemed friendly, but then suddenly they seized me and carried me off in their strange ship.

seized
(sēzd)
v. captured by force; past tense of *seize*

It was a long journey to their land and when our ship made a landing, I was shown about and exhibited as though I were some kind of animal.

exhibited
(ĭg zĭb′ ĭ tĭd)
v. presented for others to see; past tense of *exhibit*

I saw their cities, and I was shown plants and animals completely strange to me. I learned to wear their clothing and even to 30 eat their food.

They taught me to communicate in their strange and difficult tongue until I could, at times, even think in their language.

I had almost given up the hope of ever seeing my home again, but they one day put me back on one of their ships and told me that they were returning me because they wished to establish friendly relations with my people. But by now, I knew enough of them to know that this was not true. However, I nodded 40 and smiled and watched for my opportunity to escape.

When the ship landed, I went out with the first search party. It was near evening and as the darkness gathered, I edged away from them and finally I fled into the blackness and safety of the forest.

They came after me, of course, but I was hidden deep in the woods where they could not find me.

Finally they gave up and I watched their ship become smaller and finally disappear, and I 50 hoped fervently that they would never return.

> **fervently**
> (fûr´ vənt lē)
> with great emotion

But now they were back again.

THINK IT THROUGH
Why does the narrator flee from the invaders?

FOCUS
Look for clues about who the invaders are.

I felt a coldness inside of me as I watched them moving slowly through the trees. They seemed somehow different from the others who had been here before. It was not so much in their appearance as in the air about them—the way they walked, the way they looked about with speculating eyes.

Slowly and instinctively, I realized that this time
60 they were not here on just another raid for a captive or two.

This time they had come to stay.

What could we do now? Could we lure them deeper into the forest and kill them? Could we take their weapons and learn how to use them?

No, I thought despairingly. There were so many more of the invaders on the ship. And more weapons. They would come out and hunt us down
70 like animals. They would hunt us down and kill us all.

I sighed. We must find out what it was that they wanted this time and whatever it might be, we must learn to adjust and to hope for the best.

But I still retreated silently before them, afraid to approach. I watched them search the ground ahead of them and knew they were looking for footprints, for some signs of life. But there was
80 not yet enough snow on the ground to track us down.

Their strangely colored eyes glanced about warily. They were cautious, yes.

They could be a cruel race, I knew. I had seen with my own eyes how they treated their animals and even their own kind.

I sighed again. Yes, we could be cruel, too. In this respect we could not claim to be superior to the invaders.

They paused now in a clearing, their eyes gleaming
90 beneath their helmets.

captive
(kăp′ tĭv)
n. prisoner

lure
(lŏŏr)
attract in order to trick

REREAD
Why is the narrator losing hope?

It was time for me to approach them.

I took a deep breath and stepped into the open. Their weapons quickly pointed at me.

"Welcome," I said.

They stared at me, and then one of them turned to their bearded leader. "It appears that this savage can speak some English, Captain Standish."

"Welcome," I said again. But I
100 wondered what they would do to my land and my people now.

REREAD
Miles Standish is an English ship captain. How might this be a clue to what is happening?

savage
(săv' ĭj)
n. fierce, brutal person

THINK IT THROUGH

1. Who is the narrator? Who are the invaders? Review the story to find details to support your answer.
2. The narrator says, "We must learn to adjust and to hope for the best." Why do you think the narrator decides to talk to the invaders?
3. As you read, who did you think the invaders were? Were you surprised? Explain.

The True Invaders

This story is based on a real event in history. It is also based on two real people. The narrator is a combination of two Native Americans. One was Samoset. In 1620, Samoset watched newcomers land on the Massachusetts coast. These people were called the Pilgrims. Samoset welcomed the Pilgrims and introduced them to the second Native American, Squanto. Squanto was captured by English fishermen and taken to England. There he learned to speak the language. After several years, Squanto was able to escape to America.

WEAPONS OF WAR

by Shirley Jordan

In any war, the choice of weapons is important. Find out how a secret weapon helped in the American Revolution.

Connect to Your Life

You may know the saying "make the best of a bad situation." Think of an example of this saying. Share your example with a classmate.

Key to the Article

This article is about how American colonists fought in the Revolutionary War. The war began in 1775 when the 13 American colonies joined together to fight Great Britain. The colonists wanted freedom from the British. They wanted to make their own laws. The British wanted control over the American colonies. The British had a well-trained army. Most of the American soldiers were farmers. As you read, try imagine what it was like for the colonists to face an expert fighting force.

Vocabulary Preview

Words to Know

tomahawks	harbor	anchors
torpedo	deck	

Reading Coach CD-ROM selection

Colonists in America have to prepare for war. Find out some of the problems these soldiers face.

America's success in the American Revolution was a surprise to many. Mostly to King George III.

You see, the colonists were not soldiers. Few of them had done any fighting at all.

England's Redcoats, however, knew about war. They were part of a trained army.

In the early years, the colonists had no uniforms. Each man carried whatever kind of gun he might own. There were few bullets. So the colonists melted
10 pots and eating tools to make bullets.

There were few cannons or other large weapons in America. Earlier fighting in the colonies had been against the Indians. Cannons did not roll well over the rough ground. They would not fit between the trees in the forests, where the Indians hid.

In the Revolution, most fighting was done by the *infantry,* the men on the front lines of battle. The British Redcoats were well trained in this kind of battle. The Americans had no choice but to fight this way too.

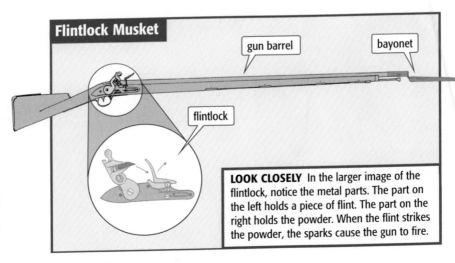

Flintlock Musket

gun barrel

bayonet

flintlock

LOOK CLOSELY In the larger image of the flintlock, notice the metal parts. The part on the left holds a piece of flint. The part on the right holds the powder. When the flint strikes the powder, the sparks cause the gun to fire.

20   In battle, both sides formed a battle line. Until
everything was ready, the line stood still. They waited
where the enemy cannons could not
reach them. Then, when the order came,
the men marched toward the enemy.
They looked just like a parade.

> **REREAD**
> Picture the battle
> scene in your
> mind.

When there was nothing else to use,
the Americans carried hunting rifles. These were not a
good weapon. They took too long to reload. And a
knife, or *bayonet,* could not be fastened to the front
30 of them.

After 1776, the colonists had uniforms and better
weapons. But there weren't always enough to go
around.

THINK IT THROUGH

The colonists had problems. In what ways were the colonists
not as ready for war as the British?

FOCUS

Read about the weapons used.

A fighting gun—the flintlock musket with a
bayonet—was the main weapon of the war. These
early muskets were six or seven feet long! And they
weighed 40 pounds!

They were loaded from the muzzle with the soldier
standing up. After each shot, the man had to reload.
40 The *flintlock* was a metal wheel that turned and set
off sparks. The sparks lit the powder in the barrel of
the gun. A soldier carried extra gunpowder and lead
balls in a leather shoulder bag.

Some officers had *breech-loading* rifles. These could be loaded from the side. Men with these fast rifles did not have to stand up to reload.

Hunting swords and small knives were worn by officers. A long, heavy weapon—the *saber*—was used by men on horses. These *cavalrymen* could
50 reach farther from their horses with the saber.

American patriots who had no bayonets often used tomahawks. The Indians had taught them how.

> **tomahawks**
> (tŏm′ ə hôks′)
> *n.* lightweight axes used as tools or weapons

THINK IT THROUGH
The colonists had a few decent weapons. What made each weapon hard to use?

FOCUS
You've seen how the colonists fought on land. Read to find out about a special weapon used at sea.

Attack from Under the Sea

This might seem strange. But America's first submarine was part of the American Revolution.

David Bushnell was a young college student with a big idea. He knew the American patriots had few ships. And that the British navy was mighty. Perhaps,
60 he thought, he could find a way to stop some of the British ships.

Bushnell built a special underwater boat of oak. It was shaped like a walnut. And it was big enough for a man to climb in and sit down.

The wood was wrapped with iron bands. Bushnell called his invention the *Turtle*.

> **REREAD**
> What are two main differences between this submarine and modern ones?

To push it through the water, the man inside turned
70 a set of blades, or *propellers*.

The plan was to get close to a British warship and drill a small hole in the side. Then the man in the submarine would stick a torpedo in the hole.

The torpedo was filled with gunpowder. After the *Turtle* left, the powder would blow up.

torpedo
(tôr pē′ dō)
n. cigar-shaped weapon that can explode

General George Washington liked the plan. The British had control of the waters around New York. If
80 the Americans could blow up a few ships, maybe the frightened British would take their other ships away.

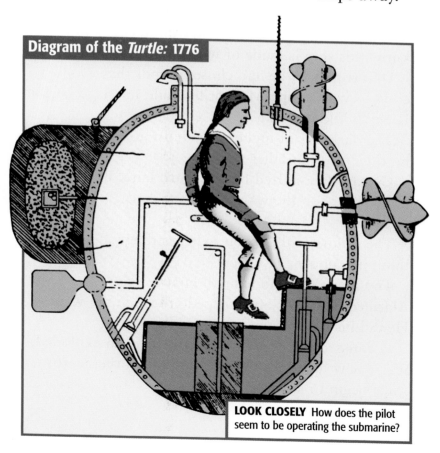

Diagram of the *Turtle*: 1776

LOOK CLOSELY How does the pilot seem to be operating the submarine?

Bushnell chose the *Eagle*. It was the largest ship in the harbor .

On the day of the attack, David Bushnell was sick. So General Ezra Lee was chosen to take his place.

Lee knew the plan. He would use a carpenter's drill attached to the front of the *Turtle*. He would stick the torpedo into the ship. And he would
90 quickly set a timer. The blast would come after the submarine had moved away.

General Lee climbed into the *Turtle*. Quietly, he moved close to the warship. Now it was time to drill a hole just deep enough to hide a torpedo. He tried. But it wasn't working.

"Why won't this work?" he wondered. "I just know this ship is made of wood!"

Unfortunately, he had chosen a spot that was covered with copper. The drill would never go in. But
100 Lee didn't know that.

The darkness of night was almost gone. There was no time to try another spot.

General Lee started back toward land. By now, sailors on the warship's deck had seen him.

The sailors said, "What is that strange thing just under the water?"

The *Eagle* sent out a small boat to see. Alarmed, Lee shot off a torpedo through the water.
110 He did his best to aim it toward the ship.

He missed the *Eagle*. But as the torpedo exploded, water flew high into the air. Men on all the nearby ships begin to shout and run about.

> **harbor**
> (här' bər)
> *n.* area of shelter where ships may anchor

> **deck**
> (dĕk)
> *n.* main level of the outside of a ship

The British were terrified. They raised their anchors. Soon, all their ships were sailing out of New York's harbor.

The Redcoats had no idea what had attacked them. And they didn't know how many of the enemy there were.

120   The *Turtle* never sank any ships. But it showed that man could attack from underwater.

A new military weapon was born!

anchors
(ăng' kərz) *n.* heavy weights attached to a connecting rope that are used to keep ships in place

THINK IT THROUGH

1. The *Turtle's* torpedo missed the ship. Why was the *Turtle* still a success?
2. Why was the *Turtle's* victory a good sign for the American fighters?
3. Look again at the diagram of the musket on page 342 and its description on page 343. Why was the gun so hard to use?

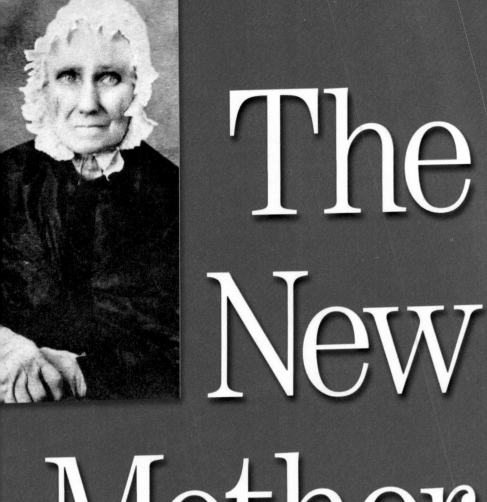

The New Mother

by Frances Cavanah

A sudden change happens in the life of young Abraham Lincoln. Discover the hope for the future that a newcomer brings.

Connect to Your Life

How well do you handle change? On a sheet of paper, draw a line like the one below.

Badly   **Well**   **Very Well**

Then place an "X" on the line to show how you react to change. Compare your line to those of your classmates.

Key to the Story

This is a work of **historical fiction,** a story that is set in the past. Historical fiction often deals with a person or event in history. It is based on fact but may include fictional, or made up, details.

Abraham Lincoln was born in Kentucky in 1809. He grew up in the deep woods of Indiana. He rose to greatness from a rough pioneer background. In 1861, he became the sixteenth president of the United States. You are about to read a story that gives details about his childhood.

Vocabulary Preview

Words to Know

huddled	distress
occurrence	reluctantly
astonishment	

 Reading Coach CD-ROM selection

349

Unexpected company arrives one night at the Lincoln cabin. Read to find out who comes to the cabin and why.

Inside the cabin the only light came from a feeble fire in the mammoth fireplace. The dirt floor felt cold under her moccasined feet as Sarah Lincoln paused in the doorway. Tom, her husband, cleared his throat in some embarrassment. He had only recently married the Widow Johnston, and he knew this home was not what she and her three children had expected.

10   "Sally, Abe, this is your new mammy," he called. "I've been back to Kaintuck to git myself a wife."

It was then that Sarah, peering through the gloom, saw the Lincoln children. They huddled on low stools near the fire, looking up at her out of frightened gray eyes. Sarah gasped at the sight of their thin soiled clothing, their dark matted hair, their pinched gray faces smudged with soot.

20   "Howdy!" She tried to smile, but they only huddled closer together. "Don't you want to meet my young'uns?"

"Mamma, I don't like it here," said Johnny Johnston.

"Sh!" Sarah warned. She nudged Betsy and Mathilda, who stopped staring long enough for each to make an awkward curtsy. Sally, after one glance at their pretty linsey-woolsey dresses and neat leather moccasins, tried to hide her bare toes under the stool.

30   Abe said, "Howdy," somewhere down inside his stomach.

mammoth
(măm′ əth)
huge

Kaintuck
the state of Kentucky

huddled
(hŭd′ ld)
v. crowded together; past tense of *huddle*

THINK IT THROUGH

Who is Sarah, and why is she there?

FOCUS

Read to see how Sarah tries to unite her new family.

From the moment Sarah laid aside her hood and shawl, things began to happen in the Lincoln cabin. First, she announced cheerfully, she and Sally would have some victuals on the table, quicker than anyone could say "Jack Robinson." Tom went out to the wagon to unhitch the horses, and when he came
40 back he was carrying a slab of bacon and a comb of honey.

> **victuals**
> (vĭt′ lz)
> food

Dennis Hanks, an older cousin who made his home with the Lincolns, brought in some firewood. Abe and Mathilda started for the spring, swinging the water pail between
50 them. A few minutes later Sally had forgotten her soiled dress and her bare feet, as she and Betsy mixed batter and set corn bread to bake on the hearth.

Keep 'em busy. Get 'em working together, said Sarah to herself. They'll soon forget they're shy.

Soon the magic smell of frying bacon filled the air. The table was rather crowded with eight people gathered around it, but no one seemed to mind. Under the influence of a hearty meal, Sally and her stepsisters chattered like old friends. Only Abe ate in silence, his eyes on the slab of bark which served him as a plate.

"I declare," said Dennis, as he sopped up some of the golden honey on his corn bread. "I ain't et like this since Cousin Nancy died."

Abe jumped up and started for the cabin door. A little choking sound escaped him.

Tom tried to hide his embarrassment in a show of anger. "Abe Lincoln, you set right down and finish your corn bread."

Abe shook his head. "I . . . I can't, Pa."

Tom was on his feet now. "This is a purty way to treat your new ma—after she goes and gits all these good victuals ready. You clean up your plate, or I'll give you a hiding."

The young Johnstons gasped. Sally, twisting the hem of her dress, cast an appealing glance at her new stepmother.

<appealing (ə pē' lĭng) begging>

Sarah's heart seemed to turn over. Abe looked so miserable and scared. He was frightened not only of his father but of the strange woman who had come, without warning, to take his mother's place. She never would get next to him if Tom was not careful.

REREAD
What do Sarah's thoughts tell about her?

"Please, let the boy be," she said.

"I won't stand for him treatin' you that way."

Sarah smiled, more brightly than she felt. "Abe and
90 I'll have plenty of chance to git acquainted. I reckon
all of us are through."

She arose, her hands on her hips, surveying the
dirty room. "Thar's a sight o' things to be
done here before we unpack my plunder
from the wagon. Fust, I'll need lots of hot
water. Who wants to go to the spring?"

Her glance rested on Abe.

"I'll go, ma'am." He grabbed the wooden
bucket and made his escape.

plunder
(plŭn' dər)
Sarah Lincoln's
name for her
household items.
Usually, *plunder*
means "stolen
items."

THINK IT THROUGH
Why is Abe so willing to get water from the spring?

FOCUS
Read to discover the other changes Sarah Lincoln brings.

100 Abe made several trips to the spring that afternoon.
Each pailful of water was poured into one of the huge
iron kettles over the fireplace. Higher and higher
roared the flames, and when Sarah wasn't asking for
more water, she was asking for more wood. She
would hear the steady chop-chop of Abe's ax in the
clearing. Every few minutes, it seemed, he was
bringing in a fresh armful of wood. His
woebegone expression was giving way to
one of curiosity—curiosity at all the strange
110 goings-on in the Lincoln cabin.

For even Dennis was working. Under
Sarah's direction he washed the cabin walls, while the
girls scrubbed the table and the few three-legged

woebegone
(wō' bǐ gôn')
deeply sad

stools. Not since Nancy died had the cabin had such a thorough going-over.

At length Sarah climbed the peg ladder to peer into the loft. "Tssch! Tssch!" she said when she saw the cornhusks and dirty bearskins on which the boys had been sleeping. "Take 'em out and burn 'em, Tom."

"Burn 'em?" he protested.

"Burn those kivers on the bed downstairs, too. We're startin' fresh in this house."

Tom sighed, but did as he was asked.

Within a few hours the cabin fairly shone. Then came the most remarkable occurrence of that remarkable afternoon— the unloading of Sarah Lincoln's plunder.

"Tom, you oughter git the walnut bureau in fust," she suggested. "I'm most perticular about that."

With much heaving and grunting Tom and Dennis carried in the bureau, setting it in the place of honor against the wall opposite the bed. "This-here bureau cost forty-five dollars," Tom announced in an undertone.

Forty-five dollars! Abe gasped. Sarah saw him run a finger over the shining dark wood. She noticed his startled expression when he saw his reflection in the little mirror which she hung above the bureau. Most likely he had never seen a looking glass before.

The wagon yielded other pieces of furniture—a larger table, chairs with real backs, a spinning wheel,

occurrence
(ə kûr′ əns)
n. event

bureau
(byŏŏr′ ō)
a dresser for holding clothes

REREAD
Read Tom's words aloud. Use your voice to show his feelings.

startled
(stär′ tld)
surprised

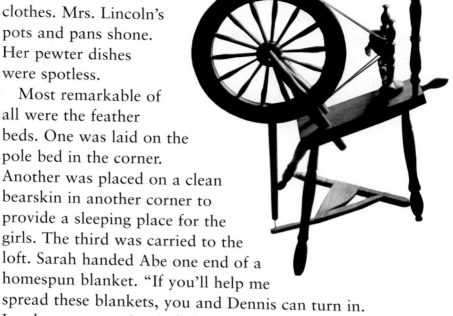

a big chest filled with clothes. Mrs. Lincoln's pots and pans shone. Her pewter dishes
150 were spotless.

Most remarkable of all were the feather beds. One was laid on the pole bed in the corner. Another was placed on a clean bearskin in another corner to provide a sleeping place for the girls. The third was carried to the loft. Sarah handed Abe one end of a
160 homespun blanket. "If you'll help me spread these blankets, you and Dennis can turn in. I reckon you won't mind if Johnny bunks with you."

"Yes'm—I mean, no'm," said Abe.

She saw his look of astonishment when he felt the warmth of soft wool between his fingers. It had been a long time since he had slept under a blanket. He almost smiled as he punched his fist into the feather bed.

Within a few minutes gentle snores could be heard
170 coming from the loft. The three girls on the makeshift bed in the corner were already asleep. Sarah sank down into one of her own chairs before the fire, a pile of sewing in her lap.

Thar's nothin' wrong with Sally that soap and water and a little lovin' won't fix, she thought. Did my heart good to hear her call me Mamma, jes' like my own young'uns. But Abe—

astonishment
(ə stŏn′ ĭsh mənt)
n. amazement

makeshift
(māk′ shĭft′)
temporary substitute

Sarah paused to thread her bone needle.

180   Abe's harder to figure out, she went on talking to herself. Thar's a lonesome place in his heart. Still a little skittish of havin' a new mammy, I reckon. Jes' have to be patient.

REREAD
Read Sarah's thoughts. What do they show about her?

The bearskin at the door was pushed aside and Tom entered, his arms filled with wood. He started to dump the whole armful on the floor near the fireplace. Then, seeming to think better of it, he arranged the logs in a neat pile.

190   "By cracky"—he gave a look around the room— "you sure did a heap of fixin' here today."

Sarah laughed softly. "Why, Tom, we ain't started yit. You won't know the place when we git through. I reckon you and Dennis will want to split and smooth some logs and lay a puncheon floor. Folks shouldn't live on a dirt floor, not this day and age."

There was a look of distress, almost of anguish, on Tom's face as his wife continued to outline the changes she 200 expected in the cabin. "But, Sairy!" he protested.

distress
(dĭ strĕs')
n. suffering

"Yes, Tom?" Sarah looked up from her sewing.

Under her level gaze, he began to squirm. "Nothin' much. I jes' figured maybe Dennis and I'll go huntin' tomorrow. That slab of bacon is all the meat we have."

THINK IT THROUGH
What things are now better because of Sarah? Use details from this section to support your answer.

FOCUS

Read to find out what Sarah learns as she turns her attention to Abe himself.

The next morning Sarah was pleased to have the men out of the house. "Abe," she said, "today I aim to make you two young'uns look more human."

210 Abe looked startled, but at his stepmother's request he carried several pails of water from the spring. He poured it into the kettles to boil. He dragged a big wooden tub inside. Then mumbling something about having to chop more wood, he disappeared through the door. Sarah smiled as the sharp, steady sound of his chopping was borne to her on the crisp air.

> **borne**
> (bôrn)
> carried

Two hours later she stood in the doorway watching the girls trip gaily down the path.
220 Sally, her hair in two neat pigtails, was wearing her stepmother's shawl over one of Betsy's dresses. She was taking her new sisters to call on one of the neighbors.

Sarah shaded her eyes with her hand and peered off into the woods. "Abe! Oh, Abe," she shouted.

The only answer was the sound of an ax biting into wood—faster and faster.

"You heerd me, Abe," she called.

He came then, reluctantly. Leaving
230 his ax by the door, he edged into the room.

> **reluctantly**
> (rĭ lŭk′ tənt lē)
> *adv.* unwillingly

"Sally's had her bath," said Sarah firmly. "Now I've got a tub of good hot water and a gourdful of soap waiting' for you. Skedaddle out of those old clothes and throw 'em in the fire—"

"I . . . I ain't got any others." Abe looked terrified.

Sarah laughed. "I don't aim to pluck your feathers without giving you some new ones. I set up late last night, cutting
240 down a pair of Mr. Johnston's old pants. I got one of his shirts, too."

REREAD

Is Sarah a tough person or a gentle one? Explain.

Abe slowly started taking off his shirt. He walked toward the fire, edging along the wall, keeping as far away as possible from the tub of hot water.

"That tub won't bite," Sarah reminded him. "Now I'm a-goin' down to the spring. When I git back, I want you to have yourself scrubbed all over."

Abe stuck one toe into the water, said "Ouch!" and
250 drew it out again. Finally, screwing up his courage, he put in his whole foot. He put in his other foot. Then he sat down in the tub. By the time Sarah returned he was standing before the fire dressed in the cut-down trousers and homespun shirt of the late Mr. Johnston.

Sarah surveyed him critically. "You look different already. Those trousers look a mite too big, but you'll soon grow into 'em."

surveyed
(sər vād')
inspected

Abe was somewhat surprised to find how good it
260 felt to be clean. "Thank you, ma'am. Now I reckon I'd better finish my chopping."

"No," said Sarah. "You set yourself down on that stool and let me git at your hair."

Sarah not only washed his hair but some of the places Abe himself had overlooked. His neck had not had such a scrubbing for more than a year. He submitted silently, only screwing up his eyes a little tighter when Sarah dug in behind his ears. But when she opened the top drawer

270 of the bureau and took out a haw comb and a pair of scissors, he jumped up in alarm.

submitted
(səb mĭt' ĭd)
surrendered to

"Thar's no call to be skeered," she told him, with another look at his mop of unruly black hair. "I'm jes' goin' to cut away some of that brush heap on top of your head."

"Then how folks know I'm me?" he asked plaintively.

plaintively
(plān' tĭv lē)
in a sorrowful way

"What do you mean, Abe?"

"When we came to Indiany, Pappy marked

280 off our claim by pilin' brush along the boundary lines. He said he wanted everyone to know this here was our farm. I figured that brush heap atop of me is my boundary line. How folks know I'm Abe Lincoln, if you clear it away?"

It was the first time Sarah had heard him say more than "Yes'm" or "No'm," and such a long speech took her by surprise. Was he joking? It was hard to tell, he was such a solemn-looking boy. Or was he still frightened? He sat

solemn
(sŏl' əm)
deeply serious

290 quietly as she snipped off lock after lock of the unruly black hair. She tried not to pull, but once he said, "Ouch!" She patted his shoulder and waited a moment before she attacked the next tangle.

"Thar!" she said at last. "It's all over. S'pose you mosey over to the lookin' glass and tell me if that's Abe Lincoln you see."

He gazed at his reflection, a pleased expression in his eyes. "It's Abe, I reckon. I still ain't the purtiest boy in Pigeon Creek. On
300 t'other hand, thar ain't quite so much of me to be ugly, now you cleared away the brush heap."

REREAD
What does Abe show about himself here?

Suddenly he grinned, and Sarah laughed in relief. "You're a caution , Abe. Smart, too. Had much schoolin'?"

caution
(kô' shən)
someone who is surprising

Abe shook his head, serious again. "I've just been to school by littles."

"Have you a mind to go again?"

"There ain't any school since Master
310 Crawford left. Anyhow, Pappy don't set much store by eddication."

set much store by
see as valuable

Sarah looked at him sharply. "Can you read?"

"Yes'm. But I haven't any books."

"Now, that's peculiarsome," said Sarah. "You can read and you haven't any books. I have books and can't read."

Abe stared at her, amazed. "You have books?"

She walked over to the bureau and came back
320 carrying four worn-looking volumes. "Books are a right good thing to have, so I brung 'em along. You set yourself down thar at the table and I'll show you."

THINK IT THROUGH
What does Sarah discover about Abe? What does he discover about her?

FOCUS

Sarah and Abe continue talking. Find out what happens as she learns more about him.

Abe, his brown cheeks flushed with pleasure, spelled out the titles: "Rob-in-son Cru-soe, Pil-grim's Prog-ress, Sin-bad the Sail-or, Ae-sop's Fa-bles. Oh, ma'am, this here book is one Master Crawford told us about."

Sarah sat down beside him and turned the pages. "The stories look like little bitty ones.
330 Could you read one of 'em to me, Abe?"

The book was open to the story of "The Crow and the Pitcher." Abe, his shorn head bent above the page, began to read. "A crow was almost dead of—of th-thirst, when he found a p-pitcher with a little water in the bottom."

It had been so long since Abe had seen a book that he stumbled over a few of the words, but he gained more confidence as he went along. "'The crow reached in his bill to take a drink. He
340 tried and tried, but he could not reach the water. He was al-most ready to give up, when he had an i-dea. He picked up a peb-ble in his bill and dropped it into the pit-cher. He picked up an-other pebble and an-other . . .

"'With every pebble that he dropped, the water in the pitcher rose a little high-er. At last the water rose so high that the crow could reach it with his bill. He took a long drink, and so was a-ble to q-q-quench his thirst and save his life.'"

350 "You read right well," said Sarah.
Abe laughed delightedly. "It says something else here. 'Mo-ral,'" he read. "'Little by little does the trick.'"

Master	teacher or schoolmaster
bill	beak
moral	(môr' əl) the lesson taught by a fable or story

Abe took the book closer to the fireplace where it was easier to see the words. He read story after story, pausing only now and then to throw
360 another log on the fire. As Sarah went about her household tasks, she watched him closely, a puzzled frown in her honest gray eyes.

This photograph of Sarah Lincoln was taken in the 1860s. At this point, her stepson had already been president.

Abe was different from what her John would ever be. He was different from any boy she had ever seen. She pulled a chair closer to the fire and picked up her knitting. "Which
370 story do you like best?" she asked.

REREAD
In what ways do you think Abe is different?

Abe looked up with a start. "The one about the smart crow that filled up the pitcher with pebbles so he could git himself a drink."

"That story sorta reminds me of you," she told him.

"How come, ma'am?"

"Didn't that Mr. Aesop say, 'Little by little does the trick'? Wall, you go to school by littles. Each time you l'arn something. I figure those little bits of l'arnin' are
380 like pebbles. Keep on pilin' 'em up higher, and you'll make something of yourself."

Abe shook his head. "I reckon I won't ever git to go to school agin."

"I wouldn't say that. Lots of new folks are a-comin' to Pigeon Creek, and the more folks, the more likely another schoolmaster is to come."

"But Pappy says I already know how to read and write and cipher. He says I have more eddication than he ever had. I—I can't help it, ma'am. I want to know more'n Pappy knows."

390

cipher
(sī' fər)
to solve number problems

"Your pappy's a good man," said Sarah, "and the next time a school keeps in these parts, I'm a-goin' to ask him to let you and the other young'uns go. That's a promise, Abe."

Again Abe could only stare.

"Meanwhile, you can l'arn right smart jes' by reading these-here books."

"I can read 'em—any time I like?"

400 "I'm a-giving 'em to you to keep."

"Oh, Mamma," said Abe. The name slipped out as though he had always been used to saying it.

Only the fire crackling softly on the hearth broke the long silence. "You're my boy now, Abe," said Sarah softly, "and I'm a-goin' to help you all I can."

Abe did not answer. He did not need to. His shining eyes told Sarah all she wished to know. And he had called her Mamma of his own free will.

THINK IT THROUGH

1. Abe and Sarah talk about stories. They discuss the moral that "Little by little does the trick." How does Sarah use the story to help Abe?

2. What kind of person is Sarah Lincoln? Support your answer with details from the story.

3. Think about the qualities young Abe Lincoln shows in this story. In your opinion, which of these qualities could be helpful to him later when he is president of the United States?

Find out how railroad worker John Henry reacts to the
coming of the steam drill.

When John Henry was about three days old,
A-sittin' on his pappy's knee,
He gave one loud and lonesome cry:
"The hammer'll be the death of me,
5   The hammer'll be the death of me."

Well, the captain said to John Henry one day:
"Gonna bring that steam drill 'round,
Gonna take that steam drill out on the job,
Gonna whop that steel on down,
10   Gonna whop that steel on down."

John Henry said to the captain:
"Well, the next time you go to town
Just bring me back a twelve-pound hammer
And I'll beat your steam drill down,
15   And I'll beat your steam drill down."

John Henry said to the captain:
"Well, a man ain't nothin' but a man,
And before I let a steam drill beat me down
Gonna die with the hammer in my hand,
20   Gonna die with the hammer in my hand."

THINK IT THROUGH

Why do you think John Henry wants to compete against the steam drill?

FOCUS

Read to discover the unforgettable actions of John Henry.

John Henry went to the tunnel,
And they put him in the lead to drive,
The rock so tall and John Henry so small,
He laid down his hammer and he cried
25   He laid down his hammer and he cried.

John Henry said to his shaker:
"Shaker, why don't you sing?
For I'm swingin' twelve pounds from the hips on
    down,
Just listen to that cold steel ring,
30   Just listen to that cold steel ring."

John Henry told his captain:
"Look-a yonder what I see—
Your drill's done broke and your hole's done
    choke',
And you can't drive steel like me,
35 And you can't drive steel like me."

Well, the man that invented the steam drill,
He thought he was mighty fine,
But John Henry drove his fifteen feet,
And the steam drill only made nine,
40 And the steam drill only made nine.

REREAD
Who won the contest?

John Henry looked up at the mountain,
And his hammer was striking fire,
Well, he hammered so hard that he broke his poor
old heart,
He laid down his hammer and he died,
45   He laid down his hammer and he died.

They took John Henry to the graveyard,
And they laid him in the sand,
Three men from the east and a woman from the
west
Came to see that old steel-drivin' man,
50   Came to see that old steel-drivin' man.

They took John Henry to the graveyard,
And they laid him in the sand,
And every locomotive comes a-roarin'
by
Says: "There lies a steel-drivin' man,"
55   Says: "There lies a steel-drivin' man."

locomotive
(lō′ kə mō′ tĭv)
train

THINK IT THROUGH

1. This poem describes a contest between a man and a machine. Who do *you* think won? Explain your answer.
2. Find details in the ballad that show the kind of person John Henry was.
3. In the ballad, John Henry died from his efforts. Machines did take over the work. In your opinion, were John Henry's actions worth doing?

from
California Gold Days

by Helen Bauer

"It's a wonderful land—but dangerous!" Many took risks to reach California. Were the risks worth it?

Connect to Your Life

Imagine you are moving to a new place. It is far from your present home. Each family member can take only a few things. What would you take with you? Make a list to show to a classmate.

Key to the Article

In 1848 in California, an ordinary worker discovered gold. This started the California Gold Rush. By 1849, the exciting news had attracted thousands to the West. Some wanted to find gold. Most simply wanted to find a new chance in life.

These fortune seekers were called "Forty-Niners." They traveled to the West in covered wagons that looked almost like sailboats. They traveled in large groups called *wagon trains.* This article gives details about the kinds of journeys the Forty-Niners had.

Vocabulary Preview

Words to Know

plains   barrels   passes

 Reading Coach CD-ROM selection

About forty thousand people came to California by sea in 'forty-nine and 'fifty. An even larger number came overland. This was a harder way to go than by ship. It did not take much money to go this way, but it took lots of courage. The trip across the plains, mountains, and desert took six months. Because of the snow, the gold seekers could not go in winter.

> **plains**
> (plānz)
> *n.* large, treeless area of land

Most of the overland gold seekers left
10 from St. Joseph or Independence, Missouri. By April 1849, the first twenty thousand people from all over the United States were waiting to start. Tents could be seen everywhere along the riverbanks. "How many miles to California from St. Joe?" could be heard on all sides. "Two thousand miles," was the answer. "They are long, hard miles too!"

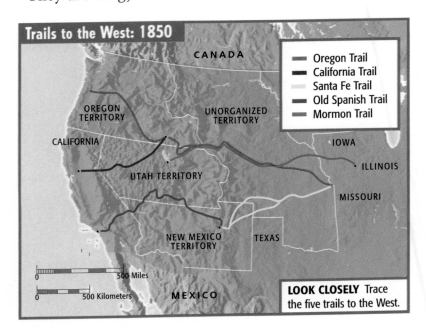

Trails to the West: 1850

- ▬ Oregon Trail
- ▬ California Trail
- ▬ Santa Fe Trail
- ▬ Old Spanish Trail
- ▬ Mormon Trail

CANADA

OREGON TERRITORY

UNORGANIZED TERRITORY

CALIFORNIA

IOWA

ILLINOIS

UTAH TERRITORY

MISSOURI

NEW MEXICO TERRITORY

TEXAS

0   500 Miles
0   500 Kilometers

MEXICO

LOOK CLOSELY Trace the five trails to the West.

All of the people were eager to start. Some of them were old; most of them were young. There were wives, mothers, children. All were going for gold.
20 More important than that, they were looking for a better life than they had known. California was to be their new home.

The trails were fairly well known by this time. For the most part, they followed the trails of early trappers and fur traders. One trail went southwest to Santa Fe (New Mexico). Here the trail made a fork. One fork led through the desert. The other went by way of South Pass in the 30 Rocky Mountains. Almost all took this trail.

> **fork**
> point at which one road divides into two

> **REREAD**
> Which colored trail from the map on page 372 did most people take?

THINK IT THROUGH

Besides money, what excites the Forty-Niners about California?

FOCUS

Find out how the Forty-Niners prepare for the journey.

The Forty-Niners made careful plans before starting. While waiting in the camps, parties and companies were formed. They agreed that it was safer to have ten to thirty wagons in a train. It would take about six yoke or pairs of oxen to each wagon. A captain would be the head of each party. His orders were to be obeyed by all. He was to guide them over the plains 40 and into California. In all ways he was to treat everyone fairly. It was his duty to keep all as well and happy as possible. Each man in the party was given certain duties. Young men would go ahead as scouts

> **yoke**
> bars connecting two working animals

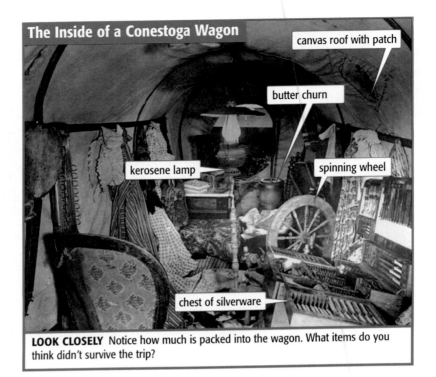

The Inside of a Conestoga Wagon

canvas roof with patch

butter churn

kerosene lamp

spinning wheel

chest of silverware

LOOK CLOSELY Notice how much is packed into the wagon. What items do you think didn't survive the trip?

to find the best trails. It would be their duty to look for good camping places each night. Each man was to take turns guarding day and night.

The camps were noisy with men trying to sell supplies and food. "Buy now—or have nothing!" they called. The Forty-Niners did not know what to
50 believe. So they bought—and bought. They took as much food as they could carry: barrels of flour, sacks of beans, rice, coffee, dried fruit. They had frying pans, buckets, axes, hammers, tools, guns. Some of the wagons were loaded with trunks and even furniture. They thought the West was wild. They must be prepared. So they took more than they should have taken.

> **barrels**
> (băr′ əlz)
> *n.* large, round containers, usually made of wood

Now it was May—and the grass showed green. It
60 was the time they had been waiting for so the cattle
would have food. All made ready to start at once.
Everyone was busy now—men, women, and children.
There was cooking, baking, packing,
hitching up of oxen and mules. Excitement
was in the air! They were headed for the
"land of gold." Different signs could be seen
on the white canvas "prairie schooners":

> **hitching up**
> (hĭch′ ĭng ŭp′)
> connecting
> animals to a
> wagon

BOUND FOR CALIFORNIA

TO THE LAND OF GOLD

70 **CALIFORNIA OR BUST**
MEET ME AT SUTTER'S FORT

They were glad to go—but it was hard to leave, too.
"Remember, there's an Indian behind every tree!" some
warned. "Be careful out there! It's a wonderful land—
but dangerous!" But no one wanted to turn back.
At last there was the creaking of the heavy white-
topped wagons. Yoke chains clanked. Oxen bawled
and moved slowly forward. Mules brayed. Men yelled
and whips cracked. "All's set! Let's get going! Keep
80 the wagons moving!" was the captain's command.
Drivers walked by their wagons. Men with guns rode
beside the wagons to keep watch for Indians. Soon
there was only a white line of wagons moving into the
distance. It looked as if a whole nation was marching
to the West!

THINK IT THROUGH

Excitement was in the air! Do the Forty-Niners seem to be
thinking clearly? Explain.

Read to find out what challenges the Forty-Niners face during their journeys.

The people seemed to enjoy the excitement of the journey at first. Meadows were covered with spring wild flowers. Grass was green and thick for the cattle. Rushing streams were beautiful but hard to cross with
90 heavy wagons. So they went slowly each day—about fifteen miles. Day after day, wagons rolled on to the West.

About sundown each day the captain blew a horn. The wagons were placed in a circle, **tongues** out. The animals were put outside to graze, with guards to watch them. The camp inside the circle was just like a fort. All felt safer that way. Then with fear forgotten, evenings were spent around the campfire
100 inside the circle. Sometimes they sang and made up their own words for songs they knew:

> **tongues**
> poles attached to the fronts of wagons

"Oh Susanna!
O don't you cry for me!
I'm on my way to Californy
With my wash-bowl on my knee!"

OR
"California!
You're the land for me!
There's plenty of gold, so I've been told
110 In Cali—for—ny—ee!"

The Indians did not bother the first parties. Those who came in 1850 had more trouble with them. But the Forty-Niners had other things to worry them.

Many of the travelers became ill; some died. The wagons were much too heavy for hard travel. Many things were thrown away along the overland trail to make the wagons lighter. Others who came later could pick up what was needed along the way—if there was room to carry it. Most of the wagons were too loaded
120 to carry anything more.

On and on across the plains went the wagons. Then they came to the buffalo country. The buffaloes had nibbled the grass short. Cattle of the overland train could not get enough to eat. They bellowed with hunger. Later trains found even less grass. Most of the grass had been eaten by the ox trains before them. Sometimes the buffalo herds came racing toward the wagons. Some of the buffaloes were killed for meat. The rest of the herd was scared away by
130 guns. If this did not work, a fire was built to drive them away. In this way, the wagon train was saved from harm.

REREAD

How does this scene contrast to the start of the trip?

Notice the weary expressions on the faces of these travelers. Days on the trail were rough.

The longer the journey, the harder it became. There was always the fear that they would be caught in the mountains by snow. Everyone was tired, but they had to keep going. Food ran low. One had to share with another. Sometimes they could find no water. All suffered as they crossed the desert. In the mountains, the passes were almost too

140 narrow to get through. It was very hard to climb these steep mountains with wagons. Sometimes it was even worse to go down the other side. Often heavy ropes were tied around the trees and the wagons let down by the ropes. The trip seemed never to end. But when the mountains were crossed, the worst was over.

passes

(păs' ĭz)

n. ways around, over, or through mountains

REREAD

Picture this challenge in your mind. What does this show about the Forty-Niners?

One party made a trip that made California history. This company was led by young William Manly.

150 When he first heard of gold, he decided to seek his fortune. On the way to California his party met a man who had a new map. It showed a shorter way to go. This they followed. In time they came to a lonely valley. The low desert valley had high mountain walls around it. There was not a blade of grass there. Not a drop of water was seen. All were hungry and thirsty— people and beast. The party went slower and slower. Food was almost gone, so they ate the oxen. What could they do next? Manly and another young man

160 agreed to go for help. Sixteen were left behind by a little spring they had found. At last Manly came to Mission San Fernando in southern California. From there the two young men started back with food. They were surprised to find any of the party still alive. Sometime after their return they started on. As they looked back at the camping place, they said,

"Goodbye, Death Valley!" And the place has had that name to this day. By the time they came to Mission San Fernando, they had been a whole year on the way. The gold fields were still six hundred miles away!

170

When the overland gold seekers finally came to the diggings, they were tired, ragged, and hungry. Hundreds had died on the way. But those who came by land were better able to stand the life at the mines. They were used to rough, outdoor life. Nothing could have been harder than the long overland trip they had taken.

THINK IT THROUGH

1. Why do you think the Forty-Niners were able to survive in Death Valley?

2. Think of the mood of the Forty-Niners before they made their trip. Think of their mood at the end. What caused the change? Use details from the article to support your answer.

3. How might the Forty-Niners have prepared themselves better for the trip? Give reasons for your answer.

RABBIT FOOT:

A STORY OF THE PEACEMAKER

RETOLD BY
JOSEPH BRUCHAC

A PEACEMAKER TELLS A VERY
STRANGE TALE. HE HOPES THIS TALE
WILL MAKE ANGRY LISTENERS STOP
AND THINK. JOIN THE LISTENERS IN
HEARING THE TALE OF RABBIT FOOT.

Connect to Your Life

Think of examples you see today of groups that fight each other. What important things does each group have to understand? What are ways both sides can try to work out their problems? List some solutions with a small group of classmates.

Key to the Oral History

This is an **oral history,** a tale that has been passed down by word of mouth. It includes both facts and imaginary details. For hundreds of years, storytellers have told the tale to celebrate a real event. The event was the coming of someone called the Peacemaker to the Iroquois (ĭr′ ə kwoi′) Indians.

Vocabulary Preview

Words to Know
culture
feuds
coiled

 Reading Coach CD-ROM selection

Several Iroquois tribes once lived in the northern section of New York. They made the worst kind of war—against each other. They attacked neighbors' villages. They stole food and took prisoners. In the 1500s, a man named Deganawida (the Peacemaker) met with the tribes. He wanted to convince them to make peace. With the help of a young chief named Hiawatha, the tribes listened. They joined together, forming the Iroquois League. They created a body of laws called the Great Law of Peace. A long period of peace followed.

FOCUS

Find out why the Peacemaker has come to the Iroquois people.

Many hundreds of years ago
before the Europeans came
the Five Nations of the Iroquois,
Mohawk and Oneida, Onondaga, Cayuga and Seneca,
were always at war with one another.

Although they had a common culture
and languages that were much the same
no longer did they remember
they had been taught to live
10 as sisters and brothers.

> **culture**
> (kŭl′ chər)
> *n.* the ideas, customs, and skills shared by a certain people

Once they had shared the beautiful land
from Niagara to the eastern mountains,
but now only revenge was in their hearts
and blood feuds had made every trail
a path leading to war.

> **feuds**
> (fyo͞odz)
> *n.* bitter fights

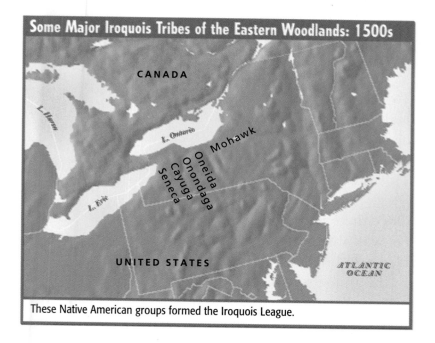

Some Major Iroquois Tribes of the Eastern Woodlands: 1500s

CANADA

L. Huron

L. Ontario

Mohawk

Oneida
Onondaga
Cayuga
Seneca

L. Erie

UNITED STATES

ATLANTIC OCEAN

These Native American groups formed the Iroquois League.

So it was that the Great Creator
sent once again a messenger,
a man who became known
to all of the Five Nations
20 by the name of the Peacemaker.

THINK IT THROUGH

How had life among the tribes changed?

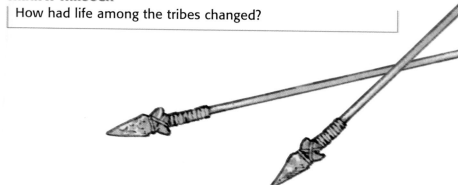

FOCUS

The Peacemaker tells a tale. Read to find out what a boy called Rabbit Foot sees.

To help the people once again
make their minds straight
he told them stories
about peace and war.
This is one of his tales.

Once there was a boy named Rabbit Foot.
He was always looking and listening.
He knew how to talk to the animals
so the animals would talk to him.

One day as he walked out in the woods
he heard the sound of a great struggle
coming from a clearing just over the hill.
So he climbed that hilltop to look down.

What he saw surprised him.
There was a great snake
coiled in a circle.
It had caught a huge frog
and although the frog struggled
the snake was slowly swallowing its legs.

coiled
(koild)
adj. wound into a series of rings

Rabbit Foot came closer
and spoke to the frog.
"He has really got you, my friend."
The frog looked up at Rabbit Foot.
"Wa'he! That is so," the frog said.

Rabbit Foot nodded, then said to the frog,
"Do you see the snake's tail there,
just in front of your mouth?
Why not do to him what he's doing to you?"

Then the huge frog reached out
50 and grabbed the snake's tail.
He began to stuff it into his mouth
as Rabbit Foot watched both of them.

The snake swallowed more of the frog
the frog swallowed more of the snake
and the circle got smaller and smaller
until both of them swallowed one last
   time
and just like that, they both were gone.

REREAD
Why do you think the snake and frog go so far?

They had eaten each other,
the Peacemaker said.
60 And in much the same way,
unless you give up war
and learn to live together in peace,
that also will happen to you.

THINK IT THROUGH

1. The Peacemaker delivers his message in the form of a tale. Why might this choice have had a stronger effect on the listeners?
2. How could the Iroquois tribes' shared culture and language help them learn to live together?
3. This tale was first told many years ago. Do you think it could be used to help other fighting groups today? Explain.

Reader's Choice

Longer Selections for Independent Reading

Unit 12
Mixed Genres

When does reading become an adventure? It can happen when you suddenly get "lost" in a strange setting. It can happen when you meet an unusual character. And it certainly happens when you find yourself at the center of an amazing event.

When you read a longer selection, your adventure can last longer, too. You get to spend more time with that interesting person. You are able to enjoy the details of the exciting event. So get ready to explore the longer pieces in this unit, and let the adventure begin!

from

HIROSHIMA

by Laurence Yep

The time is World War II. The
people of a Japanese city prepare
to defend themselves. No one
knows the destruction a secret
weapon will bring.

Connect to Your Life

Think about bombings you have heard about in your lifetime. How powerful were the bombs? What kinds of damage did they cause? Discuss your answers in a small group.

Key to the Novel Excerpt

This selection is a work of historical fiction. This means it tells a story using real events. The story takes place in 1945, toward the end of World War II. The United States and its partners, or allies, have defeated Germany. The war against Japan is not over. The United States plans to end the war quickly. The military drops an atomic (or atom) bomb on the Japanese city of Hiroshima. The bomb causes horrible damage that still affects people's lives today.

As you read, keep track of the events. The plot of this story shows the same event from two viewpoints. One shows what the pilots see as they drop the bomb. The other shows what two young girls, Riko and Sachi, experience on the ground.

Vocabulary Preview

Words to Know

routine	devastated
colonel	radioactive
anxiously	

Early one morning, a pilot makes special preparations. Read
to find out what he is getting ready to do.

The Bomb

Early in the morning of August 6, 1945, a big
American bomber roars down the runway on a tiny
island called Tinian. The pilot is Colonel Tibbets. He
has named the plane after his mother, Enola
Gay. On a routine mission, a B-29 would
carry 4000 to 16,000 pounds of bombs.
The *Enola Gay* is on a special mission. It
carries a single bomb. It is an atom bomb
that weighs 8900 pounds. Everyone hopes the atom
10 bomb will finally end a long and horrible war.

> **routine**
> (rōō tēn′)
> *adj.* regular

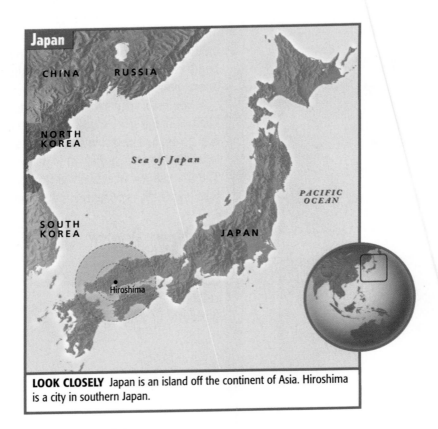

LOOK CLOSELY Japan is an island off the continent of Asia. Hiroshima
is a city in southern Japan.

Four years before, on December 7, 1941, Japanese planes attacked American ships in Hawaii without warning. Caught by surprise, many ships and planes were wrecked at the naval base, Pearl Harbor. The United States declared war on Japan and Japan's ally, Germany. With other countries, they fight a war called World War II.

By 1945, Germany has given up. Only Japan fights on. But the United States has a secret weapon—the 20 atom bomb. Nothing is as powerful and as awful. The atom bomb is so terrible that the United States hopes it will make Japan stop fighting.

Two other bombers follow the *Enola Gay.* These planes only carry cameras and special instruments to measure the explosion. Together the three bombers turn over the Pacific Ocean and speed through the darkness toward Japan.

THINK IT THROUGH
Why does the United States plan to drop the atom bomb?

FOCUS
Read to find out what is happening on that morning in Hiroshima.

The City

It is only seven o'clock in the morning, but the air is already hot and muggy in 30 Hiroshima. People go to work. Children hurry to school. Some soldiers and women go out with baskets to shop. A peddler wheels his cart carefully through the crowd. A colonel exercises his white horse.

muggy
(mŭg' ē)
damp

colonel
(kûr' nəl)
n. a military officer

There are about 320,000 people in Hiroshima that morning.

Two sisters walk sleepily in the crowd. Riko is sixteen and her little sister, Sachi, is twelve. They have stayed up all night hiding from American bombers.
40 Up until now, though, the airplanes have always bombed other cities. Some people believe that Hiroshima is so beautiful that the Americans have decided to spare it.

Riko and Sachi stop by a shrine. They say a prayer for their father, who is in the army. Looking at the calm, forgiving face of Buddha, they begin to feel at peace.

Buddha
(boo' də)
a statue of the founder of a religion practiced in Japan

• • •

An American bomber flies ahead of the *Enola Gay* and its companions. This bomber
50 is called the *Straight Flush*. It will check the weather over Hiroshima. If there are clouds over Hiroshima, the *Straight Flush* will tell the *Enola Gay* to attack another city.

The crew of the *Straight Flush* scans the sky anxiously for Japanese fighter planes. However, the Japanese are saving their airplanes for the invasion that everyone expects. So there are no Japanese planes today.

anxiously
(ăngk' shəs lē)
adv. nervously

At first, the *Straight Flush* only sees clouds. Then,
60 the crew spots a big hole in the clouds directly over Hiroshima. The sunlight pours right through the hole on to the city.

Green hills surround the city and the seven rivers shine like ribbons.

Hiroshima is a perfect target.

The *Straight Flush* tells the *Enola Gay* to continue to Hiroshima.

In the meantime, down below in Hiroshima, someone spots the *Straight Flush* and sounds the
70 alarm.

The siren shrieks in short blasts. Everywhere, people stop whatever they are doing. A streetcar rumbles to a halt. Its passengers run for the air-raid shelter.

REREAD
What do the people of Hiroshima think the *Straight Flush* is going to do?

Sachi and Riko leave the shrine and join the others. "Put on your hood, Sachi," Riko tells her. From their emergency bags, the two sisters pull out air-raid hoods. Putting them over their heads, they tie them tight. If the bombs start fires, the hoods are supposed to
80 protect them from burning sparks.

With the other people, they go down the steps to hide in the darkness.

However, the *Straight Flush* passes harmlessly over the city.

Work

When the *Straight Flush* finally leaves, the siren announces that it is safe. Breathing sighs of relief, the people leave the bomb shelters. They hurry to finish their interrupted chores. They go back to their homes to cook breakfast. The shopkeepers reopen their
90 stores. The streetcars rumble along the tracks again.

Everyone believes that they are safe now. They do not think more bombers will come so soon after the *Straight Flush*.

THINK IT THROUGH
The people in Hiroshima think they're safe. What don't they know?

A view from the air of Hiroshima before the bombing

FOCUS _____

Discover more about people's daily lives in wartime Hiroshima.

Sachi takes off her hood as soon as she is on the street. "I hate to wear it," she says and stuffs it into her emergency bag.

"We're going to be late," Riko tells Sachi. Lunches and emergency bags bouncing, the two girls start to run.

At the corner, Riko makes Sachi stop. "Don't forget
100 to wear your hood," she reminds her sister.

Sachi hurries to school and gathers in the yard with her classmates. They will not study in the classroom today. As members of the labor service corps, they have been assigned tasks outdoors to help defend Japan against the American invasion.

The older children work in the factories. Others, like Riko, record phone messages at the army headquarters, located in an old castle. They have taken the place of the
110 soldiers who are needed to fight the Americans.

REREAD
How do students help defend the city?

Sachi and her classmates work outside in the streets tearing down houses. It is a sad sight for the owners, but they know it is necessary to lose their houses to support the war effort.

Many of the Japanese buildings are wood and paper. In other cities, American planes have dropped bombs and started fires that have devastated large areas. As yet, this has not
120 happened to Hiroshima, but since no one wants to take chances, the army and city officials have decided to make fire lanes. The empty spaces will help stop the fires from spreading. The lanes will also provide avenues

devastated
(dĕv′ ə stā′ tĭd)
v. destroyed; past tense of
devastate

for fire-fighting equipment as well as escape routes for people fleeing the flames.

Sachi and her classmates help the adults wreck houses. They sort through the remains, looking for useful parts they can save and reuse, such as roof tiles. It is hot, dusty work and the muggy air makes the dust stick to their sweaty faces. To make the work go faster, the children chant in time as they wield their shovels.

REREAD
What are Sachi and her classmates doing?

Sachi's best friend pulls on white gloves to protect her hands. Several children tie headbands around their foreheads to keep the sweat from their eyes.

Everyone is busy as the *Enola Gay* approaches.

THINK IT THROUGH
What steps does the city take to defend itself?

FOCUS
How bad do you think the atom bomb will be? Read to see if you are right.

The Attack

All over Japan, there are observers who look out for the American bombers. Nineteen miles east of Hiroshima, an observer spots the *Enola Gay* and its two companions. Hurriedly, he calls the army headquarters in Hiroshima.

Riko answers the phone and takes down the report. She is shocked to learn that there are more bombers coming. Angrily, she thinks it is a sneaky trick to catch people outside the shelters.

She dials the radio station immediately and asks the announcers to warn everyone.

The *Enola Gay* is a B-29 bomber.

150   Riko thinks she is safe deep inside the ancient castle. But she prays for her mother at home and Sachi out in the street tearing down houses.

ancient
(ān' shənt)
of times long past

    In the meantime, people go on calmly with their lives. They eat their breakfasts. They begin their work. Outside their homes, the very small children begin to play. A colonel rides his horse across a bridge.

    On the *Enola Gay,* Colonel Tibbets orders,
160 "On glasses." His crew pull on goggles to protect their eyes. However, Colonel Tibbets must see clearly to steer the bomber. He does not put on goggles. Neither does the bombardier .

bombardier
(bŏm' bər dîr')
member of a bomber crew who releases the bombs

REREAD
Picture and compare these two scenes.

    Everyone is tense and excited. No one is sure if the bomb will go off. Yesterday on Tinian, Colonel Tibbets tested the gunlike device that sets off the bomb. It did not work then.

    Now the bombardier looks through his bombsight
170 and guides the *Enola Gay* the last few miles to its target.

Doors snap open on the belly of the plane.

The bombardier sees his landmark. It is a bridge shaped like a T. On the bridge, a Japanese colonel rides his horse.

The bombardier presses a button to release the bomb.

Down below, the children in the streets hear the hum of *Enola Gay*'s engines. They look up and see the *Enola Gay*. Its silver sides gleam in the sun. Fine white lines stripe the sky behind its engines. Sachi's friend calls excitedly to her and points up. "A B-29!"

"B-29! B-29!" a teacher shouts.

Sachi remembers her sister's warning. From her emergency bag, she pulls out her special hood and puts it on.

Another teacher blows a whistle. It is a signal for the children to go to the air-raid shelter.

In the *Enola Gay*, the bombardier shouts, "Bomb away!"

The huge, heavy bomb drops from the airplane. Suddenly the *Enola Gay* is much lighter, and it jerks up into the air. Colonel Tibbets is skillful. He keeps control of the airplane and swings it to the right.

The bomb whistles as it plunges down, down through the air.

On the *Enola Gay*, a crewman flips a switch on a special radio. It sends a signal to a special gun inside the bomb.

This time the gun works. It shoots a cone-shaped bullet of uranium into a larger ball of uranium.

Everything is made up of tiny particles called atoms. They are so small they are invisible to the eye. The atoms are also made up of even smaller parts.

Energy holds these parts together like glue. When the atom breaks up into its parts, the energy goes free and there is a big explosion.

Inside the bomb, one uranium atom collides with another. Those atoms both break up. Their parts 210 smash into more atoms and split them in turn.

This is called a chain reaction. There are millions and millions of atoms inside the bomb. When they all break up, it is believed that the atom bomb will be equal to 20,000 tons of dynamite. In 1945, it is the most powerful weapon ever made.

> **REREAD**
> Summarize how the atom bomb works.

As the chain reaction builds, the bomb falls faster and faster. But it does not go off over the bridge. It explodes over a hospital instead.

220   There is a blinding light like a sun.

There is a boom like a giant drum.

There is a terrible wind. Houses collapse like boxes. Windows break everywhere. Broken glass swirls like angry insects.

The wind strikes Sachi's back like a hammer and picks her up. She feels as if she has fallen into boiling oil. It tears away her special hood and even her clothes. The wind sweeps her into the whirlwind of glass.

230   There is no time to scream. There is no one to hear.

There is only the darkness. . . .

And Sachi mercifully passes out.

THINK IT THROUGH

At this point in the story, why do you think the author gives details about what happens to only one person?

This is a photograph of the mushroom cloud produced by the Hiroshima bombing.

FOCUS

Find out the other effects of this deadly explosion.

The Mushroom Cloud

The *Enola Gay* circles. The same wind that carries Sachi through the air almost knocks the bomber from the sky. Colonel Tibbets manages to right his airplane. The two companion bombers begin to take pictures and record the explosion.

> **right**
> put in upright or correct position

240 Up until then, no single bomb has ever caused so much damage or so many deaths.

Out of 76,327 buildings, over 50,000 are destroyed.

Up to 125,000 people will die on that first day or will die soon.

> **REREAD**
> Review these facts. Why was all the work done by the citizens of Hiroshima wasted?

The wind mixes their dust with the dirt and debris. Then it sends everything boiling upward in a tall purple-gray column. When the top of the dust cloud spreads out, it looks like a strange, giant mushroom.

250   The bottom of the mushroom cloud is a fiery red. All over the city fires spring up. They rise like flames from a bed of coals.

The bomb goes off 580 meters above the ground. The temperature reaches several million degrees Celsius immediately. It is so hot that the hospital below and everyone inside it disappears.

Two hundred yards away, people vanish. However, in that instant, their outlines are burnt into the cement like shadows.

260   The army headquarters and all the soldiers and Riko and her classmates are destroyed.

One mile away, the fierce heat starts fires.

Even two miles away, people are burned by the heat.

On the *Enola Gay*, the tail gunner tries to count the fires. But he gives up because there are too many.

Everyone in the crew has flown on bombers. They have helped drop tons of regular bombs. On each flight, they have seen death and destruction.

But no one has ever seen anything as
270   powerful as this one bomb.

The copilot writes a note to himself: "What have we done?"

> **REREAD**
> What might the crew be feeling at this time?

When the bomb's uranium breaks up, bits of atoms zip away. They go right through people's skin and hurt their bodies inside. This is called radiation. It will make thousands of people sick. Many will die later that day. More will fall ill and die in a year. Some will die in five years, or ten, or twenty. People are still dying today.

THINK IT THROUGH
Review the section "The Mushroom Cloud." List all of the effects of the bombing.

Destruction

280   Sachi wakes a few minutes later when she hears someone screaming. At first, there is so much smoke and dust she feels as if she is staring at a black wall. Then the smoke and dust rise like a curtain. She is stunned when she sees all the damage. One moment there was a city here. Now all the buildings are destroyed. The streets are filled with rubble and ruins. She does not know what could cause such wide destruction.

    Shocked, Sachi stumbles through the wasteland
290 until she stops upon a lawn. From the wrecked buildings, people call for help. Before she can help anyone, the buildings go up in flames.

    It is so hot around her that the grass catches fire. She crouches down and waits and hopes. The sheet of fire

The ruined city of Hiroshima a few months after the atom bomb was dropped

retreats. Flames shoot out of the nearby houses. People continue to scream. Everywhere, there is a sea of fire.

Sachi follows some people as they run into a cemetery. She jumps over tombstones. The pine trees around them catch fire with a great crackling noise.

300 Ahead she sees a river. People jump into it to get away from the fire. In the panic, some people are crushed. Others drown. Sachi cannot swim. She jumps in anyway. Then she sees a wooden bucket drifting by. She grabs it and holds on desperately.

Soon the water is full of bodies.

The hot ash from all the fires soars high, high into the sky. When the fiery ash mixes with the cold air, it causes rain. It is a horrible kind of rain.

The rain falls in drops as big as marbles.
310 The drops are black and greasy with dust.
The drops sting like falling pebbles.

The rain leaves black, oily spots wherever it falls.

The rain is radioactive . It will make people sick, too. They will also die.

> **radioactive**
> (rā′ dē ō ăk′ tĭv)
> *adj.* containing particles of radiation

> **REREAD**
> How is this rain different from regular rainfall?

After about an hour, the rain puts out the fires. Somebody finds Sachi and brings her to the hospital.

The people living just outside Hiroshima think they
320 are safe. They search through the deadly wasteland for family and friends. They do not know about radiation. Some of these searchers will also fall ill. Many of them will die.

One mother hunts all over the city for her children. Finally, she stops at a hospital.

The bodies of schoolchildren are piled up on a hallway bench. The mother looks through the bodies

from

Anne Frank:
Child of the Holocaust

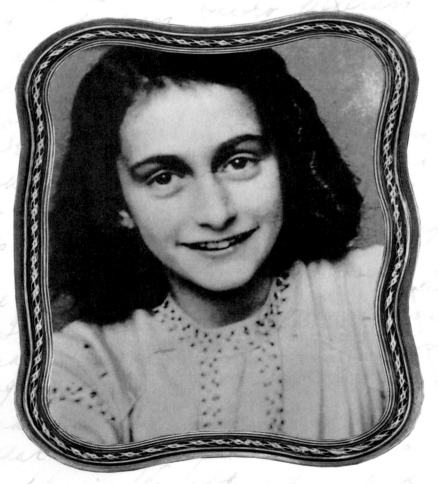

by Gene Brown

Anne was probably the most famous teenager of the last century. Here's a look at her life before she wrote the diary that moved the world.

Connect to Your Life

Think of news stories about people who become heroes. What kinds of situations make heroes out of everyday people? What qualities did the people show?

Key to the Biography

Anne Frank grew up during the 1930s and 1940s. The Nazi Party rose to power in Germany at the same time. Jewish people became the main targets of Nazi threats. Anne's family tried to escape by hiding in a secret place. While she was there, she kept a diary. The family hid successfully for two years. Then the Franks were arrested, and all were sent to prison camps. Only Anne's father survived. He published Anne's diary in 1947.

As you read the biography, notice the words in dark type. They are important words to remember about this time in history. They are defined in the text.

Vocabulary Preview

Words to Know

tolerant	torture
secure	synagogues

**Reading Coach
CD-ROM selection**

Why would anyone want to read about the most private thoughts of a 13-year-old girl? That's what Anne Frank asked herself as she wrote in her dairy in the early 1940s. She was, after all, an ordinary 13-year-old. Her parents didn't seem to understand her. She often couldn't figure out the boys she knew. And she did not care for some of her teachers.

Anne wasn't even known as a good writer. One of her teachers said that "the compositions that Anne
10 wrote in school were just ordinary, no better than average."

Yet millions of people have read Anne's diary and seen the play and movie based on it. Most were deeply moved. The diary has been translated into many languages, and Anne Frank's name is known all over the world. The place in the Netherlands where she wrote her famous diary is now a museum.

the Netherlands
(nĕ*th*' ər ləndz)
country near
Germany in Western
Europe, also called
Holland

Anne is famous because she was able to
20 write about a subject for which the world's best writers have been unable to find the right words. She was one of 6 million Jews murdered by the Nazis during World War II. She died in what we now call the "**Holocaust.**" (The word means a great fire, often used to burn a sacrifice.) Her diary tells of how she and her family hid from the Nazis and tried to keep a little hope alive when much of the world seemed to be going mad.

THINK IT THROUGH
| In what ways is Anne Frank ordinary? In what ways is she special?

FOCUS
Read to find out how Hitler came to power.

Flight from Evil

30   Anne Frank was born in Germany, the country in which the Nazis came to power. Jews had lived in Germany for hundreds of years. Often they were victims of prejudice, much like that faced by some groups such as blacks in the United States.

The family of Otto Frank, Anne's father, had lived in Frankfurt, Germany, for a long time. About 30 thousand Jews lived there—5 percent of the city's people. Only Berlin, the capital, had more Jews than Frankfurt. There was anti-Jewish feeling in Anne's
40 hometown. For example, some restaurants refused to serve Jews. Yet compared with the rest of Germany,

Anne as a baby with her father, Otto, and her sister, Margot

Frankfurt was tolerant . Otto could recall no **anti-Semitic** (anti-Jewish) incidents when he was growing up. By the early 1930s, the city even had a Jewish mayor.

Otto's family did well in the retail department store business and he decided to make it his career too. In 1908, Otto dropped out of college and spent a year in New York, working in
50 Macy's department store. The parents of a friend he had met at school owned the store.

Like other young men his age, Otto served in the German army during World War I. He joined in 1915, became an officer, and won several medals. After the war, he went into business for himself.

In 1925, Otto married Edith Hollander, whose family was also in business. Their first daughter, Margot, was born the next year. Anne was born in 1929.

60 In that year, the Great Depression began to spread through the United States and Europe. Stores closed, businesses failed, and many people lost their jobs. One out of every four persons in Frankfurt was unemployed. Those still working worried that they might be the next to become jobless.

Hard times made it easier for the Nazis and Adolf Hitler, their leader, to gain support. Many Germans were frightened. They were ready to believe anyone
70 who promised them a better and more secure life. Hitler told them that Germany didn't need freedom. It needed a leader to tell the country's people what to do— someone they should obey without question. He said he was that leader.

Hitler also played on German prejudices. He placed the blame for everything that had gone 80 wrong in their country on the Jews and on other people who were unpopular. These included gypsies, homosexuals, communists, and anyone who looked, thought, or acted differently from other Germans. Get rid of these "outsiders," he said, and 90 Germany's problems would go away. Soon, Hitler organized a movement headed by his own **Nazi Party.**

Adolf Hitler, 1934

THINK IT THROUGH

How did Hitler gain power in Germany?

FOCUS

Read to see why the German Jews became even more concerned.

The Nazis Take Control

In 1933, when Anne was four years old, the Nazis had almost complete power in Germany. The Franks watched with increasing alarm what the Nazis did. The Nazis quickly moved against their "enemies." When they found books with ideas they didn't like, they burned them. The Nazis also built **concentration camps**—large prisons—for those who opposed them. At first, people sent to these camps simply lost their

from Anne Frank: Child of the Holocaust **411**

100 freedom. Later, the concentration camps would become scenes of torture and mass killing.

Jews got the worst treatment in Germany. They could no longer hold government jobs. All Jewish officials, like the mayor of Frankfurt, had to resign. Non-Jewish Germans were ordered not to go to Jewish doctors or hire Jewish lawyers. In the schools, Jewish students were segregated—put in separate classes. Jewish teachers were fired. Jews who 110 owned stores had to mark their windows with the word "Jew." Before long, the Nazis forced Jews to sell their businesses to non-Jews. These rules affected anyone who had even one Jewish grandparent.

REREAD

What is the main idea of this paragraph? What details support it?

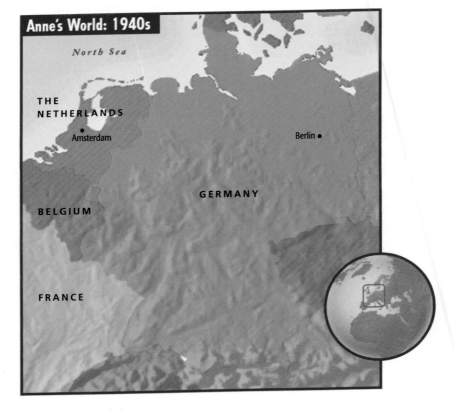

Anne's World: 1940s

North Sea

THE NETHERLANDS

Amsterdam

Berlin

GERMANY

BELGIUM

FRANCE

Few Germans spoke out against these new rules. Many believed Hitler's lies about the Jews. Those who didn't were afraid of being sent to a concentration camp if they said what they thought. Even the Catholic and Protestant churches did little to stop the 120 Nazis.

The Nazis used the Gestapo—their secret police—to scare people. The Gestapo was brutal and had spies everywhere. The Nazis also frightened people with their **storm troopers**— party members who dressed like soldiers and acted like thugs. They began to beat Jews in the street.

> Gestapo
> (gə stä′ pō)

Otto decided not to wait. He feared that conditions in Germany would get worse. Otto made up his mind to get his family out of the country. He sent Edith and 130 his daughters to live in the German city of Aachen, where his wife's family lived. Meanwhile, he got a job working for a company in Amsterdam, Holland, in the Netherlands, a country bordering Germany. About 90,000 Jews lived in Amsterdam. From there, Otto sent for his family.

Why did Otto Frank choose the Netherlands? It was close to home and, in many ways, like the area from which his family came. Jews had been treated fairly well there for many centuries, making Otto 140 think it would be a safe place. He could not have been more wrong.

THINK IT THROUGH
Why didn't other Germans try to stop the Nazis?

| Look for details that tell you more about what Anne was like. |

Another Escape

Anne Frank grew up when terrible things were
beginning to happen in the world. But her parents
could still give her and Margot a loving and secure
family life. Anne had good memories of her early
years. For example, she could recall many of her
parents' friends coming to visit on Sundays, and the
wonderful smell of the coffee and cake that was
served.

150   Anne was a slim girl with dark brown hair, intense
dark eyes, and dimples. Visitors to the Frank home
were likely to be greeted by the sight of her carrying
her cat, Moortje. The cat's hind legs almost touched
the floor as little Anne struggled to hold him.

Anne's sister, Margot, got better grades in school
and was the more serious of the two. Anne called her
"brainy." Margot was well-behaved and kept her
clothes and other things neat. Anne was messier with
her belongings. She also had high spirits. People

LOOK CLOSELY What do these pictures reveal to you about Anne's personality?

160 remembered her strong personality, which sometimes got her in trouble at school.

Margot was quiet and thoughtful, while Anne liked to say whatever was on her mind. This trait could be refreshing and honest, although at times some people found it thoughtless. Once, Anne told one of her parents' friends that his eyes were like a cat's. The friend found that very funny. But the other adults in the room considered it impolite for Anne to talk that way to an adult.

170 Anne liked attention, and she often got it by making people laugh. When she was only four years old, her mother wrote to a friend that Anne was like "a little comedian." Later, Anne loved to perform in school plays. She also enjoyed doing imitations— whether of a friend, a teacher, or even a cat.

By the time she was in grade school, Anne had many friends. Anne and her friends liked to play pingpong and a game similar to hopscotch. They also did handstands against the wall in a nearby
180 playground. Anne was a bit clumsy, though, and

sometimes fell over. No matter what Anne and her friends played, they usually went out for ice cream after the game.

The mother of a friend of Anne's once said that, even when young, Anne seemed to "know who she was." She meant that Anne had a good sense of herself, that she was mature for her age. Yet Anne could also be childish. Sometimes she swung from one way of behaving to the other: an adult one minute, a
190 child the next.

Anne had strong opinions about the people she knew. She thought that some of the other students in her school were "absolute cuckoos," and that a few of her teachers were "freaks." Her math teacher thought that she talked too much in class. To punish her, he made her write a composition about why she couldn't be quiet. That didn't silence her, so he next told her to write about what her constant talking reminded him of: "quack, quack,
200 quack." She won him over by writing, instead, a funny poem about talking.

REREAD
What does this incident show about Anne?

At age 11, most girls her age were still playing children's games. Anne and her friends, however, were already "giggling over the boys," according to one girl who knew her. Anne was very aware of her effect on the boys around her. They constantly flirted with her.

As she approached her teenage years, Anne became very interested in how she looked. She and her friends
210 often read fashion magazines. They thought of her as "stylish."

One day, a girl who knew Anne was at the local dressmaker's shop with her mother. The dressmaker was in the fitting room with a customer. "It would

look better with larger shoulder pads," they heard the customer say behind the curtain, "and the hemline should be just a little higher, don't you think?" The girl was surprised when the curtains parted and out came Anne Frank. She was the person who seemed to
220 have known just what she wanted, sounding, for a moment, like an adult.

In ordinary times, Anne might have looked forward to being a teenager much like any other girl. But these were not ordinary times. Conditions kept getting worse in Germany throughout the 1930s, especially for the Jews. Before long, the Nazis were threatening to bring their system of hate, fear, and terror to other countries around the world.

THINK IT THROUGH
In your own words, summarize the kind of childhood Anne had in ordinary times.

FOCUS _____
By the mid-1930s, the rights of Jews in Germany began to disappear. Find out the different ways in which conditions changed.

Life in Germany Grows Worse

In 1935, Germany took all political rights away
230 from its Jewish citizens. It was as if they were no longer Germans, but foreigners in their own country. Jews could no longer marry non-Jews. Many Jews, fearing for their lives, left Germany. These people had to leave behind most of their property.

In 1938, all Jewish students were ordered out of German schools. At the end of that year, the Nazis staged mass arrests of Jews, sending 30,000 to concentration camps. They also encouraged mobs to

from Anne Frank: Child of the Holocaust **417**

attack Jews throughout the country—in
their homes, shops, and synagogues . One
hundred Jews were killed as the mobs left a
path of destruction—200 synagogues and
5,000 stores were destroyed. There was so
much broken glass afterwards on the streets that the
attack became known as **"Crystal Night,"** although
the violence lasted several days.

synagogues
(sĭn′ ə gŏgz′)
n. places of
worship for Jews

The Nazis forced Jews to
wear a yellow Star of David
on the outside of their
clothing. In this way, Jews
could be easily recognized.
This meant that there was
almost no place in Germany
where Jews could be safe.

People all over the world
were horrified. There were
complaints to the German
government, but they did no

In 1941, Hitler's government forced
Jews to wear this image in public.

good. Many Jews remaining in
Germany now tried to get out. Two of Anne Frank's
aunts left for the United States. Anne's grandmother
left Aachen and went to Amsterdam to live with
Anne's family. By 1939, half the Jews who had lived
in Germany had left.

Most of the Jews still living in Germany could have
been saved, but many couldn't leave. They had
nowhere to go. Other countries, including the
Netherlands and the United States, only took in a
certain number of new people from other nations.
They might bend the rules a little for those who were
in danger, like the German Jews, but not much.

The countries that Jews wanted to move to said that they were worried about not having enough jobs for all the newcomers. Or they said they didn't have enough housing—any number of reasons were given. Often the reasons had more to do with prejudice. Jews weren't wanted because they were Jews. Anti-Semitism was everywhere, not just in Germany.

> **REREAD**
> Why didn't the countries take more Jewish newcomers?

280   Throughout the 1930s, the Nazis said that Germans needed more "room to live." In 1939, when Anne was 10, Hitler took direct action to obtain more land. His armies invaded Poland. Great Britain and France came to Poland's defense. When they declared war on Germany, they officially began World War II.

    At first, the war did not touch the Dutch, as the people of the Netherlands were called. Until 1940, the Netherlands seemed a safe place for Jews—compared to much of the rest of Europe. There were 140,000

290 Jews living in the Netherlands. About 24,000 of them had fled from Germany. There was anti-Semitism, but the Franks encountered little of it. That's why Anne could lead a fairly normal life.

> **encountered**
> (ĕn koun' tərd)
> faced

THINK IT THROUGH

Give details about daily life for Jews in Germany. Contrast this with life for Jews in the Netherlands.

FOCUS

Find out how life got worse for Jews in the Netherlands.

Amsterdam Becomes Dangerous

    On May 10, 1940, the hopes for a peaceful life in their new country were dashed. Otto Frank was at his

office that day and his face turned pale as he heard the report on the radio: the Germans had attacked the Netherlands. The Dutch fought back, but they were
300 quickly beaten. It was over in four days.

A deep shadow was suddenly cast over Anne's life—and over that of everyone she knew. The Germans used the Dutch Nazi party to help them rule the Netherlands. Gradually, the new government began to repeat what was happening in Germany.

Jews could not teach or work for the Dutch government. They couldn't go to public places like movies and libraries. Dutch Nazis began to attack Jews on the street. They also began to arrest some
310 Jews and send them to concentration camps. Soon the Nazis were regularly arresting large numbers of Jews on the street and taking them to prison.

Beginning in 1942, Jews, including children like Anne, had to wear a yellow Star of David on the left side of their coat. They had to wear the star even when they came to open their front door. When many non-Jews began to wear it in sympathy, the Germans arrested them. Dutch workers also protested the treatment of the Jews by
320 going out on strike. The Nazis broke the strike after a few days.

REREAD
How did the Dutch people try to fight back?

Jews weren't allowed to go anywhere with their non-Jewish Dutch friends. They also had a curfew: they had to be indoors by 8:00 at night.

It was hard enough being young and dealing with the usual criticism a child expects from her parents. Now Anne's mother and father had very real reasons to be concerned for her safety. One night, Anne was walking with a boy and came in a few minutes after
330 eight, making her father very angry. She wasn't used

German citizens salute a parade of German troops.

to such toughness from him, and he didn't like being so cross with her. But he knew she could have been arrested.

THINK IT THROUGH

Summarize how life changed for Jews in the Netherlands. In addition, describe how Anne's life changed.

FOCUS

Discover what Anne received that made her hardships a little easier to take.

A Wonderful Birthday Present

In the middle of this tense time, on June 12th, 1942, Anne turned 13. Her father's birthday present to her was a diary—a book with blank pages and a red-checkered hard cover. In it she could write about what happened in her life each day. She also could

record her thoughts and feelings about anything or
340 anybody.

In her first entry in the diary, Anne gave the book a
name: "Kitty." She wrote that she and the diary
would be "pals." Anne felt that she needed a friend
with whom she could share her serious thoughts, and
the diary would be it. She couldn't really do that with
any of her family or friends. Kitty, unlike others in her
life, would always be patient and willing to listen.

It would have been hard for Anne to write only
about personal things in her diary. Too many horrible
350 events were happening in the outside world. The
Nazis were rounding up Jews as if they were animals.
One Dutch woman passing a home for Jewish
orphans said she saw "the Germans were loading the
children, who ranged in ages from babies to eight-
year-olds, on trucks. When they did not move fast
enough the Nazis picked them up, by an arm, a leg,
the hair, and threw them into the trucks."

What were Jews like the Franks to do? Everyone
had to have an identification card. Besides, most
360 Dutch had blond hair and blue eyes. Jews, like Anne,
were likely to have dark hair and dark eyes. Their
appearance made them stand out.

As a result, many Jews went into hiding. They
found Dutch non-Jews who had attics, basements, or
extra rooms in which they could stay. The Dutch who
hid Jews faced arrest if they were found out.

No Place to Run

By the beginning of the summer of 1942, Anne's
parents were thinking of hiding themselves and their
children from the Nazis. They began to move some of
370 their belongings to the houses of non-Jewish friends,

who would keep them safe until after the war. On July 5, Otto told Anne that they might have to hide.

That afternoon, the Franks sped up their plan. Margot received a notice requiring that she report for forced labor in Germany. The Nazis used many young people, including Dutch non-Jews, to do work that had been done by Germans now serving in the army. If 16-year-old Margot didn't report, she would be arrested. If she did go, the Germans would make her a slave.

380

That settled it. Otto had already picked out a hiding place. It was the rooms used for storage, called the "**Annex**," above the office he managed.

> **REREAD**
>
> What event forces the Franks to go into hiding?

He had talked to one of his workers, a Dutch woman named Miep Gies, about helping him and his family remain safe there. She agreed to help. She told a few other workers at the office who promised to keep the Franks' hiding place a secret. They also would bring the family food and anything else they needed until the war ended.

> **Miep Gies**
> (mēp gēs)

390

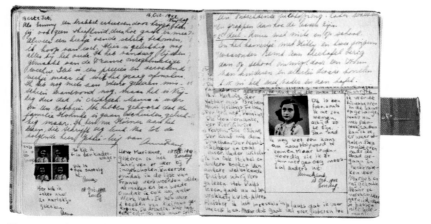

These are two pages from Anne's diary.

The Franks were to be joined in their hiding place by another Jewish family, Mr. van Daan and his wife and son. Mr. van Daan worked with Otto Frank.

Margot was in the most danger, so she went to the hiding place immediately. Anne and her parents soon followed. (Anne's grandmother had died by this time.) The van Daans came a week later.

400 Anne did not have much time to get ready, and she couldn't carry many of her belongings to the Annex because it would look suspicious. She put just a few items in her school bag. The first thing she packed was her diary. It was a warm, rainy Monday morning, but Anne wore several layers of clothing to sneak clothes into the hideout without drawing attention.

REREAD

Why do you think she packs the diary first?

Anne could not say goodbye
410 to her friends because the family's secret might have gotten out. Once safe in the hiding place, Anne wrote a letter to one of her pals explaining what had happened, but it was never mailed.

Otto Frank said that he and his family were "disappearing." Anne thought of it as a
420 "vacation." Later, she would call it an "adventure." As Miep Gies saw it, "They had simply closed the door of their lives and vanished from Amsterdam."

This bookcase hid the entrance to the Annex.

Through Her Diary, Anne Lives On

Over the next two years, Anne's diary played a major part in her life. In it, she described what happened each day in the Annex. She poured out her feelings about life in a crowded, secret place. She described fears of being discovered. Often, Anne's writings were like any teenager's. Just as often, they were filled with wisdom.

It was Miep Gies who found the diary after the family's 1944 arrest. She saved it. "I was hoping she would still come back and that I would be able to give it to her," Miep once said. "I wanted to see her smile at me." Miep gave it to Anne's father. He was the only family member to survive the concentration camps.

The diary was first published as *Anne Frank: Diary of a Young Girl* in 1947. Because of Anne's diary, the world could view a time of great suffering through the eyes of one very real person. A play based on the diary, called *The Diary of Anne Frank,* was written in 1955. Read the diary or the play. Discover more about Anne Frank's amazing life.

THINK IT THROUGH

1. What conditions forced the Frank family to go into hiding?
2. Why do you think the author gives so many details about Anne's childhood?
3. Think about Anne's personality. How do you think she handled being in hiding? Support your opinion with details.
4. Imagine that you are Anne. How would you react to what is happening around you?

from Anne Frank: Child of the Holocaust **425**

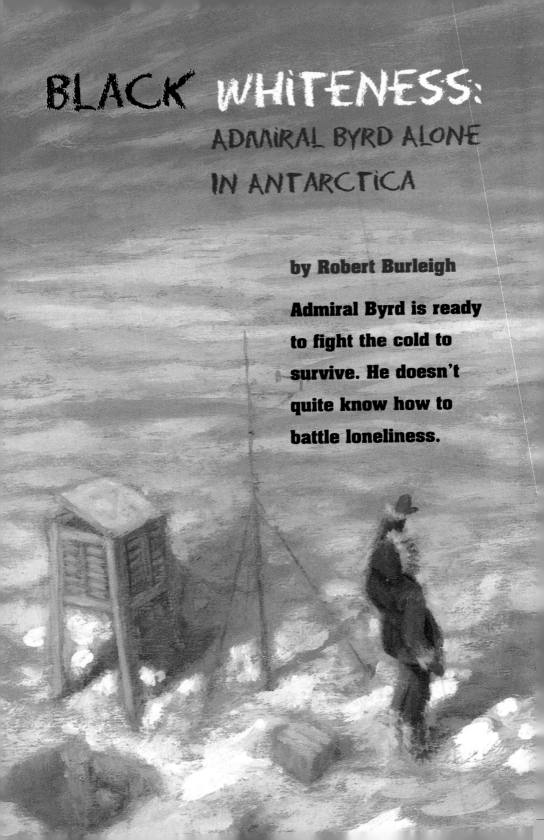

BLACK WHITENESS:
ADMIRAL BYRD ALONE IN ANTARCTICA

by Robert Burleigh

Admiral Byrd is ready to fight the cold to survive. He doesn't quite know how to battle loneliness.

Connect to Your Life

What do you dislike the most about winter? How do you react to cold temperatures? The account you're about to read is set in a place of extremely low temperatures. Think about the coldest temperature you've ever been in. Tell a classmate and discuss your experiences.

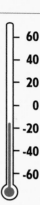

60
40
20
0
-20
-40
-60

Key to the Account

Little was known about Antarctica until Admiral Richard Byrd went there. In 1928, Byrd flew to the South Pole. He was part of two major research trips, or *expeditions.* On the first trip, he helped to set up a science research base called Little America. This account deals with Byrd's second expedition, which lasted from 1933 to 1935. During this period, he spent one long winter doing research at a base called Advance Base. He was totally alone. In Antarctica, the winter season is from May to August.

Notice the unusual form of this account. It is presented in the form of stanzas, almost like a poem. The account also includes diary entries. They are based on Byrd's own writings.

Vocabulary Preview

Words to Know

aluminum paralysis circulation
cringe nausea

Read to discover where Admiral Byrd lives at Advance Base, and what he does.

Antarctica. March 1934.
A man stands alone in the snow,
　　watching a tractor disappear over the far horizon.

Wherever he turns now,
he sees the flat whiteness roll on forever to meet the
　　sky;
he feels the things of the world "shrink away to
　　nothing."

It is midafternoon,
10　but the sun to the south is already setting.
Night is coming on,
　　pressing down with its blue-black shadow.

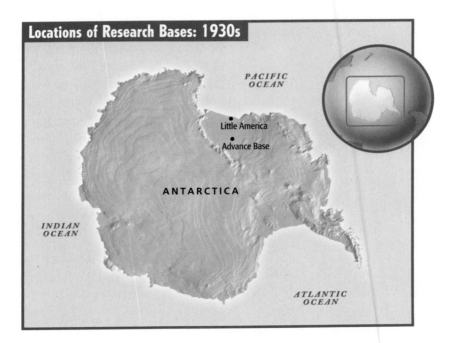

Locations of Research Bases: 1930s

PACIFIC
OCEAN

Little America

Advance Base

ANTARCTICA

INDIAN
OCEAN

ATLANTIC
OCEAN

He kneels and opens a small hatch.
Below, buried like a cave in the snow,
is the tiny shack where he will live alone for many
    months.
He puts his foot on the first rung of the ladder and
    lowers himself inside.

Admiral Richard Byrd, explorer, moves about his snug
20   house, "tidily built as a watch."
With four strides, he can cross the room:
past the bunk on a wall, a stove, shelves, hooks for
    clothes.

His narrow world is a dim one, too:
He has only a flashlight, a lantern, and a small gas
    lamp.
There are three thin windows in the roof;
the ceiling is made of aluminum
to reflect what little light there is.

> **aluminum**
> (ə loo' mə nəm)
> *n.* silvery,
> lightweight
> metallic element

30 Outside the door is a kind of porch.
The ladder to the hatch rests on it.
Leading away are two long, low tunnels.
It is here that he stores his tons of fuel and food.
His toilet is a hole at the end of one of the tunnels,
    thirty-five feet away.

The tunnels are dark as dungeons. But in the lantern light, they take on a breathless radiance. Icicles on the roof glisten like candelabra; the walls glow with a sharp, blue nakedness.

> **candelabra**
> (kăn' dl ä' brə)
> metal holder with
> arms for
> candlesticks

Advance Base is the first inland base in
   Antarctica.
There are eight weather instruments,
and each day Byrd must record the
40   information they give.
The instruments tell the wind's speed and direction.
They tell the temperature.
They tell the amount of moisture in the air.
Scientists around the world want to know these
   things.

But Admiral Byrd wants to know something else, too.
What is it like to live so completely alone?
In such intense cold and so much darkness?
Can any human being endure that?
50 Can he—Richard Byrd?

> **inland**
> (ĭn' lənd)
> located some
> distance within a
> body of land

> **endure**
> (ĕn dŏŏr')
> survive

THINK IT THROUGH
What is Admiral Byrd doing at Advance Base? What does he
want to find out?

FOCUS —————
Read about the conditions under which Admiral Byrd lives.

He keeps a diary where, at the end of each day,
he writes down his thoughts.
Writing like this, he tells himself, is like "thinking out
   loud."

Out here, in frost and darkness as complete as that of the Ice Age, I may have time to catch up, to study, and to think. I am able to live exactly as I choose, obedient to nothing but the laws of the wind and the night and the cold. That is the way I see it.

obedient
(ō bē′ dē ənt)
following the
commands

Little America, the main base, is many miles away on
   the Antarctic coast.
Admiral Byrd contacts the people at Little America on
   his radio.
He can hear their voices,
60 but he can only reply in a
   code of dashes and dots.

**code of
dashes and
dots**
special code that
is transmitted by
a telegraph
machine

The rest is mostly an eerie silence—
except for the constant ticking of the
   weather machines,
and the ceaseless blowing of the wind.

Cold, terrible cold:

kerosene
(kĕr′ ə sēn′)
oil used in
lanterns

At −50°F a flashlight dies in his hand;
at −55°F kerosene freezes;
at −60°F rubber turns brittle and snaps,
70 juice bottles shatter,
canned food from the tunnel becomes
   hard as rock.

REREAD
How do these
details help you
understand how
cold it is?

Outside, he hears his breath freeze as it
   floats away,
making a sound like firecrackers.

Sometimes the frozen breath hangs above his head
   like a small cloud;
if he breathes too deeply, his lungs burn
   with invisible fire.

80 There is also a terrible beauty:
afternoon skies that shatter "like broken goblets"
as tiny ice crystals fall across the face of the sun;
blood-red horizons, liquid twilights,
and pale green beams, called auroras,
that wind in great waves through the towering dark.

But it is April now,
and "each day more light is draining away."
Soon there will be no sun at all.
Days and days and days of total blackness.
90 The Antarctic night.

With two weeks of daylight left, the sun was just a
monstrous ball which could barely hoist itself
free of the horizon. It would sink out of sight
in the north not long after noon. I watched it
go as one might watch a departing friend.

> hoist
> raise

Mornings are the worst.
The cold in the little room lies like a thick liquid.
This morning, in the shack, it is −40°F!
(He sleeps with the stove off and the door half open,
   in order to be safe from any possible fumes.)

The slightest move sends blasts
of freezing air down his back or stomach.
The thought of his first foot on the floor
　　makes him cringe .

100　Ice coats the outside of the sleeping bag.
His clothes are so stiff
he must work them between his hands
　　before putting them on.

He pokes with the flashlight
to find a pair of thin silk gloves.
Without the gloves,
the frozen metal of the lantern would
　　tear skin off his fingers!

He strikes a match and touches it to the lantern's
110　　wick.
The flame catches and goes out,
catches and goes out.
Then it wavers , steadies, thickens:
ah, light!

It is a gloomy light, perhaps; things on the opposite
wall are scarcely touched by it. But to me the feeble
burning is a daily miracle.

In this cruel world, even the
    simple is difficult.
The snow is rough and
    brittle as white sandstone.
He cuts out blocks with a
120   saw,
then melts them in a bucket
    on the stove, slowly:
after several hours over the
    flame,
two gallons of snow make
    two quarts of water.

THINK IT THROUGH
Summarize the problems Admiral Byrd faces.

FOCUS
An unexpected danger arises at the base. Read to find out
what happens.

Sometimes, as he opens the trapdoor,
the wind sweeps down
and sucks all the heat from the house.

130 At the close of each day, standing by the stove,
he bathes a third of his body.
(Because warm air rises and cool air sinks,
it is often 20° colder at his feet!)

Finally, with all heat off,
he reads in the sleeping bed—until his hands are numb.

Patiently, he parcels out the day:
checks each instrument many times;
writes out and stores his reports;
patches the stovepipe;
140 observes the sky at intervals and notes down whatever
    he sees.
(He calls his observations "obs.")

Each afternoon he takes a long walk.
But in the black whiteness of the Antarctic winter,
he is never quite safe or sure.

One day he walks out beyond his trail
marked by bamboo sticks
and realizes he is lost.
He panics, and almost starts to run;
150 then calms himself and once more finds his way.

On another day he stumbles over a small hole.
Crawling carefully to the edge,
he points his flashlight, leans, and looks
    down—
into a deep crevasse !

At the surface the crevasse was not more than
three feet across; but a little way down it
bellied out, making a vast cave. I could see no
bottom.

crevasse
(krĭ văs')
deep crack in a
glacier

bellied out
(bĕl' ēd out')
swelled out

Blizzard.

Like an incoming tide, the snow rises:
over his ankles,
above his knees,
160 against his chest,
exploding into his eyes
"like millions of tiny pellets."

REREAD
What is happening to Byrd?

No night has ever seemed so dark.
The flashlight's beam blackens.
The trapdoor, weighted by the sudden snow, is stuck
    tight.

Terrified, Byrd rips and claws at the hatch-edge.

You are reduced to a crawling thing on the
    margin of a disintegrating world.

disintegrating
(dĭs ĭn′ tĭ grā′ tĭng)
coming apart

The drift piles up around him.
The air comes at him in white rushes.
170 If he tries to stand,
the snow wall beats him back.

He stabs at the hatch with his shovel.
Again and again and again.
He pries open an inch, forces in his fingers,
hauls it up high and higher;
and, moaning, tumbles inside.

Late May.
And suddenly,
what he had feared the most happens.

180 Gas fumes seep into one of the tunnels!
Carbon monoxide, odorless and invisible.

Unknowing, Byrd walks into the tunnel
and leans over the radio.
He feels a strange drowsiness.
His eyes flutter.
His legs grow weak.
He falls to his hands and knees on the
    icy floor.

REREAD
What is happening to Admiral Byrd at this point?

He does not remember turning the radio
190   off,
nor crawling back toward the shack,
nor butting the door open like a wounded animal.

All he would ever remember was the "skyrocketing
    pain,"
the violent beating of his heart,
and a voice inside him saying, *I must sleep.*

Only the cold was real: the numbness in the
hands and feet, creeping like a slow paralysis
through my body. I grasped for the throat of
the sleeping bag, and eased in.

paralysis
(pə răl′ ĭ sĭs)
n. the loss of the power to move or feel

He wakes at last, deathly sick.
With trembling hands,
he lights the candle above his bed.

200 When he stands on his quivery legs, he
    feels pain and nausea .
Intense hunger.
Dreadful thirst.
He nibbles on a small piece of chocolate;
he sucks on slivers of ice
until his teeth rattle from the cold.

> **nausea**
> (nô′ zē ə)
> *n.* sick feeling in
> the stomach

The candle casts its heatless, gloomy light
into the corners of the shack.
Admiral Byrd crawls back into the bag and lies there,
210 composing last letters to his loved ones in America.

There is no hope, he thinks, *no hope.*
I am going to die.

The days pass in a blur of broken images.
Yet something in him fights to stay alive.
He manages to light the stove.
He eats a little.

But his strength is gone.
He does not stand—he wobbles.
He does not walk—he creeps.

Black Whiteness: Admiral Byrd Alone in Antarctica **439**

220 Getting fuel from the tunnel is a morning's work.
Climbing the ladder to go "topside,"
he stops to rest at every rung.

Outside or inside, day or night,
he is cold to his very bones.

Talking with Little America is harder, too.

He cranks the radio by hand.
"The room at −60°, sweat pouring down
    my chest."

cranks
(krăngks) turns the handle to create power

Should he say he is sick?
230 That he is going to die?
No, an attempt to rescue him would only doom the
    men.

*I had given a hard and fast order not to come for me
until a month after the sun returns.*

Do the people at Little America,
receiving his slow, misspelled replies,
know he is not well?

Noon. June 21:
the longest night of the Antarctic year.

Richard Byrd sits in the snow, staring out.
Darkness on three sides.
240 But in the north there is a faint dab of crimson on the
　　distant horizon;
a thin pencil line of light,
like a secret message from the now-returning sun.
But beyond the weather records
(which he keeps up day after day)
he is too weak to write,
too despairing to see.

> **despairing**
> (dǐ spâr' ĭng)
> hopeless

In his struggle to stay alive,
all else falls away.
250 Uneaten food litters the floor.
Half-empty cans are flung out on the deck.
Frozen slop is dumped in the tunnels.
Spare parts are scattered about like ice chunks.
Books lie underneath their shelves,
their upthrust pages stiff as frozen sails.
A small mirror hangs on the wall.
He gazes into it.

He leans close, listens,
and thinks he hears a very tiny voice:
260 *Endure,* it says;
Live, it says.

THINK IT THROUGH
What has caused Admiral Byrd to become so weak?
How does he manage to stay alive?

FOCUS
Is there any chance for rescue? Read to find out what
happens.

July is "born in cold."
(Twenty days will be colder than 60° below!)
Yet a message arrives from Little America:
A tractor team is coming—sooner than planned.
Is it possible?
A human face again?
A living voice?

Outside, the air rains with an unbelievable coldness.
270 Ice crystals
burn as they fall on his skin,
cling to his eyelashes,
sealing his eyes half shut.

*My toes would turn cold and then dead. While I
danced up and down to restore the
circulation, my nose would freeze; by the
time I attended to that, my hand was frozen.*

circulation
(sûr′ kyə lā′ shən)
n. the flow of
blood through
veins

Inside, "nothing is left for the ice to conquer":
It covers the floor;
it climbs up the walls;
it curves around the vent pipe;
it crawls across the ceiling.

On the table in the middle of the room,
280 a piece of meat lies unthawed.
It has been there for five days.

The tractor has set out twice,
and twice been forced to turn back.
Yesterday it started again.
(It will take two full days to arrive.)
He hears this on his radio,
but what he hears means less and less:
he has ceased to believe it is coming;
he has almost ceased to care.

290 In the gloom, he thinks of the tractor men.
Will *they* survive?
He imagines them wandering past, beeping beyond
    him,
lost in the endless dark;
he imagines them tumbling down snow
    hills,
blinded by the white wind.

REREAD
What does
Admiral Byrd
show about
himself here?

With his feeble arms, he painfully pushes himself up.
Yes, there is something he can—he must—do.
300 His thoughts search among the tunnel's
    rubble.
For a moment, he feels new blood course
    through his tired veins.
In his mind, he begins to make a plan.

course
(kôrs)
move swiftly
through

*Suddenly, I had a task to do.
My job would be that of a lighthouse keeper
on a dangerous coast.*

August 10:
a night "black with threat."

Byrd stands by the open hatch,
hauling a T-shaped kite upward by a thin
   string.

310 Around its long wire tail are wads of paper
   and pieces of cloth.
He | douses | the kite's tail with gasoline,
and tries to light a match.
A dozen matches go out in his hand.

douses
(dou' sĭz)
wets thoroughly

REREAD
What is Admiral
Byrd trying to
do? Why?

Finally, a violent uprush of light almost blinds him.
He jerks on the kite string.
The kite swoops into the air, caught on a wind gust,
flapping its spidery tail, blazing against the black.
It rises and rises, skates to a height of over a hundred
320   feet.

The sight of it swaying in the night sky delights him.
This | beacon |, he knows, can be seen for
   miles and miles.

beacon
(bē' kən)
light

For five minutes the kite flames overhead.
Byrd squints. He blinks and peers northward.

Against the backdrop of the horizon,
a single fingery beam moves up and down.
Afraid to believe it is true, he turns away,
shuts his two eyes tight and waits.
330 Then he turns and looks again.

There it is, still poking at the dark!
Quickly, he lights a flare and ties it to a stick.
He holds the stick high, waving it wildly.
The flare makes "a huge blue hole in the night."

The light from the tractor grows and grows.
Treads crunch over the crusted snow.
Horns sound and the tractor stops.
Three fur-muffled figures leap out.

> **treads**
> (trĕdz)
> metal belts that
> work like wheels
> for tractors

Byrd wants to stay calm,
340 but his hands are shaking.
He wants to cry,
but he is too empty even to sob.

He tries to jest: "Come on below, boys,
I have bowls of hot soup waiting."

Then, following the men down the ladder,
he collapses on the porch.

Many weeks pass.
The men from Little America help
   Admiral Byrd regain his strength.
350 They chart the weather, cook, clean,
sleep on the floor.

> **REREAD**
> How has the
> base now
> changed?

*The darkness lifted from my heart, just as it presently
did from the Barrier.*

Admiral Richard Byrd

At last, the Antarctic spring arrives
with a great blossoming of light.
One morning Admiral Byrd climbs
up the ladder and out the hatch.
He walks slowly across the snow,
to a small airplane waiting for him.
As the plane rises into the brightening air,
he looks down at the roof of his little house for the
360   final time.

Admiral Richard Byrd will return to Antarctica.
He will tell the people of the world more
  about this beautiful but harsh continent.

He will also write a book about his time alone.
He will talk about the cold and the fear and the
  courage.
But most of all he will tell about
"the sheer beauty and miracle of being alive."

"I live more simply now," he writes at the end of his
370   book,
"and with more peace."

THINK IT THROUGH

1. Why was Admiral Byrd able to survive such a
   terrible experience so long on his own? Explain.
2. In your opinion, was Admiral Byrd a hero? Give a
   reason for your answer.
3. What lessons might today's explorers learn from
   Admiral Byrd's experience? Use evidence from the
   account to support your response.

Student Resources

Active Reading Strategies

Good readers think while they read. Every so often they stop and check their understanding. They predict what might happen next. They question what they're reading. After they finish, they think about what they read. Each strategy below happens in a good reader's mind while he or she is reading.

CONNECT
Think about your own life when you read something. Think of something similar that you have gone through, seen, or heard.

VISUALIZE
Make a picture in your mind of what the text says. Imagine you are looking at what is described.

PREDICT
Try to guess what will happen next in the story or article. Then read on to find out if your guess was correct.

QUESTION
Let questions come to your mind when you read. If something doesn't make sense, don't pass it by. Ask or write a question to yourself. Look for answers as you read.

CLARIFY
Slow down and make sure you understand what you're reading. Reread something to make sure you understood what it meant. As you read farther, expect to understand or to find out more.
These are ways you can clarify your understanding:
- Sum up what happened in your own words, or summarize.
- Identify the main idea of the paragraph, especially in nonfiction.
- Make inferences about what the author meant but didn't say. Read between the lines and use your own experience to figure it out.

EVALUATE
Form opinions about what you read as you read it. Evaluate again after you read it.

The examples on the pages that follow show how each strategy works. The examples are from "Trombones and Colleges," by Walter Dean Myers. In this story, a boy brings home a bad report card. He has to decide whether to stay in hard classes or take easier ones.

CONNECT

Think about your own life when you read something. Think of something similar that you have gone through, seen, or heard.

> "A little ability is better than none," I said. No one said anything so I figured it probably wasn't the right time to try to cheer Clyde up.

READER CONNECTS: I know how the narrator feels. Sometimes I say the wrong thing and nobody laughs or says anything. Then I really feel stupid. I wish I could erase what I said.

VISUALIZE

Make a picture in your mind of what the text says. Imagine you are looking at what is described.

> But everything else was either a C or a D except mathematics. His mathematics mark was a big red F that had been circled. I don't know why they had to circle the F when it was the only red mark on the card.

READER VISUALIZES: In my mind I can see this report card. Everything is black except this big red F with a big red circle around it. It looks like nothing matters except that big old F—as if you wouldn't see it right away anyway.

PREDICT

Try to guess what will happen next in the story or article. Read on to find out if your guess was correct.

> "I got my report card today," Clyde said. His mother stopped taking the food out and turned toward us. Clyde pushed the report card about two inches toward her. She really didn't even have to look at the card to know that it was bad. She could have told that just by looking at Clyde. But she picked it up and looked at it a long time.

READER PREDICTS: I think she'll get mad at him. She might tell him that he's stupid or lazy and ground him until his grades get better.

> First she looked at one side and then the other and then back at the first side again. "What they say around the school?" she asked, still looking at the card. . . . "Well, what are you going to do, young man?"

READER CHECKS PREDICTION: Well, she didn't get mad after all; she just asked him what he was going to do.

QUESTION

Let questions come to your mind when you read. If something doesn't make sense, don't pass it by. Ask or write a question to yourself.

> "What are you going to do, Mr. Jones?"
> "I'm—I'm going to keep the academic course," Clyde said.
> "You think it's going to be any easier this time?" Mrs. Jones asked.
> "No."

READER QUESTIONS: Why does she ask him what he's going to do? I thought she'd tell him what to do. She didn't tell him to drop the course or to study harder. She just pointed out that it wasn't going to get any easier. I also wonder why he didn't go for the easier course and save himself some hard work. I'll look for answers as I read.

CLARIFY

Slow down and make sure you understand what you're reading. Reread something to make sure you understood what it meant. As you read farther, expect to understand or to find out more.

> And he says, 'Oh, that's a trombone I'm taking back to the pawn shop tomorrow." Well, I naturally ask him what he's doing with it in the first place, and he says he got carried away and bought it but he realized that we really didn't have the thirty-five dollars to spend on foolishness and so he'd take it back the next day. And all the time he's sitting there scratching his chin and rubbing his nose and trying to peek over at me to see how I felt about it. I just told him that I guess he knew what was best. Only the next day he forgot to take it back, and the next day he forgot to take it back, and finally I broke down and told him why didn't he keep it. He said he would if I thought he should.

READER CLARIFIES: I'm not sure I understand. Clyde's dad says he's going to take the trombone back because he shouldn't have bought it. He said he was going to return it, but he didn't. I guess he wants her to tell him to keep it. Then she tells him to keep it, and he acts like it was her decision. This way, I guess he won't feel guilty.

EVALUATE

Form opinions about what you read. Think about something as you read it and then again after you read it.

> For a minute there was a faraway look in her eyes, but then her face turned into a big smile. "You're just like your father, boy. That man would never give up on anything he really wanted. Did I ever tell you the time he was trying to learn to play the trombone?"

READER EVALUATES: I really like Clyde's mother. She didn't get mad at him about his report card. In fact, she's praising him for being brave enough to take the harder classes. She makes it sound like he's brave like his father. I admire her for this.

Fiction

A work of fiction is a story that the writer made up. It could be based on a real event, or it could be totally imagined. The **elements of fiction** are the most important parts of fiction. They are the **characters, setting, plot,** and **theme.** These elements make up the skeleton of the story.

PLOT AT A GLANCE

The plot is the sequence of events in the story. Remember that the plot is about a problem that characters must solve. Most plots have the following parts.

Climax

Turning point of story; moment of most suspense. Brings a change to the main character

Rising Action

Problem (conflict) is introduced and developed; suspense builds

Introduction

Introduces characters and setting

Falling Action and Conclusion

Ties up loose ends; may resolve the conflict

The Stranger

by Sue Baugh

If you saw someone standing by the road on a cold, rainy night, would you stop to help?

FOCUS
A young man decides to help a stranger. Read to find out what he learns about her.

Late one Saturday night, a young man was driving home on a deserted stretch of road. He could hear the rain beating against the roof of his car. His headlights cut through a cold mist that clung to the trees on either side of the road. In the flashes of lightning, tree branches seemed like ghostly hands grasping for his car. He could feel the steady drumroll of thunder. What a night to be out! He
10 shivered and wished he were safe at home.
  Suddenly, as he rounded a curve, his headlights lit up a young woman standing by the side of the road. Her

clung
(klŭng)
v. held on to something; past tense of cling

TERMS IN FICTION

- **Characters:** the people or animals in the story
- **Setting:** where and when the story happens
- **Plot:** what happens. The plot grows around a problem, or conflict. The story is about how the characters deal with this problem.
- **Conflict:** the struggle between two forces. **External conflict** happens between a character and an animal, nature, or a person. **Internal conflict** happens in a character's mind, such as a hard choice or a guilty conscience.
- **Theme:** the message the writer wants to share with the reader
- **Narrator:** the voice telling the story to the reader
- **Point of view:** the way the narrator is telling the story

  First person point of view: The narrator is part of the story.

  Third person point of view: The narrator is not part of the story, but is reporting it.
- **Suspense:** the feeling of growing tension and excitement

TYPES OF FICTION

- **Short story:** a short work of fiction that can be read at one sitting. It has a few main characters and a single conflict.
- **Folk tale:** a story that was told over and over by word of mouth. The characters may be animals or people.
- **Historical fiction:** a story set in the past. It may refer to real people or events. The dialogue is usually made up.
- **Myth:** a very old story that was told by ancient people to explain the unknown. The characters often include gods or heroes.
- **Novel:** a long story that usually cannot be read at one sitting. A novel usually has many characters. The plot is complicated. A novel excerpt is one part of the novel.
- **Legend:** a story about a hero that has been told over and over. Most legends are based on a real person or event.
- **Horror story:** a short story that is meant to scare the reader

Nonfiction

Nonfiction is writing about real people, places, and events. It is mostly based on facts.

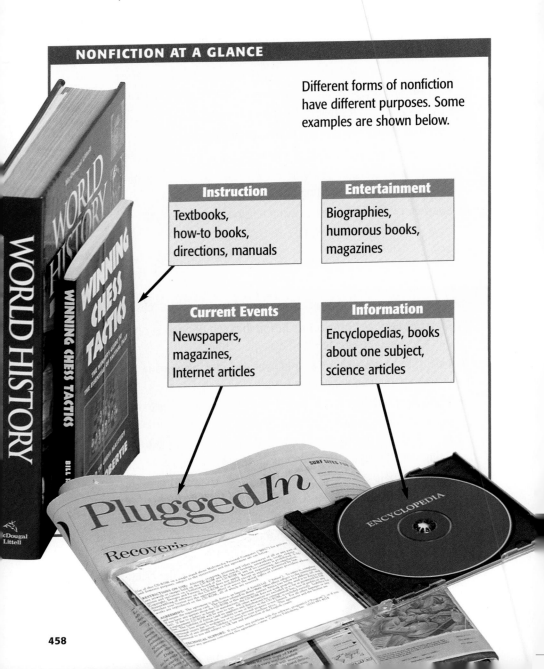

NONFICTION AT A GLANCE

Different forms of nonfiction have different purposes. Some examples are shown below.

Instruction
Textbooks, how-to books, directions, manuals

Entertainment
Biographies, humorous books, magazines

Current Events
Newspapers, magazines, Internet articles

Information
Encyclopedias, books about one subject, science articles

TERMS IN NONFICTION

- **Facts:** statements that can be proved to be true
- **Opinions:** statements of personal belief that cannot be proved
- **Chronological order:** the order or sequence in which events happen in time
- **Cause and Effect:** The cause is the reason something happens. The effect is the result, or what happens due to the cause.
- **Visuals:** diagrams, maps, charts, photos, and pictures that are part of an article. They give facts by means of pictures and sketches, with just a few words.

TYPES OF NONFICTION

- **Biography:** a true story about someone's life, written by someone else. It can cover the whole life or just one part.
- **Autobiography:** the true story of a person's life, written by that person
- **Feature Article:** an article that gives facts about a current subject. It is often found in a newspaper or a magazine. Most include visuals.
- **Informative Article:** an article that gives facts about a subject. The article might be from an encyclopedia, textbook, or book.
- **Interview:** a conversation between two people. One asks the other questions. The answers are written in the form of an interview.
- **Essay:** a piece of writing about one subject. The writer might share an opinion or make a point.
- **True Account:** an article about a real event that is told as a story
- **Narrative Nonfiction:** an article about a real event told in chronological order. It is often historical.
- **Anecdote:** the true story of a small event, usually from the teller's life. An anecdote might be funny (to entertain) or might make a point.

Drama

A drama, or play, is a story that is meant to be acted out. Actors present the play onstage. They act out the story for an audience.

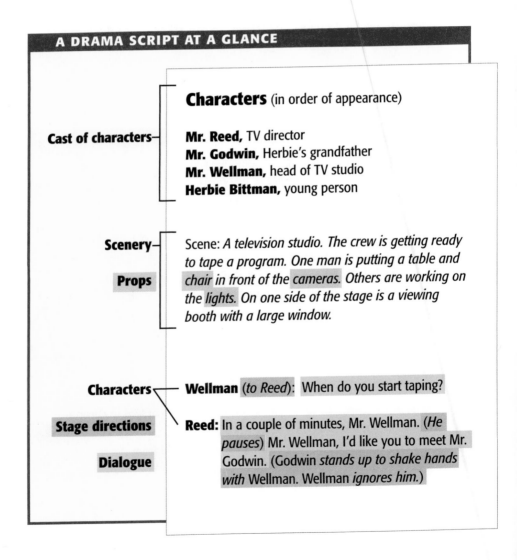

A DRAMA SCRIPT AT A GLANCE

Cast of characters—

Characters (in order of appearance)

Mr. Reed, TV director
Mr. Godwin, Herbie's grandfather
Mr. Wellman, head of TV studio
Herbie Bittman, young person

Scenery—
Props

Scene: *A television studio. The crew is getting ready to tape a program. One man is putting a table and chair in front of the cameras. Others are working on the lights. On one side of the stage is a viewing booth with a large window.*

Characters
Stage directions
Dialogue

Wellman (*to Reed*): When do you start taping?

Reed: In a couple of minutes, Mr. Wellman. (*He pauses*) Mr. Wellman, I'd like you to meet Mr. Godwin. (Godwin *stands up to shake hands with* Wellman. Wellman *ignores him.*)

TERMS IN DRAMA

- **Stage:** the platform on which the actors perform
- **Script:** the written words for the play. This is the plan that everyone reads in order to perform the play.
- **Cast of Characters:** the list of people who play a part in the story
- **Dialogue:** the words the characters say
- **Stage Directions:** the directions to the actors and stage crew. These words tell how people should move and speak. They describe the scenery—the decoration on stage.
- **Acts and Scenes:** the parts of a play. These usually change when the time or the place changes.
- **Props:** the objects used on stage in the play, such as a telephone
- **Scenery:** the background art or structures on stage to help show the setting

A Stage

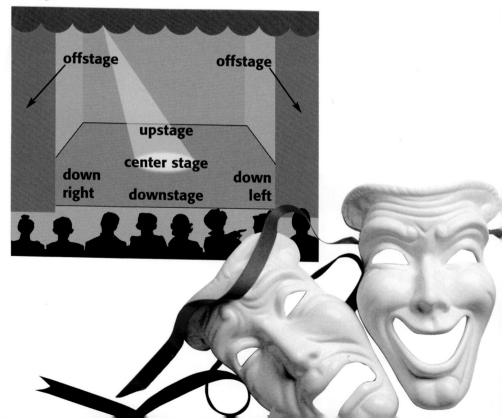

Poetry

Poetry is literature that uses a few words to tell about ideas, feelings, and images. The poet crafts the look of the poem and chooses words for their sound and meaning. Most poems are meant to be read aloud. Poems may or may not rhyme.

Some People
By Rachel Field

Isn't it strange some people make   **line**
   You feel so tired inside,   **stanza**
Your thoughts begin to shrivel up
   Like leaves all brown and dried!   **rhyming words**

But when you're with some other ones,
   It's stranger still to find
Your thoughts as thick as fireflies   **simile**
   All shiny in your mind!   **visual imagery**

Some People
By Rachel Field

Isn't it strange some people make
   You feel so tired inside,
Your thoughts begin to shrivel up
   Like leaves all brown and dried!

5   But when you're with some other ones,
     It's stranger still to find
Your thoughts as thick as fireflies
     All shiny in your mind!

Some people make you feel good and some people don't. Do you know someone who belongs in this poem?

TERMS IN POETRY

- **Form:** the way a poem looks on the page; its shape
- **Lines:** Poets arrange words into lines. The lines may or may not be sentences.
- **Stanzas:** groups of lines in traditional poetry
- **Free verse:** poems that usually do not rhyme and have no fixed rhythm or pattern. They are written like conversation.
- **Rhyme:** sounds that are alike at the end of words, such as *make* and *rake.* Some poems have rhyming words at the end of lines. Some poems have rhymes in the middle of lines too.
- **Rhythm:** the beat of the poem. Patterns of strong (´) and weak (˘) syllables make up the beat.
- **Repetition:** the repeating of sounds, words, phrases, or lines in a poem
- **Imagery:** words and phrases that appeal to the five senses—sight, hearing, smell, taste, and touch. Poets often use imagery to create pictures, tastes, or feelings in the reader's mind. For example, "The smell of sizzling bacon filled the air."
- **Figurative language:** words and phrases that help readers picture things in new ways. For example, "Snow crystals displayed a rainbow of colors in the sun."

  Simile: a comparison of two things using the words *like* or *as.* For example, "Confetti fell like rain."

  Metaphor: a comparison of two things without the words *like* or *as.* For example, "His face is a puzzle."

  Personification: a description of an animal or an object as if it were human or had human qualities. For example, "The dog smiled joyfully."

- **Speaker:** the voice that talks to the reader
- **Theme:** the message the poet gives the reader through the poem

Vocabulary Strategies

You can usually figure out a word's meaning in one of these four ways:

- by using context clues
- by analyzing the meanings of the word's parts
- by considering the meanings of related words you know
- by looking it up in the dictionary

Using Context Clues

The words and sentences surrounding an unfamiliar word often contain clues to its meaning. These are called **context clues.**

Definitions and Restatements. Often the words near an unfamiliar word define it or restate its meaning. Definitions and restatements are often signaled by the following words:

Signal Words: Definition or Restatement			
which	in other words	that is	or
this means	is, are	are called	are defined as

Punctuation marks such as commas, dashes, parentheses, or a colon may also signal this kind of context clue.

Find the definitions or restatements in the following sentences. Use them to define the words in boldface. What signals helped you know where to look?

The country's currency, or money, is similar to ours.

My brother takes sociology, which is the study of a group's beliefs and values.

The triathlon, a three-part athletic contest, is one of the most difficult events.

Examples: Writers often give examples that suggest the meanings of words.

> We may experience some turbulence, including minor bumps and sudden drops in altitude. So please keep your seatbelts fastened.

> The orchards contained a variety of citrus, including grapefruits, oranges, and lemons.

The following words often introduce examples.

Signal Words: Examples		
such as	like	for example
especially	for instance	including

Sometimes examples follow a colon or a dash instead of a word. They can come before a dash as well.

> The newspaper is known for its amazing graphics: striking photographs, colorful charts, and clean illustrations.

Comparisons and Contrasts. A **comparison clue** hints at an unfamiliar word's meaning by pointing out a similarity. In the sentences below, the comparison is signaled by *as . . . as*.

> People often say that my sister is as argumentative as a courtroom lawyer.

The comparison suggests that an argumentative person must be one who challenges or disagrees with others, like a courtroom lawyer.

A **contrast clue** suggests the meaning of an unfamiliar word by pointing out a difference.

> Ordinarily she is very stubborn, but this morning she was extremely amenable.

Since *amenable* is contrasted with *stubborn*, the words must be opposite in meaning. In other words, *amenable* must be something like "agreeable" or "cooperative."

Comparisons and contrasts are typically signaled by words and phrases such as these.

Signal Words: Comparison and Contrast			
like	similarly	but	not
likewise	in contrast to	on the other hand	unlike
as	instead of		

Cause and Effect. In a cause-and-effect relationship, one event makes another one happen. Knowing this can help you figure out an unfamiliar word.

Because she is so versatile, Maya is successful in everything she tries.

The result of being *versatile* is that Maya can do just about anything. So the word *versatile* must have something to do with the ability to do many different tasks well.

Signal Words: Cause and Effect		
because	consequently	so
since	therefore	as a result

General Context. Sometimes the general context that a word appears in provides clues to the word's meaning. Notice how the details in this passage help you understand the word *potential*.

> The Dodgers kept quiet about Roberto. They did not play him often so that scouts would not notice him and steal him away. Scouts from the Pittsburgh Pirates spotted him, though, and decided that Roberto had the potential to become a great player. They quickly signed a contract with him.
>
> — Irma Zepeda, *Roberto Clemente: Hero and Friend*

This paragraph says that Roberto did not play much. But since the Pirates quickly signed a contract with him, he must have been very talented. So *potential* must have something to do with the ability to accomplish something in the future.

Analyzing Word Parts

Sometimes you can **infer,** or figure out, the meaning of a word from the meanings of its parts. Words can have four different kinds of parts: base words, word roots, prefixes, and suffixes.

Base Words. A **base word** is a complete word that can stand alone. However, other words or word parts may be added to base words to form new words.

When two or more base words are joined to make a new word, that new word is called a **compound word.** For example, *bookend* and *searchlight* are compound words.

Prefixes and Suffixes. A **prefix** is a word part attached to the beginning of a base word or a word part. The meaning of the new word is often a combination of the meaning of the prefix and the word or word part to which it is attached. For example, the prefix *re-* means "again, back, or backward." When it is added to the word *view,* the new word, *review,* means "to examine again, look back over, or study."

Common Prefixes		
Prefix	**Meaning**	**Examples**
a-	on, in, without	aboard, ablaze, amoral
dis-	absence of, not, undo, away	dislike, disapprove, disconnect
em-, en-	in	embed, encourage
inter-	among, between	interact, interlock
over-	too much	overextended, overload
pro-	before, in place of	provision, pronoun

A **suffix** is a word part attached to the end of a base word or a word part. A suffix usually tells you the part of speech of a word. For example, by adding different suffixes to the adjective *short* you can create *shorten* (verb), *shortness* (noun), and *shortly* (adverb).

Common Suffixes

	Suffix	Meaning	Examples
Nouns	-er, -ist	doer	writer, typist
	-ation, -ment	action, process	consideration, enjoyment
	-ity, -ness, -ship, -tude	condition, quality, state	tranquility, foolishness, hardship, longitude
Verbs	-ate	to become or produce	validate
	-en	to become, to cause to have	frighten
	-ize	to cause to be	realize
Adjectives	-able, -ible	able, inclined to, worthy of	washable, sensible
	-ate	having, resembling	collegiate
Adverbs	-ly	in the manner of, like	drearily, softly

Roots. A **root** is a word part to which a prefix, a suffix, or another root must be added. Word roots cannot stand alone. Many English words contain ancient Greek and Latin roots. If you are familiar with the meaning of common roots, you can often use them to figure out the meanings of unfamiliar words.

Common Greek Roots

Root	Meaning	Examples
aster, astr	star	asterisk, astronomy
chron	time	chronicle, chronology
cycl	circle	bicycle, cyclone
dem	people	democracy, epidemic
geo	earth	geography, geology
log	speech, word	apology, monologue
physio	nature	physical, physician

Common Latin Roots		
Root	**Meaning**	**Examples**
duc, duct	lead, bring	aqueduct, conduct
fract, frag	break	fracture, fragile
ject	cast, hurl	eject, reject
mitt, miss	send, throw	emit, missile
pli	fold, bend	pliable, plier
scend	climb	ascend, descend
son	sound	sonata, unison
tract	pull, draw	distract, tractor
volv, volu, volut	roll, turn	revolution, involve

Word Families. A **word family** is a group of words that contain the same root. For example, this word family shares the Latin root *fac* or *fact*, from *facere*, meaning "to do or make."

fact   factual   factory

factor   facsimile   manufacture

artifact   benefactor   factitious

Your knowledge of word families can often help you determine the meaning of an unfamiliar word. For example here is how you can use a word family to figure out the meaning of the word *facsimile*.

Here's How	Using Word Families

- To figure out the meaning of the word *facsimile,* first look at the root: *fac, fact*

- Think of other words with the same root, such as ***factory*** and ***manufacture.***

- Figure out the meaning they share: **"to make"**

- Think about what prefixes, suffixes, or other roots add to the meaning: *Simile* is from *similis*, which means "similar."

- From these clues, you can make a guess that facsimile means **"a copy or reproduction," "something made to be similar."**

Using Reference Works

Reference tools like dictionaries and thesauruses can help you use language more accurately.

Dictionaries. **Dictionaries,** both in print and online, tell more than just the meanings of words. For example, look at the information you can learn from this entry.

brave / break	**GUIDE WORDS: FIRST AND LAST ENTRY WORDS ON THE PAGE**
brave (brāv) *adj.* **brav·er, brav·est.** Having or showing courage: *a brave defiance of danger.* —*n.* A Native American warrior. —*tr.v.* **braved, brav·ing, braves.** To undergo or face with courage: *Fire-fighters brave many dangers in the line of duty.* [First written down in 1485 in Middle English, from Old French, probably from Latin *barbarus,* like a barbarian.] **—brave'ly** *adv.* — **brave'ness** *n.*	**ENTRY WORD DIVIDED INTO SYLLABLES**
	PRONUNCIATION GUIDE
	PART OF SPEECH
	DEFINITION
Synonyms: **courageous, fearless, bold.** Antonym: **cowardly.**	**SAMPLE SENTENCE**
	ETYMOLOGY (WORD ORIGINS)
brav·er·y (brā′və rē *or* brāv′rē) *n., pl.* **brav·er·ies.** The quality or condition of being brave; courage.	**OTHER FORMS OF THE WORD**
	SYNONYMS
bra·vo (brä′vō *or* brä vō′) *interj.* An expression used to show approval, as for a musical performance. —*n., pl.* **bra·vos.** A shout or cry of "bravo."	**ANTONYM**

—adapted from *The American Heritage Student Dictionary*

Here's How Choosing the Right Definition

1. **Rule out any definitions that don't make sense.** In the sentence, "The brave began the ritual," you'd know that the definition "having courage" doesn't fit the context.

2. **Determine the word's part of speech.** In "Mountain climbers brave terrible conditions," brave is a verb, so you would choose a verb definition. In "The brave began the ritual," brave is a noun, so you would choose the noun definition.

Thesauruses. A **thesaurus** is a dictionary of **synonyms**—words that have similar meanings. Many thesaurus entries also note **antonyms**—words that have the opposite meaning—of the entry word.

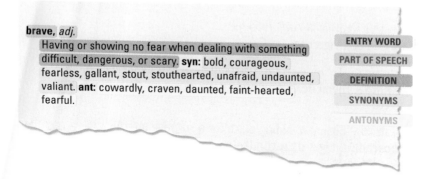

brave, *adj.*
Having or showing no fear when dealing with something difficult, dangerous, or scary. **syn:** bold, courageous, fearless, gallant, stout, stouthearted, unafraid, undaunted, valiant. **ant:** cowardly, craven, daunted, faint-hearted, fearful.

ENTRY WORD
PART OF SPEECH
DEFINITION
SYNONYMS
ANTONYMS

Not all synonyms can be substituted for each other. Some words are used only in certain ways. For example, although convey and transport have similar meanings, you wouldn't ask, "Did I transport what I meant here?"

Synonym Finders. A **synonym finder** is a tool that's often in word-processing software. It enables you to display synonyms for a highlighted word—but does not tell you as much as a thesaurus does.

Glossaries. A **glossary** is a list of specialized terms and their definitions. Many books, especially textbooks and nonfiction books, contain glossaries—usually at the back of the book.

A

advancing (ăd văn' sĭng) *v.* moving forward
avanzando *v.* adelantando

affliction (ə flĭk' shən) *n.* cause of pain
aflicción *s.* causa de dolor o pena

aggressive (ə grĕs' ĭv) *adj.* forceful
enérgico *adj.* vigoroso

aluminum (ə lōō' mə nəm) *n.* silvery, lightweight metallic element
aluminio *s.* metal de color y brillo parecidos a los de la plata, muy ligero

ambush (ăm' bōōsh) *n.* hiding place for a surprise attack
emboscada *s.* lugar de escondite para un ataque sorpresivo

anchors (ăng' kərz) *n.* heavy weights attached to a connecting rope that are used to keep ships in place
anclas *s.* pesas de hierro con ganchos que se atan a una cuerda para aferrar los barcos al fondo del mar

annoyed (ə noid') *adj.* bothered
fastidiado *adj.* molestado

anxiously (ăngk' shəs lē) *adv.* nervously
ansiosamente *adv.* de modo nervioso

apprentice (ə prĕn' tĭs) *n.* one who is learning a job
aprendiz *s.* alguien que está aprendiendo un oficio o trabajo

approve (ə prōōv') *v.* think to be right or good
aprobar *v.* considerar que algo es correcto o bien

astonishment (ə stŏn' ĭsh mənt) *n.* amazement
asombro *s.* sorpresa

audition (ô dĭsh' ən) *n.* performance to show a skill
audición *s.* actuación para demostrar una destreza

authorities (ə thôr' ĭ tēz) *n.* persons who have power
autoridades *s.* personas que tienen el poder

B

barbarians (bär bâr' ē ənz) *n.* brutal people
bárbaros *s.* personas fieras y crueles

barrels (băr' əlz) *n.* large, round containers, usually made of wood
barriles *s.* grandes recipientes redondos, por lo común hechos de madera

bizarre (bĭ zär') *adj.* strange
raro *adj.* extraño

boisterous (boi' stər əs) *adj.* active and noisy
estrepitoso *adj.* alborotado y ruidoso

bristled (brĭs' əld) *v.* stiffened; past tense of *bristle*
erizó *v.* se puso de punta; pasado de *bristle/erizar*

brutal (brōot' l) *adj.* extremely rough
brutal *adj.* extremadamente tosco; cruel

buckles (bŭk' əlz) *v.* crumples
se desploma *v.* cae

bugles (byōo' gəlz) *n.* horns that are shorter than a trumpet
corneta *n.* instrumento musical mas corto que una trompeta

bundled (bŭn' dld) *adj.* wrapped up
arropado *adj.* envuelto

C

captive (kăp' tĭv) *n.* prisoner
cautivo *s.* prisionero

cautious (kô' shəs) *adj.* very careful
cauto *adj.* muy cuidadoso

cinders (sĭn' dərz) *n.* ashes
carbonillas *s.* cenizas

circulation (sûr' kyə lā' shən) *n.* the flow of blood through veins
circulación *s.* flujo de sangre a través de las venas

clearing (klîr' ĭng) *n.* land from which trees have been removed
claro *s.* terreno al que se le han quitado los árboles

coarse (kôrs) *adj.* rough
burdo *adj.* tosco; áspero

coiled (koild) *adj.* wound into a series of rings
enroscado *adj.* enrollado

colonel (kûr' nəl) *n.* a military officer
coronel *s.* oficial militar

compassion (kəm păsh' ən) *n.* concern for the suffering of others
compasión *s.* preocupación por el sufrimiento de otros

compliment (kŏm' plə mənt) *n.* words of praise
halago *s.* palabras de elogio

comrades (kom' rădz') *n.* persons sharing an activity
camaradas *s.* personas que hacen una misma cosa

content (kən tĕnt') *adj.* satisfied
complacido *adj.* satisfecho

continent (kŏn' tə nənt) *n.* one of the seven large land areas on the earth
continente *s.* una de las siete grandes extensiones terrestres de la Tierra

contraption (kən trăp' shən) *n.* mechanical device
artefacto *s.* aparato mecánico

council (koun' səl) *n.* body of people elected to plan, discuss, or give advice
concilio *s.* quienes son elejidos para planear, discutir, o dar consejo

course (kôrs) *n.* route
curso *s.* ruta

coyotes (kī ō' tēz) *n.* small animals that are similar to wolves
coyotes *s.* pequeños animales que son parecidos a lobos

craft (krăft) *n.* ship
nave *s.* barco

cringe (krĭnj) *v.* shrink back, as in fear
menguarse *v.* encogerse, como de miedo

culture (kŭl' chər) *n.* the ideas, customs, and skills shared by a certain people
cultura *s.* ideas, costumbres y destrezas compartidas por un pueblo

cunning (kŭn' ĭng) *n.* skill in fooling others
artimaña *s.* habilidad para engañar

custom (kŭs' təm) *n.* something done regularly by a group
costumbre *s.* algo hecho con regularidad por un grupo de personas

D

dainty (dān' tē) *adj.* beautiful in a delicate way
exquisito *adj.* que tiene una gran belleza y delicadeza

daring (dâr' ĭng) *n.* boldness
arrojo *s.* atrevimiento

deceitful (dĭ sēt' fəl) *adj.* full of lies
engañoso *adj.* falso o lleno de mentiras

deck (dĕk) *n.* main level of the outside of a ship
cubierta *s.* nivel principal de la parte exterior de un barco

defy (dĭ fī') *v.* resist with boldness
desafiar *v.* atreverse; resistirse

descended (dĭ sĕn' dĭd) *v.* moved from a higher to a lower place; past tense of *descend*
descendió *v.* se rebajó a; pasado de *descend/descender*

determine (dĭ tûr' mĭn) *v.* decide
determinar *v.* decidir

determined (dĭ tûr' mĭnd) *adj.* not willing to change one's mind
resuelto *adj.* decidido firmemente

devastated (dĕv' ə stā' tĭd) *v.* destroyed; past tense of *devastate*
desoló *v.* destruyó; pasado de *devastate/desolar*

disgusted (dĭs gŭs' tĭd) *adj.* irritated and impatient
disgustado *adj.* fastidiado e impaciente

disputes (dĭ spyōōts') *n.* arguments
disputas *s.* discusiones

distracted (dĭ străk' tĭd) *adj.* not paying attention
distraído *adj.* no poniendo atencíon

distress (dĭ strĕs') *n.* suffering
angustia *s.* sufrimiento o dolor

document (dŏk' yə mənt) *n.* official report
documento *s.* informe o escrito oficial

drifted (drĭf' tĭd) *v.* wandered; past tense of *drift*
deambuló *v.* vagó; pasado de *drift/deambular*

E

elegant (ĕl' ĭ gənt) *adj.* classy
elegante *adj.* refinado

emerged (ĭ mûrjd') *v.* came into view; past tense of *emerge*
emergió *v.* salió a la vista; pasado de *emerge/emerger*

employee (ĕm ploi' ē) *n.* person who works for pay
empleado *s.* alguien que recibe un pago por su trabajo

encouraged (ĕn kûr' ĭjd) *adj.* given a sense of hope
alentado *adj.* estimulado

entangled (ĕn tăng' gəld) *adj.* twisted together
embrollado *adj.* enredado

erupt (ĭ rŭpt') *v.* explode
hacer erupción *v.* explotar

essential (ĭ sĕn' shəl) *adj.* necessary
esencial *adj.* muy necesario

exhibited (ĭg zĭb' ĭ tĭd) *v.* presented for others to see; past tense of *exhibit*
exhibió *v.* presentó para que otros vean; pasado de *exhibit/exhibir*

F

fashioned (făsh' ənd) *v.* shaped or formed; past tense of *fashion*
moldeó *v.* formó o labró; pasado de *fashion/moldear*

fasts (făsts) *n.* periods of time without food
ayunos *s.* períodos de tiempo sin comer ningún alimento

fatal (fāt' l) *adj.* deadly
fatal *adj.* mortal

feuds (fyo͞odz) *n.* bitter fights
  enemistades *s.* luchas prolongadas

G

gladiators (glăd′ ē ā′ tərz) *n.* men who fought each other as a public
  show
  gladiadores *s.* hombres que luchan entre sí en un espectáculo público

glaring (glâr′ ĭng) *adj.* staring in anger
  iracundo *adj.* que mira con rabia

H

handicaps (hăn′ dē kăps′) *n.* physical disabilities
  discapacidades *s.* impedimentos físicos

harbor (här′ bər) *n.* area of shelter where ships may anchor
  puerto *s.* lugar donde anclan los barcos

heir (âr) *n.* one who gets a person's money or title after the person dies
  heredero *s.* alguien que recibe dinero o títulos después de la muerte
  de otra persona

hilarity (hĭ lăr′ ĭ tē) *n.* fun and laughter
  hilaridad *s.* risa y animación

horizon (hə rī′ zən) *n.* line where the earth seems to meet the sky
  horizonte *s.* línea donde la tierra parece unirse con el cielo

huddled (hŭd′ ld) *v.* crowded together; past tense of *huddle*
  se acurrucó *v.* se apiñó; pasado de *huddle/acurrucarse*

I

idiotic (ĭd′ ē ŏt′ ĭk) *adj.* stupid
  idiota *adj.* estupidez o torpeza

imbecile (ĭm′ bə sĭl) *n.* silly or stupid person
  imbécil *s.* persona tonta o estúpida

impostor (ĭm pŏs′ tər) *n.* person who pretends to be someone else
  impostor *s.* persona que se hace pasar por otra

inherit (ĭn hĕr' ĭt) *v.* receive from one who has died
heredar *v.* recibir de alguien que ha muerto

instinctively (ĭn stĭngk' tĭv lē) *adj.* by natural action; without thinking
instintivamente *adj.* de una manera que es natural o espontánea

J

jealousy (jĕl' ə sē) *n.* fear of losing one's love to another person
celos *s.* temor a perder el amor de una persona a otra

M

menacingly (mĕn' ĭ sĭng lē) *adv.* in a threatening way
amenazantemente *adv.* de un modo que amenaza o desafía

mimicking (mĭm' ĭ kĭng) *n.* imitating
parodia *s.* imitación

mission (mĭsh' ən) *n.* special duty
misión *s.* deber o tarea especial

mortal (môr' tl) *adj.* extreme, almost threatening death
mortal *adj.* ser casi fatal o de muerte

motto (mŏt' ō) *n.* sentence that expresses the group's goals
lema *s.* oración que expresa las metas de un grupo

N

nausea (nô' zē ə) *n.* sick feeling in the stomach
náusea *s.* sensación de malestar en el estómago

navigator (năv' ĭ gā' tər) *n.* one who tells a pilot where to go
navegante *s.* quien le indica a un piloto en qué dirección ir

nonviolent (nŏn vī' ə lənt) *adj.* not using force as a way of getting results
sin violencia *adj.* no emplear la fuerza como medio para obtener resultados

novice (nŏv' ĭs) *n.* beginner
novato *s.* principiante

O

occurrence (ə kûr′ əns) *n.* event
occurrencia *s.* suceso

offended (ə fĕn′ dĭd) *v.* hurt; past tense of *offend*
ofendió *v.* lastimó; pasedo de *offend/ofender*

ominously (ŏm′ ə nəs lē) *adv.* in a threatening way
ominosamente *adv.* de modo amenazante

oppress (ə prĕs′) *v.* rule harshly
oprimir *v.* gobernar con tiranía

P

paralysis (pə răl′ ĭ sĭs) *n.* the loss of the power to move or feel
parálisis *s.* pérdida de la facultad para moverse o sentir

passes (păs′ ĭz) *n.* ways around, over, or through mountains
desfiladeros *s.* pasos estrechos entre montañas

plains (plānz) *n.* large, treeless area of land
planicies *s.* terreno extenso sin árboles

plantation (plăn tā′ shən) *n.* large farm in the South where workers raised crops
plantación *s.* granja grande del Sur donde los trabajadores sembraban

potential (pə tĕn′ shəl) *n.* ability
potencial *s.* habilidad

precisely (prĭ sīs′ lē) *adv.* exactly
precisamente *adv.* exactamente

prejudice (prĕj′ ə dĭs) *n.* unfair treatment, usually based on race or religion
prejuicio *s.* trato injusto por logeneral basado en raza o religión

procedure (prə sē′ jər) *n.* way of doing something
procedimiento *s.* forma de hacer algo

profile (prō′ fīl′) *n.* side view of a face
perfil *s.* vista lateral de un rostro

prospects (prŏs' pĕkts') *n.* people with possibilities
  candidatos *s.* personas con buenas posibilidades

Q

quills (kwĭlz) *n.* sharp, hollow spines, like pointed needles
  púas *s.* puntas agudas

R

radioactive (rā' dē ō ăk' tĭv) *adj.* containing particles of radiation
  radioactivo *adj.* que contiene partículas de radiación

rails (rālz) *n.* two steel bars that form train tracks
  rieles *s.* dos barras de acero que forman la carrilera del tren

reassuringly (rē' ə shŏŏr' ĭng lē) *adv.* in a way that makes one trust
  alentadoramente *adv.* de un modo que brinda confianza o tranquilidad

reins (rānz) *n.* straps used to control a horse
  riendas *s.* correas que se usan para controlar a un caballo

rejection (rĭ jĕk' shən) *n.* act of being refused
  repudio *s.* rechazo

reluctantly (rĭ lŭk' tənt lē) *adv.* unwillingly
  a regañadientes *adv.* de mala gana

required (rĭ kwīrd') *adj.* needed
  requerido *adj.* necesario

retreat (rĭ trēt') *v.* withdraw from attack
  replegarse *v.* retirarse de un ataque

revived (rĭ vīvd') *v.* refreshed; past tense of *revive*
  reavivó *v.* reanimó; pasado de *revive/reavivar*

routine (rōō tēn') *adj.* regular
  rutinario *adj.* regular

rumor (rōō' mər) *n.* unproved information spread by word of mouth
  rumor *s.* información no comprobada que va de boca en boca

S

sacred (sā′ krĭd) *adj.* holy
sagrado *adj.* bendito o divino

satellites (săt′ l īts′) *n.* man-made objects that orbit the earth
satétiles *s.* objetos lanzados para girar alrededor de la Tierra

savage (săv′ ĭj) *adj.* fiercely wild
salvaje *adj.* feroz

savage (săv′ ĭj) *n.* fierce, brutal person
salvaje *s.* persona feroz y brutal

scrolls (skrōlz) *n.* rolls of paper, usually with writing on them
volutas *s.* rollos de papel, por lo común con algo escrito

secondhand (sĕk′ ənd hănd′) *adj.* used; not new
de segunda mano *adj.* usado; que no es nuevo

secure (sĭ kyŏŏr′) *adj.* free from danger
salvo *adj.* libre de peligro

seized (sēzd) *v.* captured by force; past tense of *seize*
capturó *v.* tomó a la fuerza; pasado de *seize/capturar*

self-conscious (sĕlf′ kŏn′ shəs) *adj.* very aware of one's own actions and appearance
cohibido *adj.* que se refrena por temor a lo que otros piensen de sus acciones o apariencia

settlement (sĕt′ l mənt) *n.* small community
poblado *s.* pequeña comunidad

shimmering (shĭm′ ər ĭng) *adj.* shining with a flickering light
resplandeciente *adj.* que brilla tenuemente

spindly (spĭnd′ lē) *adj.* slender and long
larguirucho *adj.* alto y delgado

sprawled (sprôld) *v.* spread out; past tense of *sprawl*
se desparramó *v.* se extendió; pasado de *sprawl/desparramarse*

spunky (spŭng′ kē) *adj.* having spirit or courage
valeroso *adj.* que tiene ánimo o valor

stallion (stăl′ yən) *n.* adult male horse
semental *s.* caballo reproductor

stipulated (stĭp′ yə lā′ tĭd) *v.* ordered; past tense of *stipulate*
  estipuló *v.* ordenó; pasado de *stipulate/estipular*

submitted (səb mĭt′ ĭd) *v.* presented for approval; past tense of *submit*
  presentó *v.* entregó para aprobacion; pasado de *submit/presentar*

suspiciously (sə spĭsh′ əs lē) *adv.* without trust
  suspicazmente *adv.* sin confianza; con dudas

swirling (swûr′ lĭng) *v.* moving with a twisting motion
  revoleando *v.* dando vueltas; girando

synagogues (sĭn′ ə gŏgz′) *n.* places of worship for Jews
  sinagogas *s.* lugares de oración para los judíos

system (sĭs′ təm) *n.* set way of doing things
  sistema *s.* conjunto de métodos para hacer alguna cosa

T

tactics (tăk′ tĭks) *n.* methods used to get results
  tácticas *s.* métodos utilizados para obtener resultados

terrapin (tĕr′ ə pĭn) *n.* turtle
  terrapene *s.* tortuga

timber (tĭm′ bər) *n.* tree
  maderamen *s.* tronco de árbol

tolerant (tŏl′ ər ənt) *adj.* respectful of the beliefs or customs of others
  tolerante *adj.* respetuoso de las creencias o costumbres de otros

tomahawks (tŏm′ ə hôks′) *n.* lightweight axes used as tools or weapons
  tomahawks *s.* hachas livianas utilizadas como herramienta o armas
    de guerra

topple (tŏp′ əl) *v.* push over
  volcar *v.* caer

torpedo (tôr pē′ dō) *n.* cigar-shaped weapon that can explode
  torpedo *s.* arma con forma de cigarro que puede explotar

torture (tôr′ chər) *n.* the causing of physical pain as punishment
  tortura *s.* dolor físico como forma de castigo

turnover (tûrn′ ō′ vər) *n.* fruit-filled pastry
  tarta *s.* pastelito relleno de fruta

U

uninhabited (ŭn′ ĭn hăb′ ĭ tĭd) *adj.* without people
  deshabitado *adj.* sin habitantes

union (yōōn′ yən) *n.* organized group of workers
  sindicato *s.* grupo organizado de trabajadores

V

vessel (vĕs′ əl) *n.* boat
  embarcación *s.* barco

veterans (vĕt′ ər ənz) *n.* soldiers with long experience
  veteranos *s.* soldados con mucha experiencia

vulture (vŭl′ chər) *n.* bird that eats dead things
  buitre *s.* ave que se alimenta de cosas muertas

W

willful (wĭl′ fəl) *adj.* always wanting to get one's own way
  voluntarioso *adj.* que quiere que las cosas siempre se hagan a su manera

wistful (wĭst′ fəl) *adj.* dreamy
  melancólico *adj.* soñador

wits (wĭts) *n.* ability to think fast
  agudeza *s.* habilidad para pensar rápidamente

Index of Authors and Titles

Acknowledgments

Literature

UNIT ONE

HarperCollins Publishers: *Cinder Edna* by Ellen Jackson, illustrated by Kevin O'Malley. Text copyright © 1994 by Ellen Jackson. Illustrations copyright © 1994 by Kevin O'Malley. Used by permission of HarperCollins Publishers.

Harcourt: "The No-Guitar Blues," from *Baseball in April and Other Stories* by Gary Soto. Copyright © 1990 by Gary Soto. Reprinted by permission of Harcourt, Inc.

UNIT TWO

Alfred A. Knopf Children's Books: "A Slave," from *Many Thousand Gone* by Virginia Hamilton. Copyright © 1993 by Virginia Hamilton. Reprinted by permission of Alfred A. Knopf Children's Books, a division of Random House, Inc.

Carolrhoda Books: *Wilma Mankiller* by Linda Lowery. Published by Carolrhoda Books, Inc., a division of the Lerner Publishing Group. Text copyright © 1996 by Linda Lowery. Used by permission of the publisher. All rights reserved.

J. Weston Walch, Publisher: "Cesar Chavez: Civil Rights Champion," from *16 Extraordinary Hispanic Americans* by Nancy Lobb. Copyright © 1995 by J. Weston Walch, Publisher. Used with permission of J. Weston Walch, Publisher. Further reproduction prohibited.

UNIT THREE

Viking Penguin: "Trombones and Colleges," from *Fast Sam, Cool Clyde, and Stuff* by Walter Dean Myers. Copyright © 1975 by Walter Dean Myers. Used by permission of Viking Penguin, an imprint of Penguin Books for Young Readers, a division of Penguin Group (USA) Inc.

Chronicle Books: "In a Neighborhood in Los Angeles," from *Body in Flames/Cuerpo en Llamas* by Francisco X. Alarcón. Copyright © 1990 by Francisco X. Alarcón. Reprinted by permission of Chronicle Books.

Marshall Cavendish: "Mudslinging," from *Mud Matters* by Jennifer Owings Dewey. Copyright © 1998 by Jennifer Owings Dewey. Reprinted by arrangement with Marshall Cavendish.

Jesse Stuart Foundation and Marian Reiner, Literary Agent: "Another April," from *Tales from the Plum Grove Hills* by Jesse Stuart. Copyright © 1942, 1946 by Jesse Stuart, copyright renewed by Jesse Stuart and the Jesse Stuart Foundation. Used by permission of the Jesse Stuart Foundation and Marian Reiner, Literary Agent.

Random House: "On Aging," from *And Still I Rise* by Maya Angelou. Copyright © 1978 by Maya Angelou. Reprinted by permission of Random House, Inc.

UNIT FOUR

Marjorie Murray: "The Telephone," from *The Haunting of Hathaway House* by John Murray. Reprinted by permission of Marjorie Murray.

Plays Magazine: "The Prince and the Pauper" by Mark Twain, adapted by Joellen Bland, *Plays* Magazine, April 2000, Vol. 59, No. 6. Copyright © 2000 Kalmbach Publishing Co. Reprinted by permission of Plays Magazine.

UNIT FIVE

Henry Holt and Company: "Dust of Snow" by Robert Frost, from *The Poetry of Robert Frost*, edited by Edward Connery Lathem. Copyright 1923, © 1969 by Henry Holt and Co., copyright 1951 by Robert Frost. Reprinted by permission of Henry Holt and Company, L.L.C.

Curtis Brown, Ltd.: "Elevator" by Lucille Clifton. Appears in *Home: A Collaboration of Thirty Distinguished Authors and Illustrators of Children's Books to Aid the Homeless*, edited by Michael Rosen. Published by HarperTrophy, a division of HarperCollins. Copyright © 1992 by Lucille Clifton. Reprinted by permission of Curtis Brown, Ltd.

"Graffiti" by Jane Yolen, published in *Sky Scrape/City Scape: Poems of City Life*, selected by Jane Yolen. Published by Wordsong/Boyds Mills Press. Copyright © 1996 by Jane Yolen. Reprinted by permission of Curtis Brown, Ltd.

HarperCollins Publishers: Excerpts from "Haiku" by Issa from *The Essential Haiku: Versions of Basho, Buson & Issa*, edited and with an introduction by Robert Hass. Introduction and selection copyright © 1994 by Robert Hass. Unless otherwise noted, all translations copyright © 1994 by Robert Hass. Reprinted by permission of HarperCollins Publishers, Inc.

Jesús Papoleto Meléndez: "Happy Thought," from *Street Poetry & Other Poems* by Jesús Papoleto Meléndez. Copyright © 1972 by Jesús Papoleto Meléndez. Reprinted by permission of the author.

Alfred A. Knopf: "Daybreak in Alabama," from *The Collected Poems of Langston Hughes.* Copyright © 1994 by the Estate of Langston Hughes. Reprinted by permission of Alfred A. Knopf, a division of Random House, Inc.

UNIT SIX

Dutton Children's Books: "High as Han Hsin," from *Shen of the Sea: Chinese Stories for Children* by Arthur Bowie Chrisman. Copyright © 1925 by E. P. Dutton, copyright renewed 1953 by Arthur Bowie Chrisman. Used by permission of Dutton Children's Books, a division of Penguin Group(USA) Inc.

Simon & Schuster Books for Young Readers: "For Want of a Horseshoe Nail," from *The Book of Virtues for Young People: A Treasury of Great Moral Stories,* edited by William J. Bennett. Copyright © 1997 by William J. Bennett. Reprinted with the permission of Simon & Schuster Books for Young Readers, an imprint of Simon & Schuster Children's Publishing Division.

"Crash Diet," from *It's Disgusting–And We Ate It!* by James Solheim. Text copyright © 1998 by James Solheim. Reprinted with the permission of Simon & Schuster Books for Young Readers, an imprint of Simon & Schuster Children's Publishing Division.

Browne & Miller Literary Associates: "Shot Down Behind Enemy Lines," from *Incredible True Adventures* by Don L. Wulffson. Copyright © 1986 by Don L. Wulffson. Reprinted by permission of Browne & Miller Literary Associates, LLC Chicago, Illinois.

Hyperion Books for Children: *Fa Mulan: The Story of a Woman Warrior* by Robert D. San Souci. Copyright © 1998 by Robert D. San Souci. Reprinted by permission of Hyperion Books for Children, an import of Disney Book Group, LLC.

UNIT SEVEN

Hugh B. Cave: "Two Were Left" by Hugh B. Cave. Copyright © 1942 by the Crowell Collier Publishing Co. Reprinted by permission of the author.

The Jewish Publication Society: *Terrible Things: An Allegory of the Holocaust* by Eve Bunting (Philadelphia: The Jewish Publication Society, 1989). Copyright © 1980, 1989 by Eve Bunting. Reprinted by permission of The Jewish Publication Society.

Scholastic: "Speech" by Parson Martin Niemöller, from *Bearing Witness: Stories of the Holocaust,* selected by Hazel Rochman and Darlene Z. McCampbell. Copyright © 1995 by Hazel Rochman and Darlene Z. McCampbell. Reprinted by permission of Scholastic Inc.

UNIT EIGHT

Curtis Brown, Ltd.: "Ships That Could Think," from *Great Mysteries of the Sea* by Edward F. Dolan, Jr. Copyright © 1984 by Edward F. Dolan, Jr. Reprinted by permission of Curtis Brown, Ltd.

HarperCollins Publishers: Excerpt from *Earthquakes* by Franklyn M. Branley. Text copyright © 1990 by Franklyn M. Branley. Used by permission of HarperCollins Publishers.

Diana Nightingale: "Sparky," from *Earl Nightingale's Greatest Discovery* by Earl Nightingale. Copyright © 1987 by Earl C. Nightingale. Reprinted by permission of Diana Nightingale.

Penguin Group (UK): "The Roswell Incident," from *Invaders from Outer Space: Real-Life Stories of UFOs* by Philip Brooks. Text Copyright © 1999 by Philip Brooks. Copyright ©1999 by Dorling Kindersley Limited, London. Reprinted by permission of of Penguin Group (UK).

UNIT NINE

Curtis Brown, Ltd., and H. W. Wilson Company: "The Jade Stone" by Caryn Yacowitz, published by Holiday House. Adapted by Aaron Shepard, pp. 27–33, in *Stories on Stage: Scripts for Reader's Theater.* Copyright © 1992 by Caryn Yacowitz. Copyright © 1993 by Aaron Shepard. Reprinted by permission of Curtis Brown, Ltd. and the H. W. Wilson Company.

BOA Editions: "The Carver," from *Good Woman: Poems and a Memoir,* 1969–1980 by Lucille Clifton. Copyright © 1986 by Lucille Clifton. Reprinted with the permission of BOA Editions, Ltd.

Westwood Creative Artists: "The Stolen Party" by Liliana Heker, which appeared in *Other Fires: Short Fiction by Latin American Women,* edited and translated by Alberto Manguel. Copyright © 1982 by Liliana Heker. Translation copyright © 1985 by Alberto Manguel. Reprinted by permission of Westwood Creative Artists Ltd.

Blackbirch Press: "Acceptance," from *Jane Goodall: Naturalist* by J. A. Senn. Copyright © 1993 by Blackbirch Press, Inc. Reprinted by permission.

12 Photo by Sharon Hoogstraten; **14** Illustrations copyright © 1994 by Kevin O'Malley. Used with permission of HarperCollins Children's Books; **17** Illustrations copyright © 1994 by Kevin O'Malley. Used with permission of HarperCollins Children's Books; **20** Illustrations copyright © 1994 by Kevin O'Malley. Used with permission of HarperCollins Children's Books; **24** Illustrations copyright © 1994 by Kevin O'Malley. Used with permission of HarperCollins Children's Books; **26** Copyright © Yann Arthus-Bertrand/Corbis; 27 Myrleen Ferguson Cate/PhotoEdit; **29** Copyright © Stockbyte; **30** Copyright © Yann Arthus-Bertrand/Corbis; **33** Copyright © Stockbyte; **36** Photo by Barbara Seiler.

UNIT TWO

39 Copyright © Form and Function, San Francisco; **39** Copyright © Bettmann/Corbis; **40** *Into Bondage* (1936) Aaron Douglas. Oil on canvas 60 3/8" x 60 1/2". In the collection of the Corcoran Gallery of Art, Washington, DC. Museum Purchase and partial gift from Thurlow Evans Tibbs. The Evans-Tibbs Collection; **41, 43, 44, 47** detail of *Into Bondage* (1936) Aaron Douglas. Oil on canvas 60 3/8" x 60 1/2". In the collection of the Corcoran Gallery of Art, Washington, DC. Museum Purchase and partial gift from Thurlow Evans Tibbs. The Evans-Tibbs Collection; **48** Copyright © Peter Turnley/Corbis; **48** Copyright © Bettmann/Corbis; **49** Copyright © Charles Doswell III /Getty Images; **50** Copyright © Corbis; **51** Copyright © Charles Doswell III/Getty Images; **57** Copyright © Kevin Fleming/Corbis; **58** Copyright © J. Pat Carter/Liaison Agency; **60-61** Copyright © Time Life Pictures/Getty Images; **61** Copyright © Stockbyte; **65** Copyright © Associated Press; **65** AP/Wide World Photos; **68** Copyright © Bettmann/Corbis; **69** Digital Imagery copyright © 2001 PhotoDisc, Inc.; **69** AP/Wide World Photos; **72** Digital Imagery copyright © 2001 PhotoDisc, Inc.; **73** AP/Wide World Photos; **74** Copyright © Bettmann/Corbis; **77** Digital Imagery copyright © 2001 PhotoDisc, Inc.

UNIT THREE

79 Photo by Suzanne Page; **79** Copyright © Stephen Trimble; **80** Copyright © Daemmrich Photography, Inc.; **84** Digital Imagery copyright © 2001 PhotoDisc, Inc.; **88** Digital Imagery copyright © 2001 PhotoDisc, Inc.; **90** Digital Imagery copyright © 2001 PhotoDisc, Inc.; **93** Digital Imagery copyright © 2001 PhotoDisc, Inc.; **93** Copyright © Bill Bachmann; **94** Photo by Suzanne Page; **94** Photo by Suzanne Page; **94** Photo by Suzanne Page; **94** Copyright © Stephen Trimble; **97** Photo by Suzanne Page; **98** Photo by Sharon Hoogstraten; **98** Copyright © Joel Dexter/Unicorn Stock Photos; **98** Copyright © Pat O'Hara/Corbis; **98–99** Digital Imagery copyright © 2001 PhotoDisc, Inc.; **99** Copyright © Joe McDonald/Animals Animals; **100** Photo by Sharon Hoogstraten; **103** Digital Imagery copyright © 2001 PhotoDisc, Inc.; **105** Copyright © Pat O'Hara/Corbis; **105** Photo by Sharon Hoogstraten; **108** Copyright © Joe McDonald/Animals Animals; **113** Photo by Sharon Hoogstraten.

UNIT FOUR

116 Copyright © Storm Pirate Productions/Artville/PictureQuest; **116, 118, 120, 121, 122, 123, 124, 125, 127** Photo by Sharon Hoogstraten; **129, 131** Photofest; **131** Digital Imagery copyright © 2001 PhotoDisc, Inc.; **134** Photofest; **139** Giraudon/Art Resource, New York; **145** Photofest; **146** Photofest.

UNIT FIVE

159 Copyright © Aiuppy Photographs; 159 Photo by Sharon Hoogstraten; 160 Copyright © Form and Function, San Francisco; 161 Copyright © Jupiter Images; 162 Copyright © Michael Newman/PhotoEdit; 164 Art by Ingrid Hess. Photo by Sharon Hoogstraten; 164 Photo by Sharon Hoogstraten; 166 Copyright © Caroline Wood/Getty Images; 166 Digital Imagery copyright © 2001 PhotoDisc, Inc.; 168 Copyright © Ron Chapple/Taxi/Getty Images; 168 Digital Imagery copyright © 2001 PhotoDisc, Inc.; 168 Photo by Sharon Hoogstraten; 170 Copyright © Aiuppy Photographs; 171 Photo by Sharon Hoogstraten; 172, 173 Copyright © Aiuppy Photographs.

UNIT SIX

175 Copyright © David Young-Wolff/PhotoEdit; **175** Copyright © Kit Houghton Photography/Corbis; **175** AP/Wide World Photos; **176** Digital Imagery copyright © 2001 PhotoDisc, Inc.; **177** from *Fun with Kites* by John and Kate Dyson. Published by Angus & Robertson, a division of HarperCollins UK. Illustration copyright © Brian Robins; **178** Copyright © Burke & Triolo/ Artville/PictureQuest; **180** Copyright © Keren Su/Corbis; **184** Copyright © Stockbyte; **190** Copyright © Form and Function, San Francisco; **190** © Private Collection/The Bridgeman Art Library; **191** Copyright © Kit Houghton Photography/Corbis; **191** Copyright © Kit Houghton Photography/Corbis; **191** Copyright © Kit Houghton Photography/Corbis; **192** Digital Imagery copyright © 2001 PhotoDisc, Inc.; **193** Copyright © Gianni Dagli Orti/Corbis; **194** AP/Wide World Photos; **197** © Hulton Archive/Getty Images; **203** AP/Wide World Photos; **204** *background* Copyright © David Young-Wolff/PhotoEdit; **204** *Woman Sewing* (ca. 1790) Chinese. Watercolor. Victoria & Albert Museum, London/Art Resource, New York; **204–205** Copyright © The Board of Trustees of the Armouries; **207** Copyright © The Board of Trustees of the Armouries; **208** *Archer on Horse* (1290), Ch'ien Hsuan. Ink and color on paper. British Museum, London; **211** Copyright © David Young-Wolff/PhotoEdit.

UNIT SEVEN

213 Copyright © Vince Streano/Getty Images; **216** Digital Imagery copyright © 2001 PhotoDisc, Inc.; **217** Copyright © Ken Cole/Animals Animals; **217** Copyright © Vince Streano/Getty Images; **220** Illustration by Ingrid Hess; **220** Copyright © Prisma/ Superstock; **230** Copyright © 1979 by Dover Publications, Inc.; **232** bottom Digital Imagery copyright © 2001 PhotoDisc, Inc.; **232** left Copyright © Form and Function, San Francisco; **232** top Digital Imagery copyright © 2001 PhotoDisc, Inc.; **233** Digital Imagery copyright © 2001 PhotoDisc, Inc.; **237** Copyright © Jeff L. Lepore/Photo Researchers, Inc.

UNIT EIGHT

244 Illustration by Gordon Grant; **244–245** background Digital Imagery copyright © 2001 PhotoDisc, Inc.; **245** Digital Imagery copyright © 2001 PhotoDisc, Inc.; **249** Digital Imagery copyright © 2001 PhotoDisc, Inc.; **252** R.E. Wallace 34ct/ U.S.G.S. Photo Library, Denver, CO; **253** Copyright © Science VU/Visuals Unlimited; **253** Copyright © Lynette Cook/Science Photo Library/Photo Researchers, Inc.; **253** Copyright © Galen Rowell/Corbis; **254** Copyright © Science VU/Visuals Unlimited; **255** Copyright © Lynette Cook/Science Photo Library/Photo Researchers, Inc.; **256** R.E. Wallace 34ct/ U.S.G.S. Photo Library, Denver CO; **258** Copyright © Galen Rowell/Corbis; **260** Digital Imagery copyright © 2001 PhotoDisc, Inc.; 260 Digital Imagery copyright © 2001 PhotoDisc, Inc.; **262** © Hulton Archive/Getty Images; **264** Copyright © Tom Bean/Corbis; **267** Copyright © Roswell Daily Record.

UNIT NINE

269 Digital Imagery copyright © 2001 PhotoDisc, Inc.; **269** Copyright © Michael Freeman/Corbis; **270** foreground Christie's Images/ Superstock; **270, 271** background Copyright © Michael Freeman/Corbis; **273** Christie's Images/ Superstock; **273** Christie's Images/ Superstock; **274** Copyright © Vivid Details; **282** I Told Them Not To Give Me a Doll by Sonya Fe. © Sonya Fe; **282** Digital Imagery copyright © 2001 PhotoDisc, Inc.; **286, 290** Detail of I Told Them Not To Give Me a Doll by Sonya Fe. © Sonya Fe; **294** Digital Imagery copyright © 2001 PhotoDisc, Inc.; **294** Copyright © Michael Neugebauer; **294** Digital Imagery copyright © 2001 PhotoDisc, Inc.; **295** Copyright © Michael Neugebauer; **299** Copyright © Michael Neugebauer; **300** Copyright © Michael Neugebauer; **303** Copyright © George Holton/ Photo Researchers, Inc.; **304** Digital Imagery copyright © 2001 PhotoDisc, Inc.; **304** Copyright © Hulton Archive/Getty Images; **304** Copyright © Hulton Archive/Getty Images; **305** Digital Imagery copyright © 2001 PhotoDisc, Inc.; **307** Copyright © Corbis; **308** Digital Imagery copyright © 2001 PhotoDisc, Inc.; **312** Copyright © Hulton Archive/Getty Images; **315** Copyright © PhotoSpin/Artville/PictureQuest; **316** Copyright © Bettmann/Corbis.

UNIT TEN

319 Library of Congress Prints and Photographs Division; **320** Digital Imagery copyright © 2001 PhotoDisc, Inc.; **322** background Digital Imagery copyright © 2001 PhotoDisc, Inc.; **322** foreground Copyright © Joe Sohm, Chromosohm; **323** bottom Copyright © Joe Sohm, Chromosohm; **323** top Copyright © Joe Sohm, Chromosohm; **325** Copyright © Joe Sohm, Chromosohm; **328** Library of Congress Prints and Photographs Division.

UNIT ELEVEN

333 Copyright © Dorling Kindersley; **334** Digital Imagery copyright © 2001 PhotoDisc, Inc.; **341** Copyright © Lee Snider/Photo Images/CORBIS; **342** The Diagram Group; **342** The Diagram Group; **342** The Diagram Group; **348** Courtesy of the Illinois State Historical Library; **348** Photo by Sharon Hoogstraten; **349** Library of Congress; **351** Copyright © Morton Beebe, S.F./Corbis; **355** Copyright © Kevin Fleming/Corbis; **359** Copyright © Gary Hush/Getty Images; **362** Courtesy of the Illinois State Historical Library; **364** Illustration by Michael McCurdy; **366** Illustration by Michael McCurdy; **368** Illustration by Michael McCurdy; **370–371** South Dakota State Historical Society; **371** Minnesota Historical Society; **374** National Archives and Records Administration; **377** Denver Public Library, Western History Collection; **380** Copyright © Dorling Kindersley; **383** Copyright © Dorling Kindersley.

UNIT TWELVE

387 top Copyright © AFF/AFS Amsterdam, The Netherlands; bottom Reprinted with the permission of Atheneum Books for Young Readers, an imprint of Simon & Schuster Children's Publishing division from Black Whiteness by Robert Burleigh, illustrated by Walter Lyon Krudop. Illustrations copyright © 1998 Walter Lyon Krudop; **389** top Photograph returned from the U.S. Armed Forces Institute of Pathology, supplied by the Hiroshima Peace Culture Foundation; center Copyright © Bettmann/Corbis; bottom AP/Wide World Photos; **390** Digital Imagery copyright © 2001 PhotoDisc, Inc.; **393** Copyright © Bettmann/Corbis; **394** National Archives and Records Administration; **397** Copyright © Bettmann/Corbis; **400** Photograph returned from the U.S. Armed Forces Institute of Pathology, supplied by the Hiroshima Peace Culture Foundation; **402** AP/Wide World Photos; **404** Copyright © David Samuel Robbins/Corbis; **405** Copyright © AFP/Corbis; **406** left AP/Wide World Photos; **406** background Copyright © AFF/AFS Amsterdam, The Netherlands; **407** bottom Copyright © Corbis; **407** top Photo by Wil Wheeler; **409** Anne Frank Fonds, Basel/Anne Frank House, Amsterdam/Archive Photos; **411** Copyright © Bettmann/Corbis; **414** Copyright © Bettmann/Corbis; **418** Courtesy of Spertus Museum, Chicago; **421** Copyright © Corbis; **423**; Copyright © AFF/AFS Amsterdam, The Netherlands; **424** Copyright © AFF/AFS Amsterdam, The Netherlands; **426, 430, 433, 435, 439, 441, 446** Reprinted with the permission of Atheneum Books for Young Readers, an imprint of Simon & Schuster Children's Publishing division from Black Whiteness by Robert Burleigh, illustrated by Walter Lyon Krudop. Illustrations copyright © 1998 Walter Lyon Krudop; **448** The Granger Collection, New York.

McDougal Littell has made every effort to locate the copyright holders of all copyrighted material in this book and to make full acknowledgment for its use. Omissions brought to our attention will be corrected in a subsequent edition.